THE FATHERS
OF THE CHURCH

A NEW TRANSLATION

VOLUME 29

THE FATHERS
OF THE CHURCH

A NEW TRANSLATION

ROY JOSEPH DEFERRARI
Editorial Director Emeritus

EDITORIAL BOARD

EUSEBIUS PAMPHILI

ECCLESIASTICAL HISTORY

(BOOKS 6-10)

Translated by

ROY J. DEFERRARI

THE CATHOLIC UNIVERSITY OF AMERICA PRESS

Washington, D.C. 20017

Library of Congress Catalog Card No.: 65-27501

NOTE

THE PRESENT VOLUME contains the second half of the *Ecclesiastical History* of Eusebius, namely, Books 6 through 10, beginning with the persecution under Severus through the final victory of Constantine over Licinius. Book 10 is taken up largely with a discourse delivered by Eusebius in the church at Tyre and addressed to its bishop, Paulinus. This is very definitely a digression to a story which up to this point, almost the very end, has followed a carefully laid out plan. It is, however, interesting as a sample of the ecclesiastical oratory of that time in the East, being very flowery and turgid, quite characteristic of the rhetoric of this region.

CONTENTS

BOOK SIX

vii

BOOK SEVEN

BOOK EIGHT

BOOK NINE

BOOK TEN

ECCLESIASTICAL HISTORY

BOOKS 6-10

Translated by

ROY J. DEFERRARI, Ph.D.

The Catholic University of America

BOOK SIX

Chapter 1

WHEN SEVERUS[1] also was stirring up persecutions against the churches, glorious martyrdoms were achieved everywhere by the athletes of religion; they were especially frequent at Alexandria, as the athletes of God were escorted there as to a very large arena from Egypt and all the Thebais, and by the most patient endurance of different

---

1 Septimius Severus, emperor from 193 to 211, had been favorably disposed toward Christians until 202, when he issued a decree forbidding conversions to Christianity and Judaism. Cf. Spartianus, *In Severo* 16; Tillemont, *Hist. des emp.* 3.58. Any attempts to explain the change of Severus' attitude toward the Christians are purely conjectural. It is to be noted, however, that the decree was aimed only at conversions to Christianity, and may have been due to a fear that the rapidly spreading Christianity would undermine the old Roman institution. While no general and official persecution arose all over the Empire, the change in the emperor's attitude resulted in an increase of local and more open persecutions, especially in Egypt and North Africa. The principal sources of information on these are Eusebius' *Ecclesiastical History* 5.1-12, and the *De corona, Ad Scapulam,* and *De fuga in persecutione* of Tertullian.

torture and modes of death won crowns with God. Among these was Leonides, who was known as the father of Origen,[2] and who was beheaded and left behind him his son, quite young. It is not inopportune to discuss briefly how determined he was regarding the divine Word from that early age, since the story spread about him is especially widespread among the common people.

Chapter 2

Now one might say much if he tried to hand down the life of the man[1] at leisure in writing, but the treatise on him would require a special work. Nevertheless, for the

---

2 Little is known of Origen's father. He appears to have been of Greek origin, and was martyred in the tenth year of Severus (201-202). His fame was eclipsed by that of his son; hence the expression 'known as "the father of Origen."'

---

1 This present Book is the chief source of information for the life of Origen. This account suffers by the fact that Eusebius, in his effort to follow the strictly chronological method of recounting history, is thereby forced to break up his story by references to contemporary happenings. But Eusebius was very well acquainted with the life of Origen. He had collected a hundred of Origen's letters. Together with Pamphilus he wrote a *Defense of Origen* (six books), which contained not only a detailed account of his life but an explanation of his theology and a defense of the charges brought against him. Eusebius refers frequently in this Book to his *Defense*. Unfortunately, only the first book of this work is extant, and that in a translation by Rufinus. Eusebius also lived at Caesarea where Origen's library was preserved and where his memory was still fresh, and public documents were at hand. He was thus able to converse with surviving friends of Origen, and to have access to their works in which mention was made of Origen. Other sources for the life of Origen are to be found in Jerome, Rufinus, and Photius, but the information given here does not seem to be independent of Eusebius' *Defense*. St. Epiphanius (*Haeres.*, LXII and LXIV) gives anecdotes of doubtful credibility. In the *Panegyric* of Gregory the Wonder-worker we find a detailed description of

present we shall epitomize most things as briefly as possible, and shall state some few facts about him, bringing together what we present from certain letters and from the knowledge of his pupils who have remained alive even to our own time.

Information on Origen even, as it were, from his very swaddling clothes seems to me to be worthy of mention. For Severus was in the tenth year of his reign,[2] and Laetus[3] was Governor of Alexandria and of the rest of Egypt, and Demetrius[4] had recently taken up the episcopacy of the parishes there in succession to Julian.[5] Now, then, when the fire of persecution had blazed on high, and countless persons were gaining the crowns of martyrdom, such a desire for martyrdom seized the soul of Origen, although he was still quite a youth, that he was eager to come face to face with dangers and to rush forth to the conflict. Now, very little intervened and the events leading to his departure from life were not far off, had not the divine and heavenly Providence, for the benefit of the many, through his mother stood in the way of his eagerness. At any rate, she at first tried verbal entreaties, and begged him to be sparing of her motherly feelings toward him, but perceiving that, having learned that his father had been captured and was being held a prisoner,

---

Origen's method of teaching, and an account of his amazing influence over his pupils. Origen himself was the most modest of writers and almost never alludes to himself in his own works. Eusebius' account of Origen as given here reveals in a striking manner the tremendous respect and love which he had for the man. See the *Catholic Encyclopaedia* for an excellent outline of the life of Origen and bibliography.

2 A.D. 203.
3 The dates of his rule in Egypt are unknown.
4 Successor of Julianus, in 189, as the eleventh Bishop of Alexandria. Cf. Book 5.22.
5 Of this Julian nothing is known except what Eusebius tells us in Book 5.9,22.

he was entirely carried away with the passion for martyrdom, he was more determined than ever, she hid all his clothes and thus forced him to remain at home. Since he could do nothing else, being unable to be quiet because of the zeal intense beyond his years, he sent his father a most encouraging letter on martyrdom,[6] in which he exhorted him with these very words: 'Persevere, do not change your mind on our account.' Let this be recorded as the first evidence of Origen's youthful readiness and of his genuine disposition toward godliness. For he already had laid down no small foundation in his study of the faith, having been trained in the divine Scriptures even from his boyhood. Certainly he spent no ordinary amount of labor on these, for his father, in addition to the usual curriculum of studies,[7] gave these no secondary consideration. On every occasion, for example, before attending to the secular subjects he urged him to train himself in the sacred studies, requiring him each day to study and recite. And these studies were not without purpose in the boy's mind, who, on the other hand, labored so zealously at these that the simple and superficial readings of the sacred words did not satisfy him, but he sought for something more, and already at that age busied himself with deeper speculations, so that he even caused his father annoyance, as he inquired what the intent of the inspired Scripture really was. And his father seemingly rebuked him to his face, urging him not to seek anything beyond his age nor anything beyond the manifest meaning; but privately by himself he rejoiced greatly, and gave most profound thanks to God, the Author of all blessings, for having deemed him worthy to become

6 This sentence is all that has been preserved of this letter.
7 Ordinarily understood as mathematics, grammar, and rhetoric.

the father of such a boy. And it is reported that he often stood near his boy as he slept and uncovered his breast, as if the Holy Spirit were enshrined within it, and reverently kissed it, and counted himself blessed in his goodly offspring. These things and others akin to these are related to have happened to Origen while he was a boy.

But when his father had reached perfection through martyrdom, he was left destitute, when he was not quite seventeen,[8] together with his mother and six younger brothers. When his father's property was confiscated for the imperial treasury, he together with his relatives was in dire need of the necessaries of life, and he was deemed worthy of divine care and found both welcome and rest with a woman very rich in this world's goods and very renowned in other respects, yet who was offering hospitality to a famous person among the heretics of the time at Alexandria.[9] This man was an Antiochene by race, and the aforementioned woman kept him with her as an adopted son and treated him with great honor. Although Origen associated of necessity with this man, he gave clear proofs of the orthodoxy of his faith at that age, for when a great multitude, because of Paul's apparent skill in speech (for this was the man's name), was gathered together with him, not only heretics but also our own, he was never induced to associate with him in prayer, preserving the canon of the Church[10] even from boyhood, and, as he

8 In 185 or 186.
9 This Antiochene heretic, Paul, is known only from these remarks. We may assume, however, that the lady in question was a Christian in good standing. Otherwise, Origen would not have made his home with her.
10 The pseudo-Apostolic Constitutions VIII.34, say: 'Let not one of the faithful pray with a catechumen, no, not in the house; for it is not reasonable that he who is admitted should be polluted with one not admitted. Let not one of the godly pray with a heretic, no, not in the house. For, what fellowship has light with darkness.'

himself says somewhere using the very word, 'loathing' the teachings of the heresies. Being directed by his father in the studies of the Greeks and after his death having applied himself more eagerly to the study of literature, so that he had a considerable preparation in letters, not long after his father's death he gave himself over to these studies, and well supplied himself for a person of his age with the necessaries of life.

Chapter 3

While he was devoting himself to lecturing in the school, as he himself relates somewhere in writing, and no one in Alexandria was devoted to giving instruction in the faith, since all had been driven away by the threat of persecution, some of the pagans came to him to hear the word of God. Of these it is pointed out that Plutarch[1] was the first, who after having lived a noble life was decorated by a divine martyrdom; the second, Heraclas,[2] Plutarch's brother, who himself, after giving him a very abundant example of a philosophic life and discipline, also was deemed worthy of the episcopate of the Alexandrians to succeed Demetrius.

---

1 In 6.4 Eusebius says that he was the first of Origen's pupils to suffer martyrdom. This is all that is known about this Plutarch.
2 After being a pupil he became an assistant to Origen in teaching. Origen left the school to him on retiring from Alexandria to Caesarea. But Heraclas was in charge of the school for only a short while, because he was elected to succeed Demetrius as patriarch of Alexandria (233-249). He was clearly a friend of Origen in his earlier years. Heraclas did not accept all of Origen's views, and it has been said that he voted for the deprivation of his office as teacher and of his orders, and for his excommunication at the two synods held by Demetrius. It is also noted that when elected bishop he did not attempt to rescind these sentences. However, it cannot be proved that he had a hand in the condemnatory action of the synod, and that in later life he was hostile to Origen.

Origen was in his eighteenth year when he took charge of
the catechetical school,[3] and at this time also he became
prominent during the persecutions under Aquila,[4] the Governor of Alexandria,[5] when he acquired an especially famous
name among all those who were of the faith by the kindness
and good will which he displayed toward all the holy martyrs,
both unknown and known. For he was with the holy martyrs
not only while they were in prison and not only while they
were being examined up to the last sentence, but also after
this when they were being led away to death, displaying
great boldness and coming into close contact with danger;
so that, when he approached courageously and with great
boldness saluted the martyrs with a kiss, the multitude of
pagans round about often became enraged and almost stoned
him, had he not obtained the helping hand of God and
escaped marvelously; and the same divine and heavenly grace
at other times again and again—it is not possible to say how
often—preserved him[6] when he was plotted against at that
time for his excessive zeal and boldness for the word of Christ.
And so great was the war on the unbelievers against him that
they stationed soldiers, formed into groups, for his protection[7]
about the house where he remained, because of the multitude
of those who were being instructed by him in the holy faith.

---

3 In 204.
4 These persecutions took place after 203, when Origen had already
taken charge of the catechetical school, and before 211, when Severus
died. It cannot be determined whether Aquila succeeded Laetus or
became his subordinate.
5 In office in 206.
6 Scholars have engaged in much speculation as to how Origen escaped
persecution, when he was so thoroughly hated by the heathen, and
exposed himself continually. Eusebius regularly ascribes this to the
grace of God.
7 Or, 'for his capture.'

Thus the persecution against him blazed forth daily, so that
the entire city no longer had a place for him, as he went
from house to house and was driven from everywhere, because
of the multitude of those who came to the divine teaching
through his effort. For his everyday deeds included most
marvelous right actions of a very genuine philosophy. As the
saying goes, 'surely as was his speech, so was the manner of
life he displayed,' and 'as was his manner of life, so was his
speech.'[8] By this means especially, with the co-operation of
the power of God, he won countless over to his own zeal.

And when he saw still more pupils coming to him, for the
catechetical school had been turned over to him alone by
Demetrius who was in charge of the church, he considered
the teaching of language and literature at variance with
training in sacred studies,[9] and without hesitation broke off
the school of language and literature as useless and inimical
to divine learning; then with fitting reason, that he might
not have need of assistance from others, he disposed of
whatever works he had of ancient literature, although he
cherished them fondly, and was content with receiving four
obols[10] a day from him who brought them. For a great many
years he continued to live like a philosopher[11] in this manner,

8 Cf. Plato, *Republic* 400D.
9 This passage has caused some dispute as to its meaning. It probably
means nothing more than that, now that he had been given the
responsibility for the catechetical school by Demetrius, the demand
for teaching divine things was so great that he felt obliged to devote
his whole time to it and give up the teaching of secular literature.
10 An obol, a Greek coin, was equivalent to about three and a half cents
a day, barely enough even in that day for the mere necessities of life
but sufficient for Origen with his ascetic tendencies.
11 The ascetic way of life was commonly called the 'philosophical' or
'the life of the philosophers.' Cf. the works of John Chrysostom,
passim. This passage in Eusebius is probably the earliest use of the
expression.

divesting himself of all the substances of youthful desires;[12] throughout the entire day he carried on labors of discipline of no light nature, and for the greater part of the night he devoted himself to the study of the divine Scriptures; he persevered as much as possible in a very philosophical life, sometimes by exercises in fasting, sometimes by limiting his time for sleep, which he zealously managed to take never on a couch but upon the ground. And he thought that those words of the Saviour in the Gospel should especially be observed which exhort us not to have two cloaks and not to use shoes,[13] and not to be exhaustively solicitous for tomorrow.[14] He exhibited a zeal beyond his age, and by persevering in cold and nakedness,[15] and proceeding to the limit of excessive poverty, he especially astounded his followers, causing grief to a great many who desired to share their professions with him because of the labors which they saw him bestow upon the teaching of divine subjects. However, he did not relax his endurances. For example, he is said to have walked for many years without ever using a shoe; moreover, for a great many years abstaining from the use of wine and all other things unnecessary for sustenance, so that presently he fell into the danger of upsetting and injuring his constitution.[16]

By giving such proofs of a philosophic life to those who saw him he naturally roused many of his pupils to similar zeal, so that presently no ordinary persons from the unbelieving Gentiles and from the fields of education and

---

12 Cf. 2 Tim. 2.22.
13 Cf. Matt. 10.10.
14 Cf. Matt. 6.34.
15 2 Cor. 11.27.
16 The Greek *thōrax* means, properly, 'chest.' The Latin translators, e.g., Rufinus, translate *stomachum*, which is regularly *stomachus* in Greek. English translators unsatisfactorily say 'stomach.'

philosophy were brought over to his instruction. And these very persons through him received into their souls the true faith in the divine Word and really became prominent in this period of the persecution, with the result that some of them were captured and attained perfection by martyrdom.

Chapter 4

Now, the first of these was Plutarch, whom we mentioned a little above. While this man was being led away to his death, he who is the subject of this account remained with him to the very end of his life and again was almost killed by his fellow citizens, on the ground that he was clearly responsible for his death. But the will of God on this occasion also preserved him. After Plutarch, Serenus[1] was the second of Origen's pupils to show himself a martyr, giving proof through fire of the faith which he had received. The third martyr of the same school was Heraclides,[2] and after him Hero was the fourth; the former was still a catechumen, the latter but recently baptized. Both were beheaded. And still besides these a Serenus, different from the first, was proclaimed a fifth athlete of piety. Report has it that after enduring the greatest tortures he had his head taken off. And among the women, Herais, who was still a catechumen, as Origen himself says, 'received baptism by fire' and departed her life.

---

1 Two persons named Serenus are mentioned here: one was burned to death; the other, beheaded. Nothing more is known of them.

2 Authentic information on this Heraclides and the others mentioned here is limited to this passage, although they appear in the mediaeval martyrologies.

Chapter 5

As the seventh among these let Basilides[1] be numbered, who led away the clebrated Potamiaena,[2] concerning whom to this day a long story is still sung among the people of the country, for having struggled much against lovers for the purity and virginity of her body, in which she excelled (for surely her youthful beauty of body as well as her soul was in its full bloom), and for having suffered much, and finally, after tortures fearful and terrible to relate, for having been perfected through fire, along with her mother Marcella.[3] They say, indeed, that the judge (his name was Aquila), imposed severe punishments on her entire body and finally threatened to hand her over to the gladiators for bodily abuse; but, on being asked, after she had reflected a little, what her decision was, gave such a reply as, according to their opinion, contained something profane. As soon as she spoke, she received the measure of her sentence, and Basilides, who was one of those serving in the army, seized her and led her away to death. When the crowd tried to annoy her and to insult her with licentious words, he restrained the insulters and drove them away, displaying the greatest pity and kindness toward her. She accepted his sympathy for her, and bade the man be of good cheer, saying that, after she had departed, she would intercede for him with her Lord,

---

1 Eusebius' clear statement here that Basilides was one of the disciples of Origen has been doubted for no worthy reason.
2 Potamiaena (June 28), one of the most celebrated martyrs of Alexandria during the persecution of Severus, a virgin famous for her beauty, chastity, and courage. Palladius (*Historia Lausiaca* 3) gives a full account of her martyrdom with some questionable details not mentioned by Eusebius. Although Rufinus makes her a disciple of Origen, it is to be noted that Eusebius definitely does not.
3 All that is known of Marcella is recorded here.

and that after no great time he would receive a reward for
what he had done for her. After she had said this she nobly
endured the issue, when boiling pitch was poured slowly and
gradually upon the various parts of the body from the tips
of her toes even to her head. Such a contest did this maiden
celebrated in song wage. After no long time had passed,
Basilides for some reason was asked by the soldiers to swear,
and he strongly maintained that it was not at all possible for
him to swear,[4] for he was a Christian and he openly confessed
this. At first for a time he was thought to be joking, but,
when he steadfastly held to it, he was led away to the judge.
When he confessed in his presence to his opposition [to the
oath], he was committed to prison. When the brethren in
God came to him and asked the reason for his sudden and
incredible impulse, he is said to have declared that Potamiaena
three days after her martyrdom stood near him in the night
and placed a crown about his head, and said that she
besought the Lord for him and had obtained her request,
and that before long she would receive him. Thereupon, the
brethren gave him the seal[5] in the Lord, and on the next
day, after giving glorious testimony for the Lord, he was
beheaded. And many more of the people in Alexandria are
related to have gone over all at once to the word of the
Lord in the times of the persons mentioned, for Potamiaena
appeared to them in their sleep and exhorted them. But let
this suffice on this subject.

---

4 Cf. Matt. 5.33,34.
5 The Greek *sphragis* ('seal') was commonly used by the Fathers to
mean 'baptism.'

Chapter 6

Clement,[1] who succeeded Pantaenus,[2] was in charge of catechetical instruction at Alexandria until such time as Origen was one of his pupils. When Clement wrote his work *Stromateis,* he presented a chronological table in the first book, and he defined his dates[3] with reference to the death of Commodus, so that it is clear that he composed his work under Severus, whose times this present account is recording.

Chapter 7

At this time, also, Judas,[1] another writer, discoursing in writing on the seventy weeks in Daniel,[2] brought his chronology down to the tenth year of the reign of Severus. He, too, thought that the much talked about coming of the Antichrist was already near[3] at that time. Thus did the instigation of persecution against us then violently disturb the minds of the many.

---

1 Speaking of Clement here seems like an inconsistency. He has already been treated in Book 5, and if mention need be made of him in connection with Origen, it had been done better in Ch. 3, where Origen's appointment as head of the catechetical school is related. Various conjectures have been made to explain this.

2 Cf. 5.10.

3 Cf. Clement, *Stromata* 1.21.

1 Jerome (*De vir. ill.* 52) mentions the writer Judas, but merely repeats what Eusebius says here. We know nothing more about him.

2 Cf. Dan. 19.24.

3 That the second coming of Christ was in the immediate future was a common belief among the early Christians to the time of Constantine, and severe trials such as violent persecutions were regularly interpreted as the beginning of the end.

Chapter 8

At this time, while Origen was carrying on the work of catechetical instruction at Alexandria, he committed an act characteristic of an immature and useful mind, yet, notwithstanding, including abundant proof of faith and self-control.[1] For he took the words, 'There are eunuchs who have made themselves eunuchs for the kingdom of heaven,'[2] in too literal and extreme a sense, thinking both to fulfill the words of the Saviour and also, since although youthful in years he discoursed on divine subjects with women as well as with men, to avoid all suspicion of shameful slander in the minds of unbelievers, he hastened to carry out the Saviour's words by action, having planned to escape the notice of most of his pupils. But it was not possible, although he desired, to conceal such a deed. Demetrius, in fact, learned of it later, for he was in charge of the parish there, and he marveled greatly at him for his rashness, but he approved the zeal and the sincerity of his faith, and he bade him be of good cheer and urged him to apply himself more than ever to the work of catechetical instruction.

Of such a nature was he at that time. But not long afterwards the same Demetrius, when he saw that he was prospering and was great and distinguished and celebrated every-

1 That Origen performed this act and did so for the purpose of freeing himself of the baser passions in order that he might live a purer life seems quite certain from the evidence, although some scholars go so far as to argue that he never committed the act. That he believed that the Scriptures contain justification for the deed, although he repented of it later, judging from his statement in *Comment. in Matt.* 15.1, seem equally certain. Eusebius apparently did not approve of Origen's act, although he admired him for his courage and the motives that led to it.
2 Matt. 19.12.

where, was overcome by human weakness and attempted to describe the deed to the bishops throughout the world as a most foolish act, when the especially notable and distinguished of the bishops of Palestine, those of Caesarea and Jerusalem,[3] considered Origen to be worthy of privileges and the highest honor and ordained him to the presbyterate.[4] Thereupon, as he advanced greatly in reputation and earned no small reputation and fame with everyone everywhere for virtue and wisdom, Demetrius, for lack of any other accusation, made a grievous charge of the deed which he had long ago committed in his boyhood, daring to include in his accusations those who had raised him to the presbyterate.

Now this was done a little later. Meanwhile, Origen carried on his work of divine teaching at Alexandria for all, without distinction, who came to him by night and by day, devoting all his time untiringly to divine subjects and to those who attended his school.

After Severus had been in power for eighteen years, he was succeeded by his son Antoninus.[5] At this time a certain Alexander, who was among those who had played the man in the face of persecution and after their struggles for the faith by their confessions had been preserved by the providence of God, he whom we lately pointed out as bishop of the church at Jerusalem, because of his having excelled in his confessions in behalf of Christ, was deemed worthy of the aforesaid bishopric, while Narcissus,[6] who was his predecessor, was still alive.

---

3 Namely, Theoctistus and Alexander. Cf. 19.17; 27.
4 Cf. 6.23.
5 In 211. Septimius Severus died on February 4, 211, after a reign of a little more than seventeen years and eight months.
6 On Narcissus, cf. next three chapters and 5.12.

Chapter 9

Now, the citizens of the parish call to mind many other miracles, as having been handed down by the brethren in succession, and among these they describe the following wonder as having taken place through him. It is related that once at the great all-night paschal vigil the oil failed the deacons, whereupon, as a terrible despondency seized the entire multitude, Narcissus ordered those who were preparing the lights to draw water and bring it to him; that, when this was no sooner said than done, he prayed over the water, and with genuine faith in the Lord gave orders to pour it into the lamps; and that, when they had done this, contrary to all reason by a miraculous and divine power he changed the nature of water into a quality of oil, and for a very long time, from that time to our own, a small proof of the miracle of that day has been preserved by very many of the brethren there.[1]

And they record a great many other things worthy of mention in the life of this man, among which is the following. Certain wretched creatures, unable to endure the vigor and firmness of his life, out of fear of being seized and submitted to trial, since they were conscious of themselves having committed numerous evils, anticipated the event by devising a plot against him and circulated a terrible slander against him. Then, to win the confidence of those who gave heed, they confirmed their accusations by oaths; one swore that he might be destroyed by fire; another, that his body might be wasted away by a foul disease; and the third, that his

---

1 It is to be noted that Eusebius relates this story on the basis not of documents but of hearsay.

eyes might be blinded. Even so, none of the faithful paid any attention to them, although they insisted, because the sobriety and very virtuous manner of Narcissus' life was well known in every way among all. He himself, however, unable to endure the wickedness of what was said, and, besides, having for a long time cherished the philosophic life,[2] escaped the entire multitude of the church, and passed very many years secretly in deserts and obscure places.[3] The great eye of justice, however, did not remain unmoved at what was done, but most promptly let loose upon these wicked men the curses with which they had bound themselves in perjury. The first, together with his whole family, was burned to death, when, for no other reason than a small spark falling upon it, the house in which he was staying was entirely enveloped in flames during the night; the body of the second was suddenly covered from the tips of his toes to his head with the disease which he had imposed as a penalty upon himself; and the third, beholding what had happened to those before him and fearing the inevitable judgment of God who watches over all, confessed to everyone what they had concocted in common, and in his repentance was so wasted away with lamentations and was so ceaseless in his tears that both eyes were destroyed. These men suffered such punishments for their falsehood.

---

2 Cf. 6.3.
3 The date of his retirement cannot be determined.

Chapter 10

Since Narcissus had retired and it was not known where he might be, those in charge of the neighboring churches decided to proceed to the consecration of another bishop. Dius was his name, and after he had been in charge for no long time Germanion succeeded him, and Germanion was succeeded by Gordius.[1] In his time Narcissus appeared from somewhere as if come to life again,[2] and he was for a second time called to the episcopacy by the brethren, for all admired him still more because of his retirement and philosophic life and above all because of the punishment by which God had thought it proper to avenge him.

Chapter 11

Since he was no longer able to fulfill his office because of a ripe old age,[1] God's dispensation summoned the above-mentioned[2] Alexander, who was bishop of another parish,[3] to a

---

1 Nothing more is known of these three.
2 Literally, 'as if from a resurrection.'

---

1 Narcissus was now more than 110 years old. Certainly by the time of the Council of Nicaea, and probably before, the principle prevailed that no bishop was to be transferred from one diocese to another, and that no appointment was to be made of an assistant bishop, which would result in two bishops for one city. This principle in its twofold aspect was violated here in the translation of Alexander to Jerusalem. However, exceptions were made to this rule where such action was for the common good. For example, St. Augustine was quite conscious of this rule when he hesitated to allow himself to be ordained assistant bishop of Hippo.
2 Cf. 6.8.
3 It is impossible to state with certainty of what city in Cappadocia Alexander was bishop. Some on very slender evidence have given Flaviopolis or Flaviadis as the name of the city.

joint service with Narcissus, by a revelation which appeared to him at night in a vision. Thus, then, as if in response to an oracle, he made the journey from the land of the Cappadocians, where he was first thought worthy of the episcopate, to Jerusalem for the sake of prayer and an investigation of the holy places. The people there received him most kindly, and did not permit him to return home because of another revelation which appeared to them also in the night and uttered the clearest message to the most zealous among them. It pointed out that they should go forth outside the gates and receive the bishop who was foreordained by God for them. And when they had done this, with unanimous consent of the bishops who governed the churches round about, they forced him of necessity to remain. Actually, Alexander himself relates in a personal letter to the Antinoites,[4] which has been preserved among us to our own day, writing towards the end of the letter exactly as follows: 'Narcissus salutes you, who administered the office of the episcopate here before me, and now is associated with me in the prayers, having completed his one hundred and sixteenth year; and he exhorts you, and I do likewise, to be of one mind.'

Thus, then, were these matters. But when Serapion[5] died, Asclepiades,[6] who himself was distinguished for his confessions under the persecution, succeeded to the episcopacy

---

4 Antinoë, or Antinoöpolis, on the eastern bank of the Nile, was founded by Hadrian in 122, in honor of Antinous. Cf. 4.8.2. This letter was probably written between 212 and 216. The fragments of Alexander's letters are translated into English in the *Ante-Nicene Fathers*, 6.154.
5 Cf. 5.19.
6 The *Chronicon* with some certitude places the accession of Asclepiades in the first year of Caracalla, 211. This passage contains all that is known of Asclepiades.

of the church at Antioch. Alexander recalls this man's appointment, writing to the Antiochenes thus: 'Alexander, slave and
bondsman of Jesus Christ, to the blessed church of the
Antiochenes, greeting in the Lord. Light and easy for me
did the Lord make my bonds, when at the time of my
imprisonment I learned that by divine providence Asclepiades,
most suitably because of his worthy faith, had taken over the
episcopacy of the holy church of you Antiochenes.'

He indicates that he sent this letter by Clement, writing
near the end in this manner. 'My reverend brethren, I have
dispatched this letter to you by Clement,[7] the blessed presbyter,
a virtuous and esteemed person, whom you both know and will
know better, who, while he was here, under the providence
and watchfulness of the Master established and increased the
Church of the Lord.'

Chapter 12

Now, it is probable that other monuments of Serapion's
literary activity are preserved by others, but those addressed
to Domnus,[1] one who had fallen away from the faith of
Christ to Jewish will-worship at the time of the persecution,
have alone come down to us; and those to Pontius and
Caricus,[2] men of the Church, and other letters to other
persons; and another work he composed, *On the So-Called*

---

7 Clement of Alexandria. Cf. 5.11.

1 All our information on Domnus comes from this passage. The Greek
word, *ethelothrēskeia,* is worthy of note here. It is translated 'will-
worship,' and as used for the first time in Col. 2.23 means 'an
arbitrary self-imposed worship,' a worship which one affects. It may
well be that his lapse was into heresy rather than into actual Judaism.
2 Cf. 5.19.

Gospel according to Peter,[3] which he wrote when refuting the false statements in it, because some in the parish of Rhossus[4] had gone astray into heterodox teachings on the basis of the aforesaid writing. It will be well to present statements from this work, through which he presents the opinion which he holds about the book, writing as follows: 'For we, brethren, accept[5] both Peter and the other Apostles as Christ, but those false writings under their names we, as men of experience, reject, for we know we did not receive such [as genuine]. When I visited with you, I supposed that you all clung to the true faith, and, not having read the gospel they put forth under the name of Peter, I said: "If this is all that seems to cause captiousness among you, let it be read." But I have now learned that their mind lurked in the ditch of some heresy, according to what has been told me, and I shall hasten for another visit with you; so, brethren, expect me soon. But we, brethren, having discovered the nature of the heresy of Marcianus[6] (who used even to contradict himself, not understanding what he was saying, as you will learn from what has been written to you), have been ennobled by others who have studied this very gospel, that is, by the successors of those who began it, whom we call Docetae,[7] (for most of the ideas belong to their teaching),

---

3 Cf. 3.3. A large fragment of this Gospel (dated *c.* 165), discovered at Akhmin in 1866, agrees closely with Serapion's description of it given above. It is plainly docetic in its conception of Christ.

4 A city of Syria, on the Gulf of Issus, to the northwest of Antioch.

5 Cf. Gal. 4.14.

6 Any attempt to identify this Marcianus with the great heresiarch Marcion has little or no foundation. Marcianus was a leader of the Docetae at Rhossus.

7 Docetae (from Greek *dokeō* 'seem') was a term in common use, dating back to apostolic times, to indicate persons or sects who taught that Christ only 'appeared' or 'seemed' to be a man, to have been born, to have lived and suffered. Cf. *Catholic Encyclopedia,* arts. 'Docetae' and 'Doceticism.'

making use of [information supplied] by them, to go through it and discover that most of the material is in harmony with the true word of the Saviour, but some things, which we have appended for your benefit, have been added.'

Chapter 13

These, then, are the writings of Serapion.

But of Clement,[1] the *Stromateis,* the entire eight books, are preserved among us, to which he saw fit to give the following title, *Titus Flavius Clement's Stromateis of Gnostic Memoranda according to the True Philosophy,* and of equal number with these are his books entitled *Hypotypōseis,* in which he mentions Pantaenus[2] by name as his teacher, and has set forth his interpretations of Scriptures and traditions. He also has a book, the *Exhortation to the Greeks,* and the three books of the work entitled *Paedagogus,* and *Who Is the Rich Man That Is Being Saved?* (another book of his has been so entitled), and the treatise *On the Pasch,* and discourses *On Fasting* and *On Slander,* and the *Exhortation to Patient Endurance,* or *To Those Recently Baptized,* and that entitled *Ecclesiastical Canon* or *Against the Judaizers,* which he dedicated to Alexander, the bishop who has been mentioned.[3]

Now, in the *Stromateis* he has made a tapestry not only of the divine Scripture but also of the writings of the Greeks, if

---

1 Cf. 5.11. Clement of Alexandria, to be distinguished from Clement of Rome; his full name was Titus Flavius Clemens. Cf. Introduction to Clement of Alexandria, *Christ the Teacher* (New York 1954), trans. Simon P. Wood, Vol. 23 in this series.
2 Cf. 5.10.
3 8.7; 11.

he thought that they also had said anything useful, and he mentions the opinions of many, elucidating those of the Greeks as well as of barbarians, and, in addition, correcting the false opinions of the heresiarchs; and he unfolded a great history, furnishing us with a basic work of extensive erudition. With all these matters he mingles, also, the opinions of the philosophers, and thus he has properly made the title of *Stromateis* correspond with his work. And he has also made use in them of the testimonies of the disputed writings, the so-called Wisdom of Solomon, and that of Jesus the son of Sirach, and the Epistle to the Hebrews,[4] and those of Barnabas,[5] and Clement,[6] and Jude;[7] and he mentions the work of Tatian[8] *To the Greeks,* and Cassian, as having himself also composed a chronography,[9] and Philo and Aristobulus and Josephus and Demetrius and Eupolemus, Jewish historians, as having shown in writings, all of them, that Moses and the race of the Jews were earlier than the ancient origin of the Greeks.[10] The works of the man which are now being mentioned are really full of a great deal of other useful learning. In the first of these he refers to himself as having been next in succession to the Apostles;[11] and in them he promises also to make a commentary on Genesis.[12]

And in his work *On the Pasch* he acknowledges that he was forced by his companions to hand down to posterity in

4 Cf. 3.3.
5 Cf. 3.25
6 Cf. 3.16.
7 Cf. 2.23.
8 Cf. 4.29.
9 Clement, *Strom.* 21 (101.2).
10 *Ibid.* 15 (72.4); 22 (150.1); 21 (147.2; 141.1ff.); 23 (153.4).
11 *Ibid.* 1 (11.3), quoted 5.4.5.
12 *Ibid.* 3.14 (95.2); 4.1 (3.3); 6.18 (168.4).

writing traditions which he happened to have heard from the elders of old; in it he speaks of Melito and Irenaeus and certain others whose accounts he has also set down.

Chapter 14

And in the *Hypotypōseis,* to sum up briefly, he has made concise accounts of all the canonical Scripture, not even passing over the disputed writings[1]—I speak of the Epistle of Jude and the other Catholic Epistles, and that of Barnabas,[2] and the so-called Apocalypse of Peter.[3] And he says that the Epistle to the Hebrews[4] is Paul's but that it was written for Hebrews in the Hebrew language, and that Luke, after carefully translating it, published it for the Greeks, and that for this reason the same complexion is found in the expression of this Epistle and the Acts; but that 'Paul an Apostle'[5] was naturally not prefixed. 'For,' he says, 'when writing to Hebrews who had taken a prejudice against him and were suspicious of him, he wisely did not repel them at the beginning by placing his name' [there].

Then, going on, he adds: 'But now, as the blessed presbyter used to say, since the Lord, being the apostle of the Almighty,[6] was sent to the Hebrews, Paul, because of modesty, inasmuch as he had been sent to the Gentiles, did not inscribe himself as Apostle of the Hebrews both because of his respect for the Lord and because out of his abundance, he wrote to the Hebrews, being a preacher and apostle of Gentiles.'[7]

1 On the New Testament canon in general, cf. 3.25.
2 Cf. 3.25.
3 Cf. 3.3.
4 *Ibid.*
5 Cf. Gal. 1.1ff.
6 Cf. Heb. 3.1.
7 Cf. 1 Tim. 2.7; 2 Tim. 1.11; Rom. 11.13.

Again in the same books, Clement has placed a tradition of the presbyters from the beginning regarding the order of the Gospels, which goes like this. He said that the Gospels which contained the genealogies were written first, but that the Gospel according to Mark[8] had this occasion: When Peter had preached the Word publicly at Rome, and by the Spirit proclaimed the Gospel, those present, who were numerous, urged Mark, inasmuch as he had followed him for a long time and remembered what had been spoken, to write down what was said; and after he had done this he gave it out to those who requested it. When Peter discovered this, he neither energetically prevented it nor urged it on. But John, the last, being conscious that external facts[9] had been exhibited in the Gospels, on the urging of his disciples and inspired by the Spirit, composed a spiritual Gospel.[10] This is the account of Clement.

Again, Alexander, referred to above,[11] mentions Clement along with Pantaenus, in a certain letter to Origen, as men who had been well known to him, and he writes thus: 'For this also, as you know, was the will of God, that the friendship which has existed from our ancestors between us remain inviolate, but, rather, warmer and more steadfast. We know those blessed men, who trod the path before us, as fathers, with whom we shall be before long:[12] Pantaenus, the truly blessed man and master, and the holy Clement, who was

---

8 On the composition of the Gospel of Mark, see 2.15. With Peter's attitude toward its composition, compare the words of Eusebius in 2.15.2.

9 *tà sōmatiká*, lit., 'things of the body.'

10 Cf. 3.24.

11 6.8,11.

12 Thus, at the time of the writing of this letter, both Pantaenus and Clement were dead.

my master and assisted me, and every man such as these, through whom I came to know you, who are in every respect the best, and my master and brother.'[13] These matters, then, were so.

Now, Adamantius[14] (for this was Origen's name also), when Zephyrinus[15] was at that time governing the Church of the Romans, himself somewhere writes that he visited Rome, using these words, 'longing to see the most ancient Church of the Romans.' After a short stay there, he returned to Alexandria, and began to fulfill there his usual work of instruction with all zeal, for Demetrius, who was bishop there at that time, urged and all but entreated him to give his assistance without stint to the brethren.[16]

Chapter 15

But when he saw that he did not have time for the deeper study of divine subjects, both for the investigation and interpretation of sacred Scriptures, and also for the instruction of those who came to him and did not give him time to breathe, for one after the other they visited his lecture hall from morning until evening, he made a division of the

---

13 The conclusion seems obvious from this passage that Alexander was a student of Clement's and a fellow pupil of Origen's. Cf. 6.2,8.
14 Probably a second name of Origen from the beginning, with no reference to character. Adamantius by derivation means 'hard' or 'adamantine,' and several attempts were made in antiquity to connect this with some outstanding characteristic of Origen. Jerome (*Ep. ad Paulam* sec. 3) applies another name, Chalcenterus, to Origen. This name was first applied to Didymus of Alexandria for his great industry, and undoubtedly was applied to Origen for the same reason.
15 Cf. 4.28.
16 On Demetrius and Origen, see 6.8.

multitude. From among his pupils he selected Heraclas,[1] a man who was zealous in divine things and a very learned man otherwise and not unacquainted with philosophy, and he made him an associate in the work of instruction, entrusting him with the first introduction of those who were just learning the elements, but reserving for himself the instruction of those with experience.

Chapter 16

So accurate an investigation of the divine words was introduced by Origen that he learned the Hebrew language thoroughly and obtained personal possession of the original writings in the actual Hebrew characters, which were in circulation among the Jews, and he traced the editions of others who translated the sacred Scriptures besides the Seventy,[2] and in addition to the translations in constant use— those of Aquila[3] and Symmachus[4] and Theodotion[5]—he

---

1 Cf. 6.3.

---

1 Jerome (De vir. ill. 54) remarks that Origen's study of Hebrew was contrary to the custom of his day and race. However, Origen needed a knowledge of Hebrew for the study of the Old Testament and for polemical purposes, yet he obtained only a bare practical knowledge of it and often made mistakes in his use of it. He himself confessed his lack of a critical knowledge of Hebrew. Cf. Hom. in Num. 14.1; 16.4.

2 Cf. 5.8.

3 The author of a translation of the Old Testament into Greek, and reproduced by Origen in the third column of the Hexapla. He belonged to the earlier half of the second century, a Jewish proselyte of Pontus, or, according to a more definite tradition, of Sinope. Cf. Irenaeus (Adv. haer. 3.24), Eusebius (Demonst. evang. 7.1), Jerome (Ep. ad Pammach. opp. 4.2), and other Fathers. He aimed to furnish a translation which was a more accurate rendering of the Hebrew than that of the Septuagint, which was in many places loose and incorrect from the beginning and somewhat corrupted in the course of four centuries. With this purpose he made a strictly literal transla-

discovered certain others, which were being interchanged and which he traced and brought to light,[6] from I know not what recesses, after they lay hidden for a long time. With reference to these, because of their uncertainty of authorship, since he did not know to whom in the world they belonged, he indicated only this much: that he found the one in Nicopolis, near Actium,[7] the other in some different place. In the

tion, striving to give a Greek equivalent for every Hebrew word, and often disregarding rules of grammar and of idiom, thus frequently rendering his words unintelligible to those unacquainted with Hebrew. This excessively literal quality of the work has impaired its value as a literary translation, but has made it very valuable as an indication of the state of the Hebrew text from which it was made. Neither Aquila's version nor the two following are extant, but numerous fragments are preserved by the Fathers who used Origen's *Hexapla*.

4 Author of the Greek version of the Old Testament, which appears next after Aquila's and before those of the Septuagint and Theodotion. According to Eusebius (6.17) and Jerome (*Comment in Heb.* 2.3), he was an Ebionite. He wrote his version during the reign of Septimius Severus (193-211), and, like Aquila, aimed to follow the Hebrew exclusively. Unlike Aquila, he strove to avoid barbarous diction and to achieve purity of Greek style. He appears to have borrowed passages from Aquila, sometimes verbally.

5 Irenaeus (*Adv. Haer.* 3.21.1) and Epiphanius (*De mens. et pond.* 17) are probably correct in calling him a Jewish proselyte. The evidence indicates that his work was not so late as 189 or earlier than 130. Thedotion's work was not an independent version but rather a revision of the Septuagint, with its insertions usually retained, but omissions supplied by the Hebrew, apparently with the assistance of Aquila's version. Origen usually preferred Theodotion's version to the other two in filling the lacunae of the text of the Septuagint. Thus, a large part of the ordinary Greek text of Jeremias, and even more of that of Job, come from the version of Theodotion. Furthermore, Theodotion's translation of Daniel was accepted by the Christians in place of the Daniel of the Septuagint, and replaced it in all the manuscripts of the Septuagint, thus being preserved entire. It is noteworthy that Eusebius mentions the three versions in the order in which they appear in Origen's *Hexapla* and not chronologically.

6 Very little is known about these anonymous Greek versions of the Old Testament.

7 Nicopolis, a city of Epirus, on the northern shore of the Ambracian gulf, opposite the promontory of Actium, so designated to distinguish it from several other cities of the same name.

Hexapla[8] of the Psalms, however, after the four famous editions he placed not only a fifth translation, but also a sixth and a seventh, and in the case of one, moreover, he has indicated that it was discovered in Jericho in a jar in the time of Antoninus, the son of Severus. All these he brought together, and he divided them according to clauses and placed them opposite each other, together with the actual Hebrew text. Thus he has left us the copies of the so-called *Hexapla*. He prepared separately the edition of Aquila and Symmachus and Theodotion, together with that of the Seventy, in the *Tetrapla*.[9]

Chapter 17

As regards these same translators, however, we should realize that Symmachus[1] was an Ebionite. The followers of the heresy of the Ebionites, as it is called, declare that Christ was born of Joseph and Mary, and assume that He was a mere man, and strongly maintain that the Law should be observed in a more Jewish manner, as we saw somewhere above in this history.[2] Memoirs of Symmachus are in circulation to this day, in which he appears to maintain this heresy by attacking the Gospel according to Matthew.[3] Origen

---

8 The *Hexapla*, the great critical work of Origen, so called because it was arranged in six main columns, from right to left in the following order: (1) Hebrew, (2) a transliteration of it in Greek letters, (3) Aquila, (4) Symmachus, (5) Septuagint, (6) Theodotion. In certain places a fifth, sixth, and even seventh Greek version were added; these were called *octopla* for some unknown reason, not *nonapla*.
9 That is, the *Hexapla* with the first two columns omitted.

1 Cf. 6.16.
2 Cf. 3. 27.
3 All traces of this work and Symmachus' other interpretations of Scripture have disappeared.

indicates that he received these, together with other inter-
pretations of the Scriptures by Symmachus, from a certain
Juliana,[4] who, he says, received the books by inheritance from
Symmachus himself.

Chapter 18

At this time, also, Ambrose,[1] who held the views of the
heresy of Valentinus,[2] being refuted by the truth as presented
by Origen and as if his mind had been illumined by light,
assented to the true doctrine as taught by the Church. Many
others among the learned, since Origen's fame was noised
about everywhere, came to him to make trial of the man's
proficiency in the sacred books. And a great many heretics
and not a few of the most famous philosophers attended his
teaching zealously, being taught by him not only in divine
things but also in secular philosophy. For as many as he
saw were naturally gifted he introduced also to philosophical

---

4 Known to us only from this passage and from Palladius, *Hist. Laus.*
147. The latter states that Juliana was a virgin of Caesarea in
Cappadocia, who gave refuge to Origen in the time of some persecution. Since Eusebius and others are quite silent about this story
it is open to grave suspicion.

---

1 Ambrose of Alexandria, disciple and friend of Origen, a deacon
according to Jerome (*De vir. ill.* 56) , died about 250. Nothing is
known of his early life. He was of a noble and wealthy family (Origen,
Exhort. ad Mart. 14f., 49; Jerome, *loc. cit.*) , and probably held some
high official position (Epiph., *Haer.* 64.3; Origen, *Exhort. ad Mart.*
36) . He was a man of an active and critical mind, and Eusebius says
here that he embraced the heresy of Valentinian. Jerome and others
give still different reports. However, in Origen he recognized his true
teacher, and embraced the orthodox faith (cf. Epiph., *loc. cit.*) . From
then until his death by martyrdom he devoted all his time and labors
to encouraging Origen in his studies of Scripture. Furthermore, he
used his wealth to support them. Cf. 6.23.
2 A Gnostic heretic of the second century; cf. 4.11.

studies, presenting geometry and arithmetic and other pre-
liminary subjects, and leading them on into the systems of
the philosophers, explaining their works, commenting upon
and examining into each, so that the man was proclaimed a
great philosopher even among the Greeks themselves. And
many of the less endowed he urged to take up the ordinary
subjects,[3] saying that from these no little benefit would be
theirs for the examination and study of the divine Scriptures.
For this reason especially he considered the training in secular
and philosophic learning necessary even for himself.

Chapter 19

Witnesses among the Greeks themselves of his proficiency
in these subjects are the philosophers who flourished in his
time, in whose writings we have found frequent mention of
the man, sometimes when they dedicated their works to him,
sometimes when they referred their own labors to him as to a
teacher for criticism. Why need we say this, when Porphyry,[1]
who lived in Sicily in our time and wrote treatises against us,
attempting to slander the sacred Scriptures through them,
mentioned those who had made interpretations of them; and,

---

3 The cycle of the arts and sciences which every free-born youth was
obliged to go through before applying himself to any professional
studies.

---

1 One of the most distinguished of the Neo-Platonist school, born in
232 or 233, probably at Tyre. When thirty years of age he went to
Rome, where he met Plotinus, and of whom he became disciple,
biographer, and expounder. He was a man of broad learning, but
not an original thinker. It is often said that Plotinus was the greatest
master of the Neo-Platonist school, and Porphyry the chief expounder.
He composed a long work against Christianity, which Eusebius himself
answered.

since he could not in any way make a base charge against their doctrines, for lack of arguments turned to deriding and slandering their interpreters, and among these Origen in particular. He says that he knew him in his early youth, and he tries to slander the man, but he unconsciously commends him, telling the truth in some instances, when it was impossible for him to do otherwise, and in others speaking falsehoods, where he thought he would not be detected, sometimes accusing him as a Christian, and at others describing his progress in philosophic learning.

But hear now what he actually says: 'Some in their desire not to abandon the baseness of the Jewish Scripture but to find an explanation for it, resorted to explanations that were incompatible and out of harmony with what was written, and that contained not so much a defense of the strange matter as approval and praise for their own works. For, after boasting that the words which were spoken clearly by Moses were so many riddles, and ascribing divine inspiration to them as oracles full of hidden mysteries, and by their absurdity bewitching the critical faculty of the mind, they bring in their own interpretations.'

Then, after other statements, he says: 'But let the manner of the absurdity be grasped from a man who enjoyed an exceedingly great reputation, whom I met while still quite young, and who still does by reason of the works which he has left behind, Origen, whose fame among teachers of these subjects has become very widespread. For this man was a hearer of Ammonius,[2] who among the men of our time had

---

2 Ammonius Saccas, so called (sakkophóros) because he had been a porter in his youth according to Seudas (under Origen) and Ammianus Marcellinus (22.528). He was a native of Alexandria, and

achieved the greatest progress in philosophy, and with regard to the knowledge of these subjects received much help from his teacher, but as regards the proper choice of life he took the course opposite to his. For Ammonius, a Christian, reared by his parents in Christian teachings, when he took hold of thinking and philosophy, immediately changed over to a life according to the Law, but Origen, a Greek, taught in Greek subjects, plunged into barbarian recklessness.[3] While rushing into this, he hawked himself and his skill in learning, living his life like a Christian and contrary to the Law, but about material things and the Deity playing the role of Greek and covertly introducing Greek material into foreign fables.[4] He was always close to Plato, and was conversant with the writings of Numenius[5] and Cronius,[6] Apollophanes[7] and Longinus[8]

---

was born of Christian parents, but returned to paganism, according to Porphyry. Eusebius (6.19) denies this, but he is evidently confusing him with a Christian of the same name, the author of a *Diatessaron*, still extant. It seems highly unlikely that the founder of the Alexandrian school of philosophy, which Ammonius Saccas was, should at the same time be a Christian. Furthermore, Eusebius' Ammonius wrote books, and according to both Longinus and Porphyry, Ammonius Saccas wrote none. He numbered among his pupils Herennius, Longinus, the pagan Origen, and Plotinus. According to this passage, the Christian Origen studied under him for a time. Ammonius, while undoubtedly taking much from his great master, Numenius, tried to reconcile Plato and Aristotle, and thus laid the foundation of mysticism and electicism for Neo-Platonism. He is said to have died in 243.

3 Porphyry means to say that Origen was first a pagan, and was afterwards converted to Chritianity, but this universal tradition and Eusebius himself below deny. Porphyry might well have assumed that Origen had been a pagan in his youth, since his erudition in pagan learning was such as only a pagan youth would have acquired.

4 Cf. 6.12f.

5 Numenius, perhaps the first of the orientalizing Greek philosophers who were influenced by Christian ideas, and who prepared the way for Neo-Platonism. He was a prolific writer, but only fragments of his works are extant. Eusebius himself has preserved numerous fragments of his chief work, On the good, in the *Praep. Evang.* He lived in Syria about the middle of the second century.

and Moderatus[9] and Nicomachus,[10] and the distinguished
men among the Pythagoreans, and he also used the books of
Chaeremon[11] the Stoic and Cornutus,[12] from whom he learned

---

6 A celebrated Pythagorean philosopher and a contemporary of Numenius, closely related in their thinking. Cf. Porphyry, *Vita Plot.* 20.
7 This Apollophanes was a Stoic philosopher of Antioch in the third
century B.C., a disciple of Ariston of Chios. None of his works is extant.
8 A distinguished Greek philosopher and grammarian of the third
century A.D. He was brought up by his uncle Fronto, who taught
rhetoric at Athens, and so has been thought to have been a native of
that city. He later traveled widely and became acquainted with the
most famous philosophers of his age. He was a disciple of Ammonius
Saccas and Origen the pagan, and a teacher of Porphyry and others
less renowned. After spending some time at Athens, he went to the
East, and became acquainted with Zenobia of Palmyra. She made him
her teacher of Greek literature, and later her chief adviser. Under
his influence she broke off her allegiance to the Roman Empire. When
she was captured by Aurelian in 273, Longinus was put to death by
the emperor. Longinus was probably the greatest philosopher of his
age, but only a few fragments survive. The treatise, *On the Sublime,*
largely extant and commonly ascribed to him, is the work of an
earlier writer. In any case, it is written in an excellent style, and is
one of the best pieces of literary criticism in Greek.
9 Moderatus, a distinguished Pythagorean philosopher of the first
century A.D. His works, which had some influence over certain of the
Neo-Platonists, are no longer extant.
10 Nicomachus, a Pythagorean, of the first or second century A.D., famous
as a mathematician. A work of his on arithmetic and another on
music are extant.
11 Chaeremon, of Alexandria, a Stoic philosopher and chief librarian of
the Alexandrian library. He was later called to Rome, and became
the preceptor of Nero. He wrote a history of Egypt, also works on
hieroglyphics, on comets, and on grammatical subjects. His works,
except for a fragment of the first, are no longer extant.
12 L. Annaeus Cornutus, a distinguished Stoic philosopher, who was born
at Leptis in Lybia. He lived and taught in Rome during the reign of
Nero. Among his pupils and friends was the poet Persius, who
dedicated his fifth satire to him and left him his library and money.
He was banished by Nero in 68 for having criticized his literary
efforts too severely. Most of his numerous works have perished, but
his treatise *On the Nature of the Gods* has survived in a mutilated
form.

the figurative interpretation employed in the Greek mysteries and applied it to the Jewish Scriptures.'[13]

These things were spoken by Porphyry in the third of his treatises written against Christians, telling the truth about the man's training and learning but clearly speaking falsely (for what was not an opponent of Christians ready to do), when he says that he came over from the Greeks and that Ammonius fell from a religious life into the way of paganism. For, the facts of the teaching according to Christ were preserved by Origen from his ancestors,[14] and the facts of his inspired philosophy were maintained pure and unshaken by Ammonius even to the end of his life,[15] as the works of the man bear witness to the present day, for he enjoyed a high reputation among most people because of the writings which he left behind him, as, for example, the work entitled *The Harmony of Moses and Jesus,* and all the rest that are found in the possession of the lovers of good literature.

Let these things, then, be set forth to prove the calumny of the false accuser and Origen's great experience in the learning of the Greeks. On this subject he defends himself against some who rebuke him for his zeal in such matters,

---

13 The Alexandrian Jews some time before the Christian era made use of the allegorical method as they attempted to reconcile the Mosaic revelation with Greek philosophy, and to find in the former the teachings of the latter. Naturally, the early Christians, especially in Alexandria, were influenced by this existing method of interpretation, which made it possible for them to find in the Old Testament all the teachings of the Gospel. With Origen, allegorical interpretation reached its highest point of development. A threefold source of Scripture, corresponding to body, soul, and spirit, was taught by Origen. In that age allegory had permeated the atmosphere of the Church as well as that of the philosophical schools.

14 2.7ff.

15 Eusebius is certainly mistaken here. Ammonius Saccas was definitely not a Christian in later life. Cf. above, n. 2.

writing in a letter[16] as follows: 'But when, while I was devoted to the Word and the fame of our proficiency was spreading abroad, we were approached sometimes by heretics and sometimes by persons acquainted with Greek learning and especially philosophy, I decided to examine the teachings of the heretics and what the philosophers were reported to say about the truth. And we have done this, imitating Pantaeus,[17] who aided many before our time and had no small preparation in those subjects, and also Heraclas,[18] who now holds a seat in the presbytery of the Alexandrians, whom I discovered when he had already spent five years with him before I began to attend his lectures. Although he formerly used a common dress on account of his teacher, he put it aside and assumed and kept a philosopher's garb[19] until the present day, and does not cease to study the books of the Greeks according to his strength.'

So much did he say as he made his defense for his training in Greek. But at this time, while he was living at Alexandria, someone of the military appeared and gave a letter to Demetrius, the bishop of the community, and to the governor of Egypt at the time, from the ruler of Arabia,[20] to the effect that Origen should be sent with all speed for an interview with him. He presently arrived in Arabia, and, after he

---

16 Little can be said about this letter other than that it was written before Heraclas became Bishop of Alexandria and while Origen was in Alexandria and still working on the matter which he defends, probably before 216.

17 Cf. 5.10.

18 Cf. 6.3.

19 Cf. 4.11. The distinctive mantle of the Greek philosophers; in Latin, the *pallium*.

20 Probably a Roman and governor of the Roman province of Arabia, established by the Emperor Trajan in 106. Cf. 33 and 37, where it is recorded that Origen was summoned there twice to settle doctrinal difficulties.

accomplished the purpose of his visit in a short time, he returned again to Alexandria. And after some time intervened and no small war[21] broke out in the city, he left Alexandria, went to Palestine, and took up his residence in Caesarea. And there the bishops of that land asked him to preach and expound the divine Scriptures publicly in the church, although he had not yet received ordination to the presbyterate.[22] This should be clear from what Alexander,[23] Bishop of Jerusalem, and Theoctistus,[24] Bishop of Caesarea, wrote regarding Demetrius. They defend themselves somewhat as follows: 'And he added to his letter that this had never been heard of, nor taken place up to now—that laymen preach in the presence of bishops. I do not know how he comes to say what is clearly untrue. For example, when people are found suited to give aid to the brethren, they are urged by the holy bishops to preach to the laity, as in Laranda, Euelpis by Neon;[25] and in Iconium, Paulinus by Celsus; and in Synnada, Theodore by

---

21 In 215 Caracalla ordered the massacre of the inhabitants of Alexandria. Scholars were special objects of his fury. The occasion was a number of satirical and cutting remarks on the murder of his brother Geta which had come from Alexandria.

22 It was unusual for the laity to preach in the church even as early as this. Origen was evidently aware of it, but seems to have felt justified in doing so, since it was at the invitation of the bishops. Demetrius, however, felt otherwise, considering the public preaching of an unordained man forbidden at any time and in any place. This seems to have been the beginning of strained relations between Demetrius and Origen.

23 Cf. 6.8.

24 Theoctistus, Bishop of Caesarea, one of the most influential bishops of the East; probably dead when Xystus was bishop of Rome, and was succeeded by Domnus. Cf. 7.14.

25 Neon, Bishop of Laranda in Lycaonia; Celsus, Bishop of Iconium; and Atticus, Bishop of Synada in Phrygia; the laymen Euelpis, Paulinus, and Theodore are known only by name.

Atticus, our blessed brothers. It is probable that this happens
in other places and that we are unaware of it.'

The aforementioned person, while still a young man, was
honored in this way not only by his fellow countrymen but
also by the bishops in a foreign land. When Demetrius again
summoned him by letter and by men who were deacons to
return to Alexandria, he came back and resumed his work with
customary zeal.

Chapter 20

There flourished in the Church at this time more learned
men, whose letters, written to one another, can easily be
found still extant today. These have been preserved even to
our own time in the library at Aelia,[1] which was established
by Alexander who then ruled the Church there. From this
library we ourselves also have been able to gather material for
this very work at hand.

Of these, Beryllus[2] has left behind, along with letters, varied
and beautiful works. He was bishop of the Arabians at
Bostra. So also Hippolytus,[3] himself at the head of another
church somewhere.

And there has come to us, also, a dialogue by Gaius,[4] a
very learned man, which was in circulation at Rome during

---

1 Aelia, the city built by Hadrian on the site of Jerusalem; cf. 4.6.
2 Beryllus, Bishop of Bostra in Arabia; cf. 6.33.
3 Hippolytus, presbyter and antipope, greatest scholar of the Western
Church in the first three centuries, lived from c. 160 to c. 236. Most of
his works have been lost or are known only through scattered fragments, while much has survived only in old translations into Oriental
and Slavic languages; other writings are freely interpolated. For a
brief treatment of the many problems connected with the life and
activity of Hippolytus, cf. *Catholic Encyclopedia.*
4 On Gaius and Proclus, see 2.25.

the time of Zephyrinus,[5] against Proclus who championed the heresy of the Phrygians. When in this work he curbs the rashness and boldness of his opponents in composing new scriptures, he makes mention of only thirteen Epistles of the holy Apostle, not reckoning with these the one to the Hebrews, for even to this day among the Romans some do not consider it to belong to the Apostle.

Chapter 21

Macrinus succeeded Antoninus,[1] who had ruled for seven years and six months, and, after he had continued as ruler for a year, still another Antoninus undertook the government of the Romans. In the first year of his reign, Zephyrinus,[2] Bishop of Rome, departed this life, after holding his office for eighteen full years. After him Callistus[3] was entrusted

---

5 Bishop of Rome from 198 to 217; cf. 5.28.

1 Otherwise known as Caracalla, son of Septimius Severus and his second wife Julia Domna; born at Lyons 188; emperor from 211 to 217, when he was slain on April 8. After four days, Marcus Opellius Macrinus, prefect of the praetorians, was declared emperor. He reigned for fourteen months, and was defeated and succeeded by Varius Avitus Bassianus, a cousin of Caracalla. The latter is commonly known as Elagabalus, since he was a priest of the Phoenician sun god. When he became emperor he assumed the offical name of Marcus Aurelius Antoninus.

2 In 222; cf. 5.28.

3 In 217 or 218. All our information about Callistus comes from Book 9 of the *Philosophumena* or *Refutation of All Heresies,* of Hippolytus, his very bitter opponent, and from Tertullian. According to Hippolytus, Callistus was the slave of Carpophorus, a Christian of the household of Caesar. Being entrusted by his master with large sums of money, he started a bank in which brethren and widows deposited funds. All of this Callistus lost. He was punished for this dishonesty, and then courted death by insulting the Jews at their synagogue. He was then haled into court, and sent to the mines in Sardinia. After

with the episcopate, and when he had continued in life for five years he left his office to Urban.

After this, Alexander succeeded to the Roman rule, when Antoninus had continued in office for only four years.[5] At this time, also, Philetus[6] succeeded Asclepiades[7] in the church of the Antiochenes. The emperor's mother, Mamaea[8] by

various other adventures, when Zephyrinus became Pope, Callistus was recalled and set over the cemetery belonging to the Church. It has ever since borne his name. He became archdeacon and, after the death of Zephyrinus, pope. This sensational and for the most part scandalous story has been completely demolished by Dollinger and Rossi. For a good brief account, see the *Catholic Encyclopaedia,* art. 'Callistus I.' If we knew more about Callistus from Catholic sources, he would probably be considered one of the greatest popes. He died a martyr about 223.

4 Urban I, Pope (220-230). The date of his birth is unknown. He died on May 23, 230. According to the 'Liber Pontificalis,' Urban was a Roman and his father's name was Pontianus. According to Eusebius here, he was elected Bishop of Rome on the death of Callistus I, October 14, 222, and was head of the Church for eight years. We have no reliable information on his life and character.

5 After a reign of three years and nine months, Elagabalus was slain in March, 222. He was succeeded by his cousin, Alexianus Bassianus, who took the names Marcus Aurelius Alexander Severus but was known as Alexander Severus.

6 Philetus became Bishop of Antioch between 216 and 218, and was succeeded by Zebinus in 227. Nothing is known of the life and character of Philetus.

7 Cf. 6.11.

8 Julia Mamaea (or Mammaea), the daughter of Julia Moesa, and niece of Julia Domna, the wife of the Emperor Septimius Severus; also the mother of the Emperor Alexander Severus by the Syrian Gessius Marcianus. On the election of her nephew Elagabalus as emperor, she went with him and her son Alexander, then thirteen years of age, to Rome. On the death of Elagabalus, and the election of her son by the Pretorian Guard, she attained great power. In the midst of an extremely corrupt court, she exercised an excellent influence over the emperor and her son, and thus some effort has been made to declare her a Christian. However, even though Eusebius calls her a very religious woman, her religion, like that of Alexander's, seems to have been quite eclectic, including many Christian principles. Her leanings toward Christianity were exhibited especially when she was with the emperor in Antioch and invited Origen to visit her as

name, a very religious woman if ever there was one, since Origen's fame was so noised about that it even reached her ears, held it of great importance to obtain a sight of the man and to make a test of his understanding of divine things which was admired by all. When staying at the time in Antioch, she summoned him with a military escort. After he had stayed with her for a time and had shown her a great many things for the glory of the Lord and of the excellence of His divine teachings, he hastened back to his customary duties.

Chapter 22

At that time, too, Hippolytus,[1] besides composing very many other memoirs, finished the work *On the Pasch*,[2] in which he presents a chronological table and sets forth a certain paschal canon of sixteen years, bringing the time down to the first year of the Emperor Alexander. Of his other treatises, those that have come down to us are as follows: *On the Hexaëmeron*,[3] *On What Followed the Hexaëmeron*,[4]

---

described by Eusebius here. The date of this visit is hotly disputed, but the evidence seems to point to some time in the reign of Elagabalus, probably before 231. Mammaea shared her son's fate when the troops revolted and murdered him in Gaul. Her last hours were embittered by her son's reproaches for the pride and avarice which had caused their common ruin.

---

1 Cf. 6.20 n. 3.
2 A chronological work on the Passover, containing a cycle for determining the date of the festival; mentioned also by Jerome, and given in the list on the statue.
3 *On the Six Days of Creation*, mentioned also by St. Jerome, but in the list on the statue. No longer extant.
4 No fragments of this work have been identified; not mentioned in the list on the statue. Jerome speaks of a commentary *In Genesim*, which may be identical with this work mentioned by Eusebius.

Against Marcion,[5] *On the Canticle,*[6] *On Parts of Ezechiel,*[7] *On the Pasch,*[8] *Against All the Heresies,*[9] and a great many others, also, you might discover preserved by many.

Chapter 23

That time also marked the beginning of Origen's commentaries on the divine Scriptures, when Ambrose[1] urged him not only by countless verbal exhortations and incentives but also by furnishing abundant means. For, as he dictated, he had at hand more than seven shorthand writers, who relieved one another at appointed times, and copyists no fewer in number, as well as girls trained in beautiful penmanship. For all these Ambrose supplied the necessary means in abundance. Nay, even more, in his study and zeal about the divine oracles he brought to bear upon Ambrose an inexpressible enthusiasm by which he especially urged him on to the composition of the commentaries.

---

5 Mentioned also by Jerome, but not in the list on the statue. No fragments are extant.

6 This commentary on the Canticle of Canticles is also mentioned by Jerome, but does not appear in the list on the statue. Four fragments survived, published in Lagarde's edition of the works of Hippolytus.

7 This partial commentary on Ezechiel is mentioned nowhere else. A fragment of questionable authenticity is given by Lagarde.

8 Both Jerome and Eusebius mention a work *On the Passover,* besides the chronological work mentioned above. The list on the statue speaks only of the chronological one. Several fragments are extant.

9 Of his polemics against heretics the most important is the *Philosophumena,* the original title of which was *A Refutation of All Heresies.* The first book had long been known; Books 4-10 were discovered and published in 1851. The first chapters of Book 4 and all of Books 1-3 are still lost.

---

1 On Ambrose and Origen, cf. 6.18.

While these matters were taking place thus,[2] Pontianus succeeded Urban,[3] who had been bishop of the Church at Rome for eight years, and Zebenus[4] followed Philetus[5] as [bishop] of the church of the Antiochenes. In their time, Origen, because of a pressing necessity in ecclesiastical affairs, journeyed to Greece through Palestine, and received ordination to the presbyterate in Caesarea at the hands of the bishops there. Now, the matters that were agitated concerning him on this account and what was decided in the matters agitated by those in charge of the churches, and all the other contributions that he made on the divine Word while in his prime require a separate treatise, and we have described them moderately in the second [Book] of the *Apology* which we have prepared in his behalf.[6]

---

2 For the dates of the Roman bishops from Peter to Urbanus, Eusebius is our best source; for the dates of Pontianus through Liberius, he is very unreliable, and other sources, especially the Liberian catalogue, have to be used. Pontianus became bishop in 232 (cf. 6.21), and reigned until Sept. 28, 235, when he was banished to Sardinia. His body was returned to Rome and buried there during Fabian's episcopate, which began in 236. Nothing is known about the life and character of Pontianus.

3 On Urban, Bishop of Rome, cf. 6.21 n. 4.

4 Zebinus, according to information supplied by Eusebius, became bishop before 231. His successor was Babylas, who died in the Decian persecution (cf. 6.39), and so Zebinus must have died before that. Eusebius (6.29) places his death in the reign of Gordian (238-244). Nothing is now known of the character and life of Zebinus.

5 On Philetus, cf. 6.21.

6 The reference here is to the *Defense of Origen*, prepared by Origen and Pamphilus, and now lost.

Chapter 24

But we should add the following to that information: that in the sixth [Book] of his *Expositions* on the [Gospel] according to John[1] he points out that he composed the first five while he was still in Alexandria, but of this work on the entire self-same Gospel only twenty-two tomes have come down to us; that in the ninth of those *On Genesis*[2] (there are twelve altogether) he shows that not only those before the ninth were composed at Alexandria, but also those on the first twenty-five Psalms,[3] and, in addition, those on Lamentations,[4] of which five tomes have come down to us, in which mention is also made of those *On the Resurrection*.[5] These, too, are two in number. Moreover, he wrote his *De Principiis*[6]

1 This *Commentary*, the first fruits of his labors at Alexandria, is probably the most important of Origen's exegetical works. Still extant are Books 1, 2, 6, 10, 13, 20, 28, 32, small portions of 4 and 5, and the greater part of 19. Although a milestone in theological thought because of its originality, it is greatly marred by an extensive use of the method of allegory.

2 Of this commentary on Genesis we have only some fragments from Books 1 and 3, some extracts, and seventeen homilies (nearly complete) in a Latin translation by Rufinus. The commentary proper covered only the early chapters of Genesis; the homilies, various parts of Genesis.

3 A complete commentary, brief notes, and homilies. Now extant are numerous fragments in Greek, and nine homilies in the Latin translation of Rufinus. St. Jerome mentions forty-six books of notes and 118 homilies.

4 All sources agree on five books. Some selections are extant.

5 Jerome speaks of two books and two dialogues on the Resurrection. Some fragments remain.

6 The first effort to establish a system of Christian doctrine. It was written before Origen left Alexandria, and we still have fragments in Greek, short passages of a translation by St. Jerome, and a complete but garbled translation by Rufinus. The four books were divided as follows: Books 1 on God and creation, Books 2 and 3 on creation and providence, on man and redemption, and Book 4 on holy Scripture.

before his departure from Alexandria, and those books entitled *Stromateis,*[7] which are ten in number, he composed in the same city in the reign of Alexander, as the notes entirely in his own hand in the front of the tomes show.

Chapter 25

Now, when he expounded the first Psalm, he made a presentation of a catalogue of the sacred Scriptures of the Old Testament, writing somewhat in the following words: 'It should be known that, according to Hebrew tradition, there are twenty-two canonical books, the same as the number of the letters in their alphabet.'

Then, further on, he adds in these words: 'The twenty-two books according to the Hebrews are these: That which among us is called Genesis, but among the Hebrews from the beginning of the book, *Brēsith,* that is, "In the beginning"; Exodus, *Ouelle smōth,* that is, "These are the names"; Leviticus, *Ouïkra,* "And he called"; Numbers, *Ammes phekōdeim;*[1] Deuteronomy, *Elle addebareim,* "These are the words"; Jesus, son of Nave, *Iōsoue ben noun;* Judges, Ruth, with them in one book, *Sōphteim;*[2] of Kingdoms I, II, with them one, *Samuel,* "The called of God"; and of Kingdoms, III, IV, in one, *Ouammelch David,* that is, "The Kingdom of David";

---

7 Jerome (*Ep. ad Magnum* 4) states that Origen wrote ten books of *Stromata,* imitating Clement's work. In it he compares the thinking of Christians with that of Greek philosophers, attempting to confirm Christian teachings by appealing to Plato and others. Only three fragments of a Latin version are extant.

---

1 Namely, 'the fifth book of the precepts' or 'of the mustered man.'
2 'Judges,' a translation of the Hebrew.

of the Chronicles, I, II, in one, *Dabre iamein*, that is, "Words of Days"; Esdras, I, II, in one, *Ezra*, that is, "Helper"; Book of Psalms, *Sphar thalleim*; Proverbs of Solomon, *Melōth*; Ecclesiastes, *Kōelth*; Song of Songs (not, as some suppose, Songs of Songs), *Sir assireim*; Esaias, *Iessia*; Jeremias with Lamentations and the Letter, in one, *Jeremia*; Daniel, *Daniēl*; Ezekiel, *Ezekiēl*; Job, *Job*; Esther, *Esthēr*. And besides these there are the Maccabees, which are entitled *Sar bēth sabanai el.*'[3]

These matters, then, he places in the above-mentioned work. But in the first of his *Commentaries on the Gospel according to Matthew,*[4] defending the canon of the Church, he testifies that he knows only four Gospels,[5] writing somewhat as follows: 'For I learned by tradition concerning the four Gospels, which alone are indisputable in the Church of God under heaven, that first there was written that according to the one-time tax-collector and later Apostle of Jesus Christ, Matthew, who published it for those who from Judaism came to have the faith, being composed in the Hebrew language;[6] secondly, that according to Mark, which he wrote as Peter[7] guided him, whom also Peter acknowledged as son in his Catholic Epistle, speaking with these words: "The church that is in Babylon, elected together with you, salutes you: and so does my son

---

3 There is a textual difficulty here. The word probably means: 'The history of the house of the warriors.'

4 Cf. 6.36, on Origen's *Commentary on Matthew*. This fragment alone is extant of Book 1 of the *Commentary*.

5 The essentially universal tradition in the early Church is that the number of true Gospels was four. Some, as Irenaeus (*Adv. Haer.*), attempted to show that the number could neither be more nor less than four. Cf., also, the Muratorian fragment, Tertullian's *Adv. Marc.* 4.2, and others.

6 Cf. 3.24.

7 Cf. 2.15.

Mark";⁸ and thirdly, that according to Luke, who composed
this Gospel, which was praised by Paul,⁹ for Gentile converts;
and in addition to them all, that according to John.'¹⁰

And in Book of his *Expositions on the Gospel according to
John* the same writer speaks as follows regarding the Epistles
of the Apostles:¹¹ 'But he who was made fit to become a
minister of the new testament, not in the letter but in the
spirit, Paul,¹² who replenished the Gospel from Jerusalem
round about as far as unto Illyricum,¹³ did by no means write
to all the churches which he had taught, but even to those to
which he wrote he sent only a few lines.¹⁴ And Peter, on
whom the Church of Christ is built, against which the gates
of hell shall not prevail,¹⁵ has left behind one acknowledged
Epistle, and perhaps also a second, for it is questioned.¹⁶ Why
need I speak of him who leaned on the breast of Jesus,¹⁷
John, who has left behind one Gospel, while confessing that
he could compose so many that not even the world itself
could contain them;¹⁸ who also wrote the Apocalypse,¹⁹ when
he had been ordered to keep silence and not to write the
words of the seven thunders? He has left behind also an
Epistle of very few lines, and perhaps also a second and a

8 1 Pet. 5.13.
9 Cf. 3.4; also, cf. 2 Cor. 8.18.
10 Cf. 3.24.
11 This fragment of Book 5 of Origen's *Commentary on John* is pre-
    served here alone.
12 Cf. 2 Cor. 3.6.
13 Cf. Rom. 15.19.
14 Cf. 3.24.
15 Cf. Matt. 16.18.
16 On the first and second Epistles of Peter, cf. 3.3.
17 Cf. John 13.25.
18 Cf. John 21.25.
19 Cf. Apoc. 10.3,4; cf., also, above, 3.3.

third—for not all say that these are genuine—but the two together do not contain a hundred lines.'

Besides these he comments as follows on the Epistle to the Hebrews[20] in his *Homilies* upon it; 'That the character of the diction of the Epistle entitled "To the Hebrews" does not possess the Apostle's rudeness of speech, who acknowledged that he was rude in speech,[21] that is, in style, but the Epistle is better Greek in the composition of its diction, as anyone who knows how to distinguish differences of phraseology would admit. And yet again, that the thoughts of the Epistle are admirable, and not inferior to the acknowledged writings of the Apostle, this also anyone would agree to be true who gives attention to reading the text of the Apostles.'

Further on he adds to this when he says: 'But I would say, if giving my opinion, that the thoughts are those of the Apostle, but the phraseology and the composition are those of someone who recalled to mind the teachings of the Apostle and who, as it were, had made notes on what was said by the teacher. If any church, then, holds this Epistle to be Paul's let it be commended for this, for not without reason have the men of old handed it down as Paul's. Who the author of the Epistle is God truly knows, but the account that has reached us from some is that Clement, who was Bishop of the Romans, wrote the Epistle; from others, that Luke, who wrote the Gospel and the Acts, is the author.'

---

20 On the Epistle to the Hebrews, and Origen's treatment of it, cf. 3.3. The only fragments of Origen's *Homilies on the Epistle to the Hebrews* extant are these quotations by Eusebius. Nothing is known of the extent or of the date of composition of these homilies and commentaries.

21 Cf. 2 Cor. 11.6.

Chapter 26

But let this suffice on these matters. This was the tenth year of the above-mentioned reign[1] in which Origen made his departure from Alexandria for Caesarea, and left the catechetical school of that city to Heraclas. And not much later Demetrius, the bishop of the church of the Alexandrians, died, having fulfilled the duties of his office for forty-three complete years,[2] and Heraclas succeeded him.

Chapter 27

At this time Firmilian,[1] Bishop of Caesarea in Cappadocia, was prominent, displaying such esteem for Origen that on one occasion he summoned him to his land to give aid to the churches, and on another, himself journeyed to Judaea and spent some time with him for his own improvement in divine matters. Yet Alexander,[2] who was in charge of the Church in

1 In 231, the tenth year of Alexander Severus.
2 In 232.

1 Firmilian, Bishop of Caesarea in Cappadocia, died about 269. According to Eusebius (6.26,27), he already occupied his see in 232. He was a friend of Origen, as is seen from the next chapter. He took part in a council called to consider the schism of Novatian, and also in other councils to study the case of Paul of Samosata. At Tarsus, while on his way to Antioch to attend one of these latter, he died. He was Bishop of Caesarea for at least thirty-four years. He was one of several bishops excommunicated by Stephen for rebaptizing heretics (cf. below, 7.2), and he wrote a letter to Cyprian on the subject, when questioned by Cyprian. This letter in a translation by Cyprian himself is extant (Cyprian, *Ep.* 75). To his contemporaries, his nearly forty years of influential reign as bishop, Cyprian's appeal to him, and his censure of Stephen made him seem the most conspicuous personage of his time.
2 On Alexander, Bishop of Jerusalem, cf. 6.8.

Jerusalem, and Theoctistus,[3] who was in charge at Caesarea, waited patiently the whole time upon him[4] as their only teacher, and yielded to him the task of interpreting the divine Scriptures and of performing the other matters of the Church's instruction.

Chapter 28

Now, the Roman emperor, Alexander, having brought his reign to an end after thirteen years, was succeeded by Maximin Caesar.[1] Because of his hatred for the house of Alexander, which consisted for the greater part of believers, he raised a persecution and ordered that the leaders of the Church alone be put to death for being responsible for the teaching according to the Gospel. Then Origen composed his work *On Martyrdom*,[3] dedicating the work to Ambrose and Protoctetus,[4] a presbyter of the parish of Caesarea; for extraordinary hardships fell upon them both during the persecution, in which the record holds that these men were

---

3 On Theoctistus, Bishop of Caesarea in Palestine, cf. 6.19.
4 To Origen, whom these bishops had ordained a presbyter, they gave full liberty to preach and teach within their dioceses.

---

1 Alexander Severus was murdered in 235. The Thracian Maximinus (Caius Julius Verus Maximinus), his commanding general, succeeded him.
2 I.e., the whole court, servants and all. Maximin's hostility toward the Christians seems to have been due not to religious feelings but to hatred for his predecessor and all that he favored. In addition, the people were roused by the belief that current earthquakes and disasters were due to the existence of the Christians. Under Maximin, also, all had free rein, whenever they felt inclined, to persecute as they pleased. Although Eusebius says nothing on the subject, from Palladius (*Hist. Laus.* 147) it is presumed that Origen was given refuge in Cappadocian Caesarea by Juliana.
3 Still extant; very beautiful and inspiring.
4 Cf. 6.18, on Ambrose. Protoctetus is known only from this reference.

pre-eminent in confession, as the reign of Maximin continued
for no more than three years. Origen has noted this particular
time for the persecution in the twenty-second of his *Commentaries on the Gospel according to John* and in different
letters.[5]

Chapter 29

After Maximin, Gordian[1] succeeded to the sovereignty over
the Romans, and Anteros[2] succeeded Pontianus[3] after he had
been bishop of the Church of Rome for six years, and Fabian[4]
succeeded him, after he had exercised his office for a month.
It is reported[5] that Fabian came from the country with others
after the death of Anteros and was staying at Rome when
he came into the office by a most marvelous display of divine
and heavenly grace. For, when all the brethren had assembled
to select him who was to succeed to the episcopacy and many

5 Cf. 6.24. No fragments are extant of Book 22 of the *Commentaries*,
and none of these epistles.

1 The younger, grandson of Gordian I and nephew or, perhaps, son of
Gordian II. In July 238, when Balbinus and Pupienus were murdered,
he became emperor at the age of fifteen in 244, he was murdered by
his soldiers and was succeeded by Philip. Only two or three months
elapsed between the death of Maximin and the succession of Gordian;
hence, Eusebius calls him a direct successor.
2 Nothing is known of his life and character.
3 Cf. 6.23. Pontianus was succeeded by Anteros in 235, three years
earlier than the date assigned by Eusebius.
4 Other sources than Eusebius are to be followed in determining the
dates of Fabian. His accession was in January 236, and his martyrdom
in January 250, after a reign of fourteen years and ten days. Cf. the
Liberian catalogue, and for his martyrdom cf. Jerome's *De vir. ill.* 54,
and Cyprian's *Epistles* 3 and 30. Eusebius 6.39 agrees with this last.
According to Cyprian, he was a person of great ability and virtue.
Tradition, however, has bequeathed many unfounded stories about
him to posterity.
5 Rufinus (6.21) tells the same story about Zephyrinus.

renowned and famous men were in the thoughts of many, Fabian, although present, came into no one's mind, but they relate that then suddenly a dove flew down from on high and settled upon his head, clearly imitating the descent of the Holy Spirit in the form of a dove upon the Saviour.[6] Thereupon, all the people, as if roused by one divine Spirit, with all eagerness and with one soul shouted that he was worthy, and without delay took and placed him upon the episcopal throne.

At that time, when the Bishop of Antioch, Zebennus,[7] also departed this life, Babylas[8] succeeded to the rule; and in Alexandria, Heraclas[9] received the episcopal office after Demetrius,[10] and Dionysius[11] succeeded to the leadership of the catechetical school there. The latter had also been one of Origen's pupils.

Chapter 30

While Origen was performing his customary duties at Caesarea, not only did many of the natives come to him but also numerous students from foreign lands who had left their

6 Cf. Luke 3.22.
7 Cf. 6.23.
8 Babylas was the twelfth Bishop of Antioch. He made a firm confession of faith during the Decian persecution (250), and was cast into prison where he died of his sufferings (6.39). Chrysostom inaccurately states that he died from violence. The existing *Acta Babylae* are spurious. Honorable mention is made of him by many of the fathers, e.g., John Chrysostom *(De Sancto Babyla contra Julianum et contra Gentiles)*, Jerome, Epiphanius, Sozomen, Theodoret, and others.
9 Cf. 6.3.
10 Cf. 5.22.
11 Cf. 6.40.

own countries. Especially celebrated among these we know to have been Theodore, who was himself that famous bishop of our own day, Gregory,[1] and his brother Athenodore. Since they were deeply enamored of Greek and Roman learning, he instilled in them a passion for philosophy and urged them to exchange their former zeal for theology. They remained with him for five years, and made such progress in divine matters that both, while still young, were thought worthy of the episcopacy of churches in the Pontus.

1 Gregory of Neo-Caesarea, known as Thaumaturgus (the Wonder-worker), born at Neo-Caesarea in Pontus (Asia Minor) about 213 and died there between 270 and 275. He holds a very prominent place among those bishops of Asia Minor who built up the Church and extended its influence. His pastoral work is only slightly known, and his theological writings are only partially preserved, but his fame and personality was widespread among his contemporaries and following generations. The sources for our knowledge of Gregory are accordingly numerous but not all reliable. Eusebius mentions him here and in 7.14,18. We possess Gregory's *Panegyrical Oration* in praise of Origen, which is the first attempt at biography in Christian literature. Gregory of Nyssa nearly a century later wrote a life of the Wonder-worker, but it is not trustworthy. St. Jerome (*De vir. ill.* 65) gives a brief biography, including a list of his writings. Arriving at Caesarea, in Palestine, on his way to Berytus, where he and his brother Athenodore were to study law, he met Origen, and he was so fascinated by him that he remained there for five years to study various subjects, especially theology. The brothers then returned to Pontus, and later were made bishops: Gregory of his native Neo-Caesarea, and Athenodore of some unknown city. He was undoubtedly an outstanding scholar, and was universally respected and loved for his genuine piety and ability, but he was famous chiefly for the reports of his miracle-working. It is noteworthy that Eusebius is silent about this phase of his career. His chief extant works are: the *Panegyrical Oration* in praise of Origen, given before a great multitude on Gregory's departure from Caesarea; a paraphrase of the Book of Ecclesiastes; only one of several epistles referred to by St. Jerome; and a trinitarian creed given by Gregory of Nyssa in his *Vita*.

Chapter 31

At this time Africanus[1] also, the author of the books entitled *Cesti,* was well known. A letter of his, written to Origen, is extant, in which he is at a loss as to whether the story of Susanna in Daniel is spurious and fictitious. Origen made a very detailed reply to this. Other works by the same Africanus which have come down to us are the five books of *Chronographies,* very laboriously and accurately achieved. In these he says that he himself made a journey to Alexandria because of the great fame of Heraclas, who, we have indicated,[2] excelled exceedingly in philosophic studies and other Greek learning and was entrusted with the episcopacy of the church there. Another letter by the same Africanus to Aristides is extant on the supposed discord between the analogies of Christ in Matthew and Luke. In this he establishes very clearly the harmony of the Evangelists according to an account which had come down to him and which I have already set forth in its proper place in Book 1 of the present work.[3]

---

1 Julius Africanus, so called by Jerome, was one of the most learned men of the pre-Nicaean period. He is the father of Christian chronography. Little is known of his life (*c.* 160-*c.* 240) and little is preserved of his work. He is important chiefly through his influence on Eusebius and on all the later writers of Church history among the Fathers and on Greek chroniclers in general. His writings are: the *Chronicle* in five books, which covers the time from the Creation (5499 B.C. according to his calculation) to the third year of Elagabalus (A.D. 221) ; the *Cesti* ('embroidered girdles' or 'puzzles') , a kind of encyclopedia of the sciences, full of curious anecdotes and illustrations; two letters, one to Origen in which he questions the authenticity of the story of Susanna, the second to a certain Aristides in which he discusses two possible genealogies of our Lord; and other writings are mentioned but they are not extant.
2 Cf. 3.2; 15; 19.13f.; 26.
3 Cf. 1.7.

Chapter 32

And at this time also the *Commentaries* on Isaias[1] were being composed, and at the same time also those on Ezekiel.[2] Of the former of these, thirty books on the third part of Isaias, up to the vision of the beasts in the desert, have come down to us;[3] and on Ezekiel twenty-five, the only ones which he has composed on the entire Prophet. While he was at Athens[4] at this time, he finished the commentaries on Ezekiel, and began those on the Song of Songs,[5] bringing them forward to the fifth book. After he returned to Caesarea he brought these also to completion, to the number of ten books. Why should we compose the exact catalogue of the man's works at the present moment, since it requires a special study? We did compose this in our account of the life of Pamphilus, the holy martyr of our own time, in which, while setting forth how great was Pamphilus'[6] zeal for divine things, I presented

---

1 Jerome refers also to homilies and notes on Isaias. Today, only two short fragments of Books 1 and 8 of the *Commentary,* and nine homilies in a Latin translation by Jerome, are extant.

2 Jerome declares that Origen wrote twenty-nine books of a *Commentary on Ezekiel.* Today, only the fragment of Book 20 in Greek referred to above, and fourteen homilies in a Latin translation by Jerome, and a few extracts are preserved.

3 Cf. Isa. 30.6.

4 The cause or date of this visit are unknown. Eusebius would place it in the reign of Gordian (238-244). He apparently stayed at Athens for some time, and had leisure for study, for while there he finished his *Commentary on Ezekiel* and completed five books of his *Commentary on Canticles.*

5 Jerome's catalogue mentions ten books on Canticles, also two books written early, and two homilies; the *Philocalia* (ch. 7) speaks of a small book on Canticles written in Origen's youth; and Eusebius notes a *Commentary on Canticles,* of which five books were written in Athens, and five more in Caesarea. Of these, Rufinus has preserved the prologue and five books in a Latin translation; Jerome, a Latin translation of two homilies; and Procopius, some Greek quotations.

6 On Pamphilus, cf. Introduction, Vol. I.

the items in the library that he had brought together of the works of Origen and of other ecclesiastical writers. From these it is possible for anyone who pleases to obtain the most complete knowledge of the works of Origen that have come down to us. But we must proceed now with the continuation of our history.

Chapter 33

Beryllus,[1] whom we mentioned a little above as Bishop of Bostra in Arabia, perverted the Church's standard and tried to introduce matters foreign to the faith, daring to say that our Saviour and Lord did not pre-exist in a form of being peculiar to Himself before His sojourn among men, nor has He a divinity of His own, but only that of the Father dwelling in Him. Thereupon, when a great many bishops had carried on investigations and discussion with the man, Origen, being invited together with others, first entered into a conference with the man, attempting to discover what his mind was, and, when he knew what he meant, he corrected his unorthodox thinking, and persuaded him by reasoning, and he established

---

1 Cf. 6.20. Beryllus, Bishop of Bostra in Arabia (erroneously called Bishop of Philadelphia by Socrates), one of the most learned teachers of the Church, was known chiefly for his heretical views as to the Person of Christ. A synod was called at Bostra in 244 to consider this, and the bishops unanimously condemned his teaching, declaring that Christ at His Incarnation was endowed with a human soul (cf. Socrates, *H.E.* 3.7). However, they were unable to convince Beryllus of his error. Origen, who was residing at Caesarea at the time, having been excommunicated at Alexandria, convinced him of his error and won him back. According to Eusebius, Beryllus wrote numerous treatises and epistles, which were available to him. Jerome (*De vir. ill.* 60) says: 'He wrote various little works and especially letters among which he gives thanks to Origen.' Jerome also says that epistles of Origen to Beryllus were extant in his time, as well as a dialogue between Origen and Beryllus. Nothing of any of these works remains.

him in the truth regarding the doctrine, and restored him to his former sound opinion. And there are still extant down to this very day written records both of Beryllus and of the synod that was held on his account, which include the questions put to him by Origen and the discussions that were carried on in his parish and the details of what happened at that time. Now, the older men of our time have handed down countless other things about Origen, which I think it best for me to pass over, since they have no connection with the work at hand. But, all those matters about him which it was necessary to know one may also gather from the *Apology* written in his behalf by us and that holy martyr of our day, Pamphilus. We composed this zealously, collaborating with each other, because of his fault-finders.

Chapter 34

After Gordian had held sway over the Romans for six full years, Philip together with his son Philip succeeded to the power.[1] Story holds that this man,[2] being a Christian, wished

---

1 In 244. The younger Gordian was murdered by the soldiers. His pretorian prefect, Philip of Arabia, taking the name Marcus Julius Philippus, succeeded him, and reigned until 249, when he was overcome and succeeded by Decius. His son Philip, seven years old at the time of his father's accession, was at once proclaimed Caesar and then received the title of Augustus. He adopted the full name of Marcus Julius Philippus Severus, and was slain at the same time as his father.

2 It is to be noted that Eusebius here merely gives an oral tradition of his day. In his *Life of Constantine*, however, he calls Constantine the first Christian emperor. Jerome (*De vir. ill.* 54) definitely states that Philip was the first Christian emperor, and this became the general tradition of the Church. He probably was merely repeating as definite what Eusebius states as possible. The sources do not support Jerome's statement.

on the day of the last paschal vigil to share with the multitude
in the prayers at the church, but was not permitted to enter
by the one[3] who was presiding at the time until he had
confessed and had numbered himself among those reckoned
to be in sins and occupying the place of penance;[4] otherwise,
had he not done so, he would never have been received by
him because of the many charges made against him. He is
said to have complied even eagerly, displaying by action his
genuine and pious disposition toward the fear of God.

Chapter 35

It was the third year of this emperor when Heraclas[1]
departed this life after a reign of sixteen years over the
churches of Alexandria, and Dionysius[2] took up the episcopacy.

Chapter 36

At this time, then, as was fitting, when the faith was
spreading and our doctrine was being boldly proclaimed

---

3 According to Chrysostom *(De S. Bab. c. Gentes)* and Leontius of
Antioch (quoted in *Chron. pasch.*), this bishop was Babylas of
Antioch.

4 In the early Church, Christians who had committed serious transgressions were excluded from communion, and, before they were
received again into the Church, had to undergo a course of penance
according to the offense.

---

1 In 247. On Heraclas, cf. 6.3 n. 2.

2 On Dionysius, cf. 6.40.

before all, it is said that Origen, who was over sixty years old,[1] since he had acquired great facility from long practice, permitted shorthand writers to take down the discourses delivered by him in public, which he had never before permitted to be done.

At this time, also, he composed the works, eight in number, in answer to the treatise written against us, and entitled *True Discourse of Celsus*[2] *the Epicurean,* and the twenty-five volumes on the Gospel according to Matthew,[3] and those on the twelve Prophets, of which we have discovered only twenty-five.[4] And there is extant also a letter by him to the Emperor Philip[5] himself, and another to his wife Severa, and various others to various persons. As many of these as have been preserved here and there and we have been able to gather

---

1 Origen was born in 185 or 186, and so this must have been as late as 245. Probably all of Origen's homilies which are now preserved were delivered after this time, and, as Eusebius says, were taken down by stenographers. The Christians were becoming increasingly bold because of their unusually comfortable condition under Philip.

2 Celsus was the first great literary opponent of Christianity. Nothing certain is known of his personal history. The *True Discourse*, no longer extant, can be reconstructed for the most part from Origen's reply to it. The entire work of the *Reply* was composed by Origen in eight books.

3 As Eusebius says here, Origen wrote the commentary on Matthew toward the end of his life. Extant are a single fragment from Book 1 (cf. 6.25) ; one from Book 2 (cf. *Philocalia* 6) ; and Books 10-17 entire, in Greek, treating Matt. 13.16-22.33. Numerous notes, some from the commentary and others from the homilies, and a Latin version of the commentary covering Matt. 16.13-27, are also extant.

4 Jerome mentions also twenty-five books on the twelve Prophets; he had found a copy of this, transcribed by the hand of Pamphilus (*De vir. ill.* 75) , in the library of Caesarea. Only one fragment of the *Commentary on Osee* is extant (cf. *Philocalia* 8) .

5 The epistles to Philip and to Severa, his wife, are not extant, nor is any means at hand of finding an adequate notion of their contents.

together,[6] we have arranged in separate bookcases that they may no longer be scattered; they surpass a hundred in number. He also wrote to Fabian,[7] Bishop of Rome, and a great many other rulers of churches, with regards to his orthodoxy. You have these facts also established in Book 6 of the *Apology* we wrote in the man's behalf.

Chapter 37

Again in Arabia[1] at the above-mentioned time others arose to introduce a doctrine foreign to the truth, who stated that human souls at the determined time perish for a while together with the bodies at their death, but that at the time of the resurrection will be revived with them. Then, when a synod of no small size was assembled, Origen was again invited and there roused discussion publicly on the subject in question, and he was of such influence that the opinions of those who had formerly been deceived were changed.

---

6 Eusebius' collection of Origen's epistles is no longer extant. Jerome in his catalogue speaks of 'eleven books of letters in all; two books in defense of his works.' Only the epistle to Julius Africanus (6.31) and that to Gregory Thaumaturgus (6.30) are preserved entire. Only several additional fragments are extant.

7 On Fabian, cf. 6.29 n. 4. The date of this letter is unknown. Its contents can only be conjectured to have had some connection with suspicions of Origen's heterodoxy.

---

1 It is difficult to determine the exact nature of the heresy described by Eusebius here. As to the time of the synod mentioned here we can only say that it was after the one concerned with Beryllus, and thus toward the close of Philip's reign.

Chapter 38

At that time also the so-called heresy of the Helkesaites[1] began another distortion of the truth, but it was extinguished even as it began. Origen mentions it in a public homily on Psalm 82,[2] speaking somewhat as follows: 'Someone[3] has come just now bragging about his ability to champion an atheistic and most impious opinion which is called "of the Helkesaites" and has recently risen against the churches. Such evils as that opinion speaks shall be presented to you that you may not be swept away by it. It rejects some things from every Scripture; again, it has made use of the texts of all the Old Testament and the Gospels; it rejects the Apostle[4] entirely. It says that to deny is a matter of indifference and that he who is wise will deny under necessity with his mouth but not with the heart. And they present a certain book which they

---

1 Helkesaites (Elcesaites), a sect of Gnostic Ebionites, whose religion was a wild medley of pagan superstitions and Christian doctrines with Judaism. Hippolytus (*Philosophumena* 9.13-17) says that a cunning individual called Alcibiades, a native of Axamea in Syria, came to Rome, bringing a book which he said had been received from Parthia through a just man named Helkasai. Others derive the name not from a person but the book. The sect taught circumcision, that Christ was born like others, that he had many times been born on earth of a virgin, that he devoted himself to astrology, magic, and incantations. For all sins of impurity, even against nature, a second baptism is enjoined 'in the name of the great and most high God and in the name of His Son the great King,' with an adjuration of the seven witnesses written in the book, sky, water, the holy spirits, the angels of prayer, oil, salt, and earth. This heresy does not seem to have played any important part in history, although it lasted a long time in the East. Cf. art. 'Elcesaites,' in *Catholic Encyclopedia*.
2 The only portion of Origen's homily on Psalm 82 extant.
3 According to Hippolytus, this was Alcibiades.
4 St. Paul.

say fell from heaven and that he who has heard it and believes[5] will receive remission of his sins, another remission in addition to that which Jesus Christ has granted.'

Chapter 39

Decius[1] succeeded Philip who had reigned for seven years.

---

5 Although Hippolytus describes the baptism of the Helkesaites with some detail, Origen does not mention it. Perhaps, according to Origen, receiving the book itself involved the peculiar baptism which it taught.

---

1 Philip, 'the Arabian', a native of Bostra in Trechontis. After being made pretorian prefect, he won the affections of the soldiers who deposed the younger Gordian and put him to death in March 244. Philip then succeeded to the throne. After making peace with Sapor the Persian king, he went on to Rome. In 248 the games to celebrate the thousandth anniversary of the founding of Rome were celebrated with great splendor. In the summer of 249 Philip was defeated by Decius near Verona and slain. Decius (Caius Messius Quintus Trajanus Decius), emperor from 249 to 251, was born near Sirmium in Pannonia of a Roman or Romanized family. Practically nothing is known of his career, not even the date of his birth, but he appears to have spent most of his life in the army. He was the first of the great soldier-emperors from the Danubian provinces under whom the senatorial regime ended and the government became an absolute monarchy. Decius, apparently a sincere Roman patriot, looked with dismay upon the terrible state of corruption and decay into which the Roman Empire had fallen. He was convinced that the only way to save the Empire was to restore the ancient Roman customs and to strengthen the ancient religion. He believed, moreover, that the ancient purity of the state religion might be more fully restored if the Christians were literally exterminated. This he attempted to do, and he has the dubious distinction of being the first to have attempted such a feat. He proceeded to his work systematically, and the persecution which followed was both universal and far more terrible than any which had preceded it. The edicts published by Decius early in 250 are no longer extant, but they are fully described in the writings of the Fathers, especially of Cyprian and Dionysius. It appears that at first every effort was made to induce the Christians to return to the paganism of the state, and when many refused the awful persecution

Decius, because of his hatred for Philip, stirred up a persecution against the churches, during which, when Fabian[2]
was perfected by martyrdom at Rome, Cornelius[3] succeeded
to the episcopacy.

In Palestine, Alexander,[4] bishop of the Church in Jerusalem,
again appeared for Christ's sake before the courts of the
governor and distinguished himself with a second confession.
He suffered the trial of imprisonment, crowned with the
hoary locks of ripe old age. When this man after his brilliant

---

began. But because of the suddenness of the attack and the wide
spread laxity and corruption which had manifested itself during the
long peace of the Church preceding, many apostacized. To those who
had offered sacrifice (*sacrificati*) or burned incense (*thurificati*)
tickets were issued attesting to the fact, while others, without actually
performing these rites, purchased certificates through the venality
of the magistrates which falsely attested their renunciation (*libellatici*).
From these circumstances arose the problem of deciding on what
conditions those who had fallen away (*lapsi*) should be admitted to
the Church and what weight was to be placed upon the pardon of
confessors.

2 Cf. 6.29.
3 Cornelius, Pope from 251 to 253, according to the Liberian catalogue,
reigned two years, three months, and ten days. His predecessor,
Fabian, was martyred by Decius on January 20, 250. Rome was
without a bishop for about fourteen months. About the beginning of
March 251, the persecution slackened because the emperor was obliged
to leave Rome to face two rivals. Sixteen bishops assembled at Rome,
and elected Cornelius against his will. A few weeks later the Roman
priest Novatian made himself antipope, and the entire Christian world
was in a turmoil over the schism. But through the loyalty of Cyprian,
the hundred bishops of Africa supported and recognized Cornelius,
and St. Dionysius the Great, Bishop of Alexandria, brought the East
within the fold in a few months. In the meantime, Decius was killed,
and his successor Gallus renewed the persecution. Cornelius fled with
a large part of the Church to Civita Vecchia, where he died in the
summer of 253. Eight epistles from Cyprian to Cornelius and two from
Cornelius to Cyprian are extant. Eusebius (6.43) quotes extensively
from an epistle from Cornelius to Fabius of Antioch, and mentions
others which are lost; he also makes mention (6.46) of one addressed
to Dionysius of Alexandria against Novatian, also lost.
4 Cf. 6.8.

and illustrious testimony in the governor's courts fell asleep in prison, Mazabanes[5] was proclaimed his successor to the episcopacy in Jerusalem. When, at Antioch, Babylas[6] in a manner similar to that of Alexander departed this life in prison after confession, Fabius[7] was placed over the Church there.

Now, how many and of what nature the experiences were which came to Origen during the persecution, and what was the nature of their result, when the evil demon arrayed himself with all his army in combat against the man, and maneuvered with every device and power against the man, and, above all, those who were being warred against at that time attacked him especially, and how many and of what nature were the sufferings which the man endured for the word of Christ, bonds and tortures of the body, and torments under iron and in the recesses of a prison, and how for a great many days, with his feet stretched four spaces[8] in that instrument of torture, the stocks, he steadfastly bore threats of fire, and all the other things inflicted by his enemies, and the nature of the outcome of his torments, as the judge strove

5 Alexander's death took place in the persecution of Decius, and he was succeeded without interval by Mazabanes. No definite date can be set. Mazabanes died no later than 265.
6 Cf. 6.29.
7 Very little is known of the life and character of Fabius. He acceded to the bishopric in Antioch on the death of Babylas during the persecution of Decius. He served as Bishop of Antioch while Cornelius was Bishop of Rome (cf. 6.43). He died while Cornelius was still bishop, before the summer of 253 (cf. 6.46).
8 The outmost limit for torture; cf. 8.10.
9 A tradition arose later that Origen died in the persecution of Decius, but this is definitely erroneous. We feel safe in following Eusebius here. Origen was imprisoned and cruelly tortured, but he held firm, and from his prison wrote letters in the spirit of the martyrs (6.36). He was still alive on the death of Decius (251), but only lingering. He died, probably as a result of the sufferings during the persecution (253 or 254), at the age of sixty-nine (7.1).

eagerly with all his might not to destroy him, the kind of saying he left behind after this, and these full of help for those who need comfort, the man's own many letters reveal both truthfully and precisely.[9]

Chapter 40

As for what befell Dionysius,[1] I shall quote from his letter

1 Dionysius of Alexandria, 'the Great,' bishop from 247-8 to 264-5, after St. Cyprian, the most eminent bishop of the third century; less a great theologian than a great administrator. He was born toward the close of the second century, studied under Origen, and succeeded Heraclas as chief of the catechetical school in Alexandria in 231 or 232 (cf. 63 and 29). In the third year of Philip's reign (246-247) he succeeded Heraclas as Bishop of Alexandria (cf. 6.35). Some believe that he continued to preside over the catechetical school even after he became bishop. He took an active part in all the controversies of the time, in the Novatian problem in which the readmission of the lapsed was the chief question; in the controversy over the rebaptism of heretics; and in the difficulty of Paul of Samosata (cf. 6.44; 7.5,7f.; 7.27). From the present chapter we learn that he was taken prisoner during the Decian persecution, but made his escape. The Emperor Valerian acceded in 253, but did not persecute until 257. In that year St. Cyprian was banished to Curubis, and St. Dionysius to Kephro in the Mareotis. He himself relates the firm answers which he gave the prefect, when writing to defend himself against the charge of a disgraceful flight made by a certain Germanus. He returned to Alexandria as soon as toleration was declared by Gallienus in 260. His writings are chiefly epistles, written for some practical purpose. Numerous fragments of these are preserved chiefly by Eusebius. Besides his epistles Eusebius (7.24,25,28) refers to a work *On Promises;* also, a commentary on the beginning of Ecclesiastes (7.26), and a work in four books against Sabellius, addressed to Dionysius, Bishop of Rome, defending himself against the charge of tritheism. He was able to clear himself of all suspicion of heresy in this matter. Athanasius defended his orthodoxy in a special work, *De Sententiis Dionysii.* When the heresy of Paul of Samosata, Bishop of Antioch, began to trouble the East, Dionysius wrote to the Church at Antioch on the matter, for he was obliged to decline the invitation to attend a synod there because of the infirmities of old age. He died soon thereafter.

to Germanus,[2] where, while speaking of himself, he relates as follows: 'I, too, speak before God, and He knows whether I lie; I have not taken flight driven in my own interests or without thought of God, but formerly, also, when the persecution under Decius was publicly proclaimed, within that very hour Sabinus[3] sent a *frumentarius*[4] to search for me, and I remained within my house for four days, expecting the arrival of the *frumentarius*; but he went about examining everything, the roads, the rivers, the fields, where he suspected I was hiding or going about, but he was smitten with blindness and did not find the house, for he did not believe that I when being pursued was tarrying at home. And after the fourth day, when God bade me depart and miraculously made a way, I and the boys[5] and many of the brethren set out together with difficulty. And that this was the work of the providence of God was shown by subsequent events, in which perhaps we were useful to some.'

Then, after some intervening statements, he shows what happened to him after the flight, adding the following: 'At about sunset I and those with me fell into the hands of soldiers. We were brought to Taposiris,[6] but Timothy[7] by the

---

2 Germanus, a bishop of some unknown see (cf. 7.11), who accused Dionysius of cowardice in the face of persecution. The letter of Dionysius quoted here and in 7.11 is a formal defense against the charge. It is addressed as much to the general public as to Germanus. The present fragment is devoted to the persecution of Decius, the later one to that of Valerian.

3 Sabinus, otherwise unknown, probably prefect of Egypt at this time.

4 *Frumentarius miles,* a military commissary, employed in various kinds of service, under the emperors usually as a secret spy.

5 Either the pupils or the servants of Dionysius; perhaps even the sons.

6 Near the coast, about thirty miles southwest of Alexandria.

7 Dionysius addressed his work *On Nature* to him according to Eusebius (7.26), where he is referred to as 'boy' (*ho pais*). Accordingly, some conclude that Timothy was Dionysius' scholar, others his son, assuming that Dionysius would not dedicate one of his works to a servant.

providence of God happened not to be on hand and escaped capture; he returned later and discovered the house deserted and servants guarding it, and ourselves reduced to slavery.'

And after other remarks he says: 'And what was the method of His wonderful arrangement? For the truth will be told. One of the countryfolk met Timothy as he fled in distress, and inquired the reason for his haste. And he spoke out the truth, and when the man heard it (he was on his way to a marriage feast, for it was their custom to spend the night at such gatherings), he went and told those reclining at the table. And they with a single impulse, as if at a preconcerted signal, all rose up, and moving on the run came quickly, and rushing in upon us gave a shout, and when the soldiers who were guarding us took to immediate flight they came upon us just as we were, lying upon cots without coverings. And I— God knows that at first I thought that they were robbers coming for spoil and plunder—remained on the bed, and I was naked but for a linen garment, and the rest of my clothes that lay beside me I held out to them. And they urged me to get up and go out very quickly. And then under-standing why they were come, I cried out, begging and beseeching them to go away and to leave us alone, and, if they wished to do us a good turn, I begged them to anticipate those who were leading us away, and to cut off my head themselves. While I was so shouting out, as my companions and those who shared everything with me know, they made me rise by force. And I let myself fall on my back upon the ground, but they seized me by the hands and feet, and dragged and brought me out. And the witnesses of all this—Gaius,

Faustus, Peter, and Paul[8]—followed me, who also seized and
carried me out of the village hastily, and, making me mount
the bare back of an ass, led me away.'[9] These things does
Dionysius tell about himself.

Chapter 41

The same writer, in a letter to Fabius,[1] bishop of the
Antiochenes, relates the struggles of those who suffered
martyrdom under Decius as follows: 'It was not with the
imperial decree that the persecution began among us, but the
persecution preceded it by a whole year,[2] and that prophet
and author of evils for this city, whoever he was, first stirred
up and roused the masses of the heathen against us, rekindling
the flame of their native superstition. And they, being roused
by him and seizing upon every authority for their unholy
action, considered this kind of worship of their gods, the
thirsting for our blood, as only a form of piety.

8 These four names are known to us only as companions of Dionysius
   during the persecution of Decius. From here and also from 7.11 the
   following bits of information are gleaned: after being carried away by
   the rescuing party mentioned here, Caius and Peter were alone with
   Dionysius in a desert place of Libya; Faustus was a deacon, ac-
   companied Dionysius during the persecution of Valerian, and suffered
   martyrdom at an advanced age in the persecution of Diocletian.
9 According to 7.11, he was taken to a desert place in Libya, where he
   remained with two companions until the persecution passed.

1 Cf. 6.39 n. 7.
2 Since the edict of Decius was issued early in 250, the persecution in
   Alexandria, according to this statement, began in 249, during the
   reign of Philip. This apparently was a local persecution, since Philip
   was quite favorable toward Christians.

'First they seized an old man, Metras[3] by name, and ordered him to make atheistic remarks. When he did not obey, they struck his body with clubs, and pierced his face and eyes with sharp reeds, and taking him into the suburbs they stoned him.

'Then they took a woman of the faith, called Quinta, to their idol temple, and tried to force her to worship; and when she turned away in disgust, they bound her by the feet and dragged her through the entire city over the rough pavement, the big stones bruising her, and at the same time they flogged her; and bringing her to the same place they stoned her to death. Then with one accord they all rushed to the homes of the pious, and, whomever they each knew as neighbors, falling upon them they led them forth, and despoiled and plundered them; appropriating the more valuable of the treasures, but scattering the poorer things and such as were made of wood and burning them in the streets, they created the appearance of a city captured by enemies. But the brethren turned away and gradually retired, and like those to whom Paul also bore witness took with joy the plundering of their possessions.[4] And I do not know whether anyone, unless someone somewhere who fell into their hands, up to this time denied the Lord.

'Further, they then seized the very marvelous virgin, an old lady, Apollonis, and they beat her jaws, knocking out all her teeth, and, heaping up a pyre in front of the city, they threatened to burn her alive if she should not join them in speaking declarations of infamy. But she begged off

---

3 The various martyrs and confessors mentioned here are otherwise unknown.
4 Cf. Heb. 10.34.

a little, and on being released eagerly leaped into the fire and was consumed.

'Serapion they seized at his house, and, after tormenting him with severe tortures and breaking all his joints, they cast him headlong from the upper story.

'There was no road, no thoroughfare, no alley passable for us, either by day or by night, since always and everywhere all cried out that, if anyone should not take part in their blasphemous speech, he must immediately be dragged off and burned. Actions of this sort flourished for a long time. But sedition and civil war in turn came upon the wretched people and directed their fury against us upon one another,[5] and for a little while we breathed again, since they did not take time to indulge their anger against us, but straightway the change from that rule[6] which was rather kind to us was announced, and the fear of threatened punishment against us loomed large. And presently the decree arrived, almost like that foretold by our Lord, little short of the most terrible of all, such as, if possible, to cause even the elect to stumble.[7] At any rate, all cowered with fear. And many of the more eminent came forward immediately in some instances through fear; others who held public positions were forced to do so by their official duties; still others were drawn on by those about them. As they were called by name they approached the impure and unholy sacrifices, some pale and trembling, as if not to perform a sacrifice, but themselves to be sacrifices

---

5 The closing months of the reign of Philip were disturbed by seditions in various places. This particular one has been identified with that described by Zosimus as having been caused in the Orient by excessive taxation and the bad government of Philip's brother.

6 Of Philip.

7 Matt. 24.24. Eusebius reads *skandalisai,* but Matthew *planásthai.*

and offerings for the idols, so that mockery was heaped upon them by the great crowd that stood around and it was clear that they were naturally cowardly in every respect, both as to dying and as to sacrificing; but some others ran to the altars more boldly, maintaining stoutly by their boldness that they had never been Christians even formerly, and concerning these the Lord's prediction is most true that they shall "hardly" be saved.[8] Of the remainder, some followed each of these; others fled; some were caught, and of these some went so far as "bonds and prisons";[9] some, too, after they had been confined for more days, then abjured themselves even before they came to trial; and still others, after remaining firm for a time against the tortures, subsequently renounced their faith.

'But the firm and blessed pillars of the Lord, being strengthend by Him, and obtaining power and steadfastness in accord with and worthy of the mighty faith that was in them, became wonderful martyrs of His kingdom. Of these, the first was Julian, a man afflicted with gout and unable to stand or to walk. He was brought up with two others who carried him, of whom the one immediately denied, but the other, Cronion by name, but surnamed Eunus, and the old man Julian himself, confessed the Lord, and were carried on camels through the entire city, which was very large, as you know, and thus elevated were beaten. Finally, when all the populace had gathered around, they were burned in quick-lime. A soldier who stood by them as they were being led off

---

8 Cf. Matt. 19.23; also, Mark 10.23; Luke 18.24. From this passage it is clear that Dionysius was willing to leave a possibility of salvation even to the worst on repentance. In this respect he is in full agreement with Cornelius, Cyprian, and the totality of Roman and Carthaginian churches.

9 Cf. Heb. 11.36.

and who opposed those who were insulting them, the most
noble warrior of God, Besas, when the people cried out, was
brought up, and after excelling in the great war of piety
was beheaded. And a certain other one, a Libyan by race,
true both to his name and the benediction [of the Lord],
Macar,[10] although much pressure was brought upon him by
the judge for a denial, was not induced and so was burned
alive. After these, Epimachus and Alexander, after they had
remained a long time as prisoners, endured countless agonies
from scrapers[11] and scourges, and they, too, were consumed
in quicklime.

'And with them four women: Ammonarion, a holy virgin,
when the judge tortured her very vigorously for a long time,
since she had declared beforehand that she would speak
nothing of what he ordered, having made her promise true,
was led away. As for the rest, the most revered aged woman
Mercuria, and she of many children, although she loved her
offspring more than the Lord, Dionysia, when the governor
became ashamed to carry on tortures to no avail and to be
worsted by women, met death by the sword, although they
had no further trial of tortures, for the champion Ammonarion
had taken these on in behalf of all.

'Hero and Ater and Isidore, Egyptians, and with them a
youth of about fifteen years, Dioscorus, were delivered up.
And at first when [the governor] tried to deceive the boy by
words, as one easily led astray, and to force him by tortures,
as one easily yielding, Dioscorus neither obeyed nor gave way.
He very savagely tore the rest in pieces, and when they
endured gave them also over to the fire. But, since he

10 'Blessed.' Cf. Matt. 5.10,11.
11 Of iron, designed to tear the flesh.

admired Dioscorus, who was so brilliant in public and answered most wisely to his questions in private, he dismissed him, saying that he granted him a respite for repentance because of his youth. And now the most marvelous Dioscorus is with us, having remained for a longer contest and a more lasting conflict.

'A certain Nemesion, he, too, an Egyptian, was falsely accused as an associate of robbers, but when he had cleared himself before the centurion of this charge so contrary to the truth, being informed against as being a Christian, he came bound before the governor. He most unjustly maltreated him with twice as many tortures and scourges as he did the robbers, and burned the blessed man between the robbers, thus honoring him by the likeness to Christ.[12]

'A whole band of soldiers, Ammon and Zeno and Ptolemy and Ingenuus, and with them an old man Theophilus, had taken their stand before the tribunal. When a certain man was being tried as a Christian and was inclined toward denial, they, standing by, gnashed their teeth, and made signs with their faces, and stretched out their hands, and gestured with their bodies. When the attention of all was directed toward them, before any could otherwise seize them, they rushed up first to the bench, saying that they were Christians, so that the governor and his assessors became fearful, and those who were being tried appeared most courageous in the face of what they were about to suffer, while their judges were afraid. And these paraded from the court, and rejoiced in their testimony,[13] as God led them in triumph gloriously.'[14]

---

12 Cf. Matt. 27.38; Mark 15.27; Luke 23.33; John 19.18.
13 Eusebius' language perhaps admits a twofold interpretation. The soldiers were either released or suffered martyrdom, probably the latter.
14 Cf. 2 Cor. 2.14.

Chapter 42

'And a great many others in cities and villages were torn to pieces by the heathen, of whom I shall mention one as an example. Ischyrion[1] was in the service of one of the rulers as a hired steward. The employer bade this man offer sacrifice; when he did not obey, he insulted him; when he remained steadfast, he abused him foully; since he still held out, he took a very large stick, drove it through his entrails and vital organs, and thus killed him.

'Why need we speak of the multitude of those who wandered in deserts and mountains,[2] and who perished from hunger and thirst and frost and diseases and robbers and wild beasts? Those of them who survived are witnesses of their election and victory, but I shall select one of their deeds as an illustration. Chaeremon,[3] a very old man, was bishop of the so-called city of Nilopolis. This man fled to the Arabian mountain, together with his wife,[4] and did not return, nor were the brethren able to lay eyes either on them or their bodies again, although they searched many places thoroughly. Many on that very Arabian mountain[5] were made slaves by the barbarian Saracens, some of whom were ransomed with difficulty for large sums of money; others have not yet been up to the present.

'I have related these things, brother, not without a purpose,

---

1 Known only from this passage.
2 Cf. Heb. 11.38.
3 Bishop of Nilopolis or Nilus, located on an island in the Nile, some distance south of Memphis. Nothing more is known about him.
4 *Súmbios*, a common word for husband or wife in later Greek.
5 The name, *tò Arábion óros*, was given by Herodotus to the mountains which separate the territory west of the Arabian Gulf from the Nile valley.

but that you may know the nature and the extent of the terrible things that happened to us. Those who have had greater experience in these matters would know more.'

Then to this, after a little, he added saying: 'So the divine martyrs themselves among us, those who are now assessors of Christ, and share His kingdom, and take part in His judgments, and make decisions with Him,[6] received some of the brethren who had fallen away and had become answerable to charges of sacrificing; and seeing their conversion and repentance, and thinking that it could be acceptable to Him who does not wish at all for the death of the sinner but for his repentance, received them back, and gathered them together, and met with them,[8] and had fellowship with them in prayers and feasts. What then do you counsel us, brethren, regarding these men? What must we do? Shall we be of the same opinion and of the same mind as they, and shall we observe their decision and charity and be merciful to those whom they pitied, or shall we hold their decision unjust, and establish ourselves as judges of their opinions, and cause grief to goodness, and to overturn their order?'

These words Dionysius very properly added when bringing up the consideration of those who had been weak in the time of the persecution.

6 Cf. Matt. 19,28; 1 Cor. 6.2,3; Apoc. 20.4.
7 Cf. Ezech. 33.11; 2 Peter 3.9.
8 The *consistentes*, or bystanders, the highest order of penitents, admitted to the Eucharistic prayers, but debarred from Holy Communion.

Chapter 43

For Novatus,[1] a presbyter of the Church at Rome, lifted up by arrogance against these, as if they no longer had hope of salvation, not even if they should perform everything in accord with a genuine conversion and a pure confession, became the leader of a special heresy of those who in the pride of their mind called themselves Puritans.[2] Thereupon, a very large synod was assembled at Rome,[3] sixty bishops in number, and still more presbyters and deacons, and individually in the remaining provinces the local pastors deliberated about what should be done. A decree was unanimously passed that Novatus, together with those who had joined him in

---

1 Cyprian and the Latins write the name Novatianus, but Eusebius and later Greek writers say Novatus. He was the founder of the Novatianists or Katharoi, the Novatianist sect. This was the first great schism in the Church not on a matter of dogma but on a question of discipline. In contrast to Cornelius, made Bishop of Rome in 251, who held that the lapsed on doing proper penance should be received back in the Church, Novatian was strongly opposed to their absolution and restoration. He was chosen Bishop of Rome in 251 in opposition to Cornelius. Fabius of Antioch was inclined to support him, but the other ecclesiastical leaders were loyal to Cornelius. On being excommunicated, he founded an independent church, and baptized all who came over to his side. According to the tradition of his followers and Socrates (*H. E.* 4.28), he suffered martyrdom under Valerian. His sect, spreading through East and West, lingered on into the sixth century. Contemporary sources for a knowledge of Novatian and his schism are: ten epistles of Cyprian, and the epistles of Dionysius and Cornelius, as quoted by Eusebius in 6.43-45; 7.8. Novatian, according to Jerome (*De vir. ill.* 10), wrote the following works: '*De Pascha, De sabbato, De circumcisione, De sacerdote, De oratione, De cibis Judaicis* (still extant), *De iustantia, De Attalo multaque alia, et De Trinitate grande volumen* (still extant).'

2 *Katharoi*, 'pure.'

3 The same as that mentioned by Cyprian in his letter (51.6) to Antonianus, held soon after the Carthaginian Synod (spring of 251), in which the problem of the *lapsi* was first discussed. It accepted the decisions of the Carthaginian Synod. It was held in October, 251.

arrogance, and those who chose to agree with the man's brother-hating and very inhuman opinion, be considered as outside the Church, and that those of the brethren who had fallen into the misfortune[4] be healed and treated with the medicines of repentance.

Now there has come to us a letter[5] of Cornelius, Bishop of Rome, to Fabius, of the church of the Antiochenes, disclosing what happened at the Synod of Rome and what was decided upon by those in Italy and Africa and the regions thereabout, and again another of Cyprian and of those with him in Africa,[6] composed in the Latin language, through which it was disclosed that they agreed with the necessity of those who had suffered trial obtaining succor, and with the reasonable need of the leader of the heresy and likewise all who were led away with him, being excommunicated from the Catholic Church. A certain other letter of Cornelius was joined to these concerning the resolution of the synod, and still another[7] concerning what Novatus did. Nothing should prevent me from quoting parts of this last letter, that those who read this work may know about him. So, when informing Fabius what sort of a man Novatus was as to character, Cornelius writes these very words: 'I wish to speak, in order that you may know that this marvelous fellow long before

---

4 The Carthaginian Synod held that no offense was beyond the regular power of the Church for remission.

5 The Greek text has the plural here, although the Latin translators have the singular. This translation of Eusebius' indefinite plural to Latin definite singular is probably accurate.

6 Jerome transforms these epistles from Cyprian and the African bishops into a single letter from Cornelius to Fabius, 'De Novatiano, de his qui lapsi sunt.' However, no epistle of African bishops addressed to Fabius is extant.

7 None of the letters mentioned here is extant, although a long fragment of the last is quoted below. Because Fabian was inclined to side with Novatian, Cornelius had many occasions to write him.

desired[8] the episcopacy, and succeeded in concealing this mad desire of his within himself, making use as a cloak for his insanity the fact that he had the confessors with him from the beginning. Maximus,[9] one of our presbyters, and Urban,[10] who twice had reaped the highest renown by confession, and Sidonius[11] and Celerinus,[12] a man who by the mercy of God, after enduring all kinds of torture most bravely and strengthening by the strength of faith the weakness of the flesh, overcame his adversary mightily—these men, then, having found him out and detected the craftiness and duplicity in him, and the perjuries and the falsehoods and his unsociability and cruel friendship, returned to the holy Church, and made known in the presence of a number of bishops and presbyters and a great many laymen all his crafty tricks and wickedness which he had secretly kept within himself, weeping and repenting because they had been won over by the treacherous and malicious beast and for a short time had left the Church.'

Then, after a little, he says: 'It is inconceivable, beloved brother, how great a change and transformation we have seen take place in him in a short time. The most illustrious man, even though he bound himself by some fearful oaths

---

8 1 Tim. 3.1.
9 A presbyter and one of the party of Roman confessors who were so active in the controversy over the lapsed. Cyprian in his letters tells us much about Maximus and those mentioned with him. Although at first they went over to Novatian, they were finally reconciled to Cornelius, and received back into the Church with rejoicing.
10 According to Cyprian, Urban was a confessor only, and not a presbyter or deacon.
11 A confessor.
12 One of the most celebrated confessors of his time, and a member of a family of martyrs (cf. Cyprian, *Ep.* 33). There is a letter written by him to Lucian, the Carthaginian confessor (cf. Cyprian, *Ep.* 21). Nothing more is known of Calerinus and these other confessors than what is told us by Cyprian.

never in any way to seek the episcopacy,[13] suddenly appears as a bishop, as if hurled into our midst from some sort of machine.[14] This dogmatist, champion of the Church's doctrine,[15] when he was attempting to grasp and to seize the episcopacy which was not granted him from above, chose for himself two companions who had despaired of their own salvation, that he might send them to a small and very insignificant part of Italy, and entice from there by some sham device three bishops, rough and very simple men, asserting and affirming vigorously that they must come quickly to Rome, on the ground that any rebellion whatsoever that had arisen there they might dissolve, joining with other bishops as mediators. When they had arrived, since, as we have already said, they were rather simple men with respect to the crafts and artifices of the wicked, they were shut up by certain disorderly men like himself, and at the tenth hour, when they were drunk and sick therefrom, he compelled them by force by a counterfeit and vain imposition of the hands to confer the episcopate upon him, which he assumed in vengeance by treachery and villainy, since it had not fallen to his lot. One of these bishops not long afterwards returned to the Church, lamenting and confessing his sin, with whom we communed as if he were a layman, all the laity present interceding in his behalf. And of the other bishops we ordained

---

13 Cf. 1 Tim. 3.1. Novatian was the logical head of the rigoristic party, and might well have been forced to take up its leadership. The account as given by his enemies may well be discounted in favor of the information given by Dionysius (6.25). Many prominent ecclesiastical leaders in Rome favored the rigoristic principles, and would have been ready to consecrate Novatian bishop of Rome.

14 *Mánganon,* probably a reference to the method of raising the cages with wild beasts to the level of the arena.

15 It has been suggested that this is a reference to Novatian's *De Trinitate.*

successors, and sent them into the places where they were.

'This guardian[16] of the Gospel, then, did not know that there should be one bishop in a Catholic church,[17] in which he was not ignorant (for how could he be?) that there were forty-six presbyters, seven deacons, seven sub-deacons, forty-two acolytes, fifty-two exorcists, readers together with door-keepers,[18] more than fifteen hundred widows with persons in

---

16 Probably another sarcastic allusion to Novatian's avowed pride in his orthodoxy.

17 The principle that only one bishop should be established in a single city was proclaimed as early as at the beginning of the second century, and was the common opinion of the Christian world. The problems of these perilous times, however, required a formal statement of it. The Council of Nicaea made it canon law.

18 The narrative of Acts 6.1-6 describes the first institution of the office of deacon, and sets the number at seven. This has been the constant tradition of the Catholic Church. It was enacted into law early in the third century in Canon 15 of the Council of Neo-Caesarea. This, however, was by no means universal, especially in Alexandria and in Constantinople. St. Isidore of Seville (seventh century) in his letter to Leudefredus thus summarizes the various functions of deacons: 'To the deacon it belongs to assist the priests and to serve in all that is done in the sacraments of Christ, in baptism, to wit, in the holy chrism, in the paten and chalice, to bring the oblations to the altar and to arrange them, to lay the table of the Lord and to drape it, to carry the cross, to declaim the Gospel and Epistle, for as the charge is given to lectors to declaim the Old Testament, so it is given to deacons to declaim the New. To him also pertains the office of prayers and the recital of the names. It is he who gives warning to open our ears to the Lord; it is he who exhorts with his cry; it is he also who announces peace.'

The subdeacons are the lowest of the sacred or major orders. Their duties are to serve the deacon at Mass; to prepare the bread and wine and sacred vessels for the Holy Sacrifice; to present the chalice and paten at the Offertory, and pour the water into the wine for the Eucharist; to chant the Epistles solemnly; to wash the sacred linen. In the Greek Church, they prepare the chalice at the Prothesis and guard the gates of the sanctuary during the Holy Sacrifice. The general opinion of theologians today is that the subdiaconate was not instituted by Christ nor does convincing evidence show that it had an apostolic origin. The subdeacons are first mentioned here, in this letter of Cornelius and in various letters of Cyprian.

distress, all of whom the grace and kindness of the Master supported. Not even this great multitude, so necessary in the Church, the number through God's providence rich and multiplying together with a very great and countless laity, turned him from such despair and failure, and recalled him to the Church.'

And again, after others statements, he adds to these the following remarks: 'Come, now, let us say next by what deeds and by what conduct he was encouraged to aspire to the episcopate. Was it because he was raised from the beginning in the Church, and had waged many battles in its behalf, and had been in many great dangers for the sake of religion? This is not so. The occasion of his having accepted the faith was Satan, who entered him and dwelt in him for a long time; when he was being healed by the exorcists he fell into a severe illness and, being considered as all but dead, received

---

Acolytes, one of the inferior orders of the clergy, are first mentioned here and in Cyprian's epistles. Their chief duties are to light the candles on the altar, to carry them in procession and during the solemn singing of the Gospel; to prepare wine and water for Mass; and to assist the sacred ministers of the Mass and other public services of the Church.

Exorcists, one of the minor orders of the Western Church, are, in general, those who exorcise demons (cf. Acts 19.3). Exorcism is frequently referred to by the Fathers of the second century, but this is the earliest distinct reference to it.

Readers or Lectors, still another of the minor orders, was already a distinct office in Tertullian's time (cf. *De praescrip.* 41). The first mention of a Christian liturgical reader is by Justin Martyr in 1 *Apol.* 67.3,4. The primary purpose for establishing a special class of readers was the need of some persons sufficiently educated to be able to read the books in church.

Doorkeeper or Janitor, first mentioned here, was frequently referred to in the fourth century. The guarding of the door of the church during the service, according to the apostolic constitution, was the duty of the deacons and subdeacons. The doorkeepers exercised their function only when the service was not being held.

baptism by affusion on the very bed where he lay,[19] if, indeed, one should say that such a man received it. However, he did not receive the other things, after he had escaped his illness, which one must share according to the canon of the Church, including the being sealed by the bishop. Since he did not obtain these, how could he have obtained the Holy Spirit?'

And again, after a little, he says: 'he who through cowardice and love of living in the time of persecution denied that he was a presbyter. For, when he was asked and entreated by the deacons to come out of the chamber in which he had enclosed himself, and give aid to his brethren as is right and possible for a presbyter to aid brethren who are in danger and need assistance, far from obeying the exhortations of the deacons he departed and left even in anger. He said that he did not wish to be a presbyter, since he was enamored of another philosophy.'[20]

Passing over a few things, he again adds to this, saying: 'This illustrious man, having abandoned the Church of God in which, when he had the faith, he was deemed worthy of the presbyterate by the favor of the bishop who laid his hand upon him for the clerical office of presbyter, and who, on being opposed by all the clergy and also many of the laity, on the ground that it was not possible for one who had been

19 Novatian clearly received baptism of the sick or clinical baptism (*baptismus clinicorum*), but this is not a valid argument in support of the contention that he was of pagan parentage, because of the widespread custom at this time on the part of Christians of postponing baptism as long as possible in order to avoid all sins after baptism. Whether his parents were pagans or Christians is unknown.
20 Novatian, although a presbyter, withdrew from active life, and lived as an ascetic. It is to this, as some scholars think, that Cornelius refers.

baptized by affusion in bed[21] because of sickness as this fellow to be ordained to an order, asked that he be permitted to ordain this one alone.'

Then he adds something else to this, the worst of all the man's offences, saying thus: 'When he had made the offerings, and as he distributes to each his part[22] and gives it, he forces the wretched men to swear instead of giving a blessing, holding in both of his hands those of the one who had received, and not releasing them until they say under oath (for I shall use the man's words): "Swear to me by the Blood and Body of our Lord Jesus Christ never to desert me and turn to Cornelius." And the miserable person does not taste until he first has called down a curse upon himself, and as he receives that bread, instead of saying Amen, he says, "I will not return to Cornelius." '

And after other remarks, he again says the following: 'But now know that he has been made bare, and that he has become desolate, as the brethren leave him every day and return to the Church. And Moses, also, the blessed martyr who lately bore a noble and marvelous testimony among us, while he was still in this world, when he saw his boldness and rashness, had no communion with him and the five presbyters who, together with him, had cut themselves off from the Church.'

And at the end of the letter he has made a catalogue of the bishops who were present in Rome and who had con-

---

21 Because the usual mode of baptism in the early Church was by immersion, clinic baptism (*baptismus clinicorum*), by pouring water, was looked upon with suspicion by some. In fact, many persons denied that it was baptism at all. The Church, however, refused to uphold this opinion. Cf. Cyprian, *Ep.* 75.

22 I.e., of the Sacrament.

demned the stupidity of Novatus, indicating at once both the names and the parishes over which each one of them presided; and of those who were not present at Rome, but who expressed their agreement with the aforesaid in writing, he gave the names as well as the cities in which each lived and from which he set out.[23] These things Cornelius pointed out and wrote to Fabius, Bishop of Antioch.

Chapter 44

To this same Fabius, when he was inclining somewhat toward the schism, Dionysius of Alexandria also wrote, relating many other things about repentance in his letter[1] to him, and describing the struggles of those who lately suffered martyrdom at Alexandria. Along with the rest of the story he tells an incident full of wonder, which very incident must be handed down with this work. It is as follows: 'This one example which happened among us I shall set forth to you. There was a certain Serapion[2] among us, an old man full of faith, who had lived most of his life blamelessly, and had fallen in the trial. This fellow sought [absolution] often, and no one paid any attention to him, for he had sacrificed. But when he had fallen ill, for three consecutive days he continued speechless and unconscious. Having recovered a little, on the fourth day he summoned his daughter's son and said, "How long do you hold me back, my child? I beg you,

---

23 These lists are no longer extant.

---

1 From the words which follow, we see that this epistle is the same as that from which Eusebius has quoted extensively in 6.41,42. These are the only portions of the letter extant.
2 This Serapion is known only from this chapter.

hasten, and release me quickly; call some one of the presbyters to me." And after he had said this, he was again speechless. The boy ran to the presbyter. But it was night, and he was ill, and was unable to come. However, since an order had been given by me that those departing life, if they requested it, and especially if they had made supplication before, be absolved, that they might depart in good hope, he gave the little boy a small piece of the Eucharist, bidding him soak[3] it and let the drops fall in the old man's mouth. The boy returned, bringing this, and when he was near, before he entered, Serapion revived a little and said, "Have you come, my child? The presbyter could not come, but do quickly what he ordered and let me depart." The boy soaked it, and at the same time poured it into his mouth, and after the man had swallowed a little he immediately gave up the ghost. Was he not clearly preserved, and did he not remain until he was released and, when his sin was blotted out, could be acknowledged for the many good deeds which he had done?'

Chapter 45

These things did Dionysius relate. Let us see what sort of a letter the same person wrote to Novatus,[1] when he was

3 The text does not specify the liquid in which the bread was to be soaked. Some assume that it was wine and others water. It is to be noted that the bread was soaked by the boy in the sick man's house, where presumably there was no consecrated wine. Furthermore, there is no indication that wine was given him for the purpose by the presbyter. In all probability the soaking was merely to enable the weak old man to receive the Sacrament easily. This is a very early instance of Communion in one kind.

1 Dionysius evidently believed that Novatian had himself sought the position of anti-pope. This is open to grave doubt. Cf. 6.43.1.

disturbing the Roman brotherhood of that time. When, then, he was making some of the brethren an excuse for apostasy and schism, on the ground that he had been forced to go that far, behold how he writes to him: 'To Novatian, brother, greetings. If you have been led on unwillingly, as you say, you will show this by retiring willingly. One ought to suffer anything at all rather than split the Church of God, and martyrdom to avoid schism would not be less glorious than martyrdom to avoid the worship of idols, but in my opinion more so. In one case one suffers martyrdom for the sake of one soul, his own; in the other, for the sake of the whole Church. And if now you should persuade or compel the brethren to come to unanimity, your right action will be greater than your fall, and the one will not be reckoned, the other will be praised. But, if you should be powerless over the disobedient, when saving save your own soul.[2] I pray that you be well, holding to the peace in the Lord.'

Chapter 46

These things also did he write to Novatus. And he also wrote a letter to the people in Egypt *On Repentance,*[1] in which he has presented his views on those who had fallen, defining the classes of transgressions. And to Colon[2] (this man was bishop of the parish of the Hermopolitans) a private

2 Gen. 19.17 (Septuagint).

1 The burning question of the time in connection with the lapsed; probably written at the same time as those to Fabius and Novatian above. No part of it has survived.
2 Mentioned also by Jerome (*De vir. ill.* 69); probably written at the same time as the preceding.

letter of his is extant *On Repentance;* another, of reproof to his flock in Alexandria. Among these is also the letter written to Origen *On Martyrdom;*[3] and to the brethren at Laodicea[4] over whom Thelymidres presided as bishop, and to those in Armenia,[5] over whom Meruzanes was bishop, he likewise wrote *On Repentance.* Besides all these he also wrote to Cornelius in Rome, after he had received his letter against Novatus,[6] to whom he pointed out clearly that he had been invited by Helenus,[7] Bishop at Tarsus of Cilicia, and by the rest of the bishops with him, Firmilian[8] in Cappadocia and Theoctistus[9] in Palestine, to attend the Synod of Antioch, where some were trying to confirm the schism of Novatus. Furthermore, he writes that he was informed that Fabius[10] had fallen asleep, and that Demetrian[11] was appointed his successor to the episcopacy at Antioch. And he writes also about the Bishop of Jerusalem, speaking with these very words: 'The wonderful Alexander,[12] while confined in prison, went happily to his rest.'

---

3 Written while Origen was in prison during the persecution of Decius (cf. 6.39), and intended to comfort and encourage him. It is no longer extant. Certain existing fragments are spurious.

4 This epistle is no longer extant; like so many others, it probably dealt with the question of discipline. Thelymidres is otherwise unknown.

5 We know nothing more about the epistle to the Armenians or of Bishop Meruzanes.

6 On Cornelius, cf. 6.39. The correspondence between Cornelius and Dionysius is entirely lost.

7 Helenus must have been bishop as early as 252, and died after 265. He took a prominent part in the discussion over the rebaptizing of heretics, joining most of the Oriental bishops in demanding it, and in the controversy over Paul of Samosata. Cf. 7.28-30.

8 Cf. 6.26.

9 Cf. 6.19.

10 On Fabius, Bishop of Antioch, cf. 6.39.

11 Successor of Fabius, and predecessor of Paul, as Bishop of Antioch. Cf. 7.5,14,27,30. The dates of his bishopric cannot be set with any great degree of accuracy.

12 Cf. 6.8.

Besides this, a certain other diaconal[13] letter is extant to those in Rome through Hippolytus.[14] And to the same people he composed another letter *On Peace,* and also *On Repentance,*[15] and again still another to the confessors there who were still in agreement with the mind of Novatus.[16] And to these same persons he wrote two others after they had returned to the Church. And he communicated with many others, also by letter, and has left behind a source of varied benefits for those who still today hold esteem for his writings.[17]

---

13 The meaning of *diakonikē* is uncertain; Rufinus translates as *'epistola de ministeriis',* i.e., 'concerning the duties of the diaconate,' 'diaconal.' Some, with Archbishop Benson, would translate 'serviceable,' which certainly is no improvement. Various suggestions have been made to explain why Dionysius should write an epistle on this subject to the Roman Church. The most attractive explanation is the following. It was customary for deacons to offer prayers for peace, *eirēnika;* this letter, like the others, discussed the Novatian schism and was an appeal for peace.

14 This Hippolytus, who cannot be identified, seems to have been the bearer of the letter. Nowhere else does Eusebius mention the name of a letter carrier, but it seems useless to speculate why he does so here.

15 Only the titles of these two letters as given here by Eusebius are known.

16 On these confessors and their return to the Church, cf. 6.43. Nothing is known of Dionysius' epistles addressed to them.

17 For at least the titles of a number of other letters of Dionysius, cf. Book 7, especially ch. 26. Even with these Eusebius does not pretend to know and to have mentioned all.

BOOK SEVEN

IN WORKING OUT Book 7 of the *Ecclesiastical History*, the great bishop of the Alexandrians, Dionysius,[1] will again join us with his own words, describing individually by means of the letters which he has left behind everything that was done in his time. My account will make its beginning with them.

Chapter 1

Gallus succeeded Decius who had not reigned for an entire period of two years[1] when he was straightway murdered

---

1 Cf. 6.35,40.

---

1 C. Messius Quintus Trajanus Decius, emperor from 249 to 251, was born at Bubalia in Pannonia. When sent by Philippus in 249 to restore order in the army of Moesia, he was compelled by the troops to accept the purple. Although he still assured Philippus of his fidelity, the latter did not trust him, and hastened to meet him in battle. Philippus was defeated and slain near Verona. Decius spent most of his short reign warring against the Goths. He, together with his son, Herennius Etruscus, fell in battle against them (251) in the marshes near Forum Trebonii in Moesia. Another son, Hostilianus, was associated with Decius' successor, Gallus, but he died soon afterwards either from the plague or by the treachery of Gallus. The exact relationship of Hostilianus to Decius is in question. He may have been not a son but a nephew or son-in-law. Eusebius here in speaking of more than one son is a witness to the former relationship, which is usually accepted.

together with his sons. At this time Origen[2] died, having
completed seventy years save one of his life. Dionysius, writing
to Hermammon[3] about Gallus,[4] has the following to say:
'Not even Gallus recognized the wickedness of Decius, nor
did he consider what caused him to fall, but he stumbled
against the same stone though it was before his eyes; when
his reign was faring well, and his affairs were proceeding
according to his mind, he drove off the holy men who were
praying to God for his peace and health. Therefore, along
with them he banished the prayers in his behalf also.'

Chapter 2

So much, then, regarding him. But in the city of the
Romans, when Cornelius[1] had brought his episcopacy to an

2 On Origen's life, cf. 6.2.
3 Nothing certain is known of this Hermammon. He was probably a
bishop of some church in Egypt. Eusebius quotes from a letter to him
from Dionysius here and in 7.10,23. These quotations seem to belong
to a single letter treating of the attitude of successive emperors toward
the Christians. The date of the epistle, given at the end of 7.23, is the
ninth year of the Emperor Gallienus, namely, August 261 to August
262.
4 C. Vibius Trebonianus Gallus was emperor from 251 to 254. On the
death of Decius and his son Herennius, he was elected emperor with
Hostilianus, the surviving son of Decius, as his colleague. In 253, the
Goths, who had again invaded Roman territory, were driven back by
Aemilianus, whose troops proclaimed him emperor in Moesia. Gallus
and his son Volusianus were put to death by Gallus' own troops.
During his reign the Roman Empire was harassed not only by barbarians but by a deadly plague which broke out in 252 and continued
for fifteen years. While Decius persecuted the Christians for political
reasons, Gallus may be said to have done so for religious reasons. The
plague was attributed to the wrath of the gods occasioned by the
Christians and their worship.

1 On Cornelius, cf. 6.39.

end after about three years, Lucius[2] was established as his successor; but after the latter had fulfilled his duty for less than eight months, he died and gave over his office to Stephen.[3] For him Dionysius composed the first of his letters on baptism,[4] since no small controversy had been stirred up at that time as to whether it was necessary to purify through baptism those who were turning away from any heresy what-

---

2 Since Eusebius (6.39) made Cornelius' episcopate a year too long, he dates the accession of Lucius a year too late. The period of Lucius' episcopate was most probably from June 253 to March 254. Nothing is known of his life before his elevation. He was sent into exile soon after his consecration but, very shortly, presumably when Valerian was made emperor, was permitted to return. He died in the beginning of March, 254. The struggle with respect to the lapsed, begun under Cornelius, continued while Lucius was bishop. Lucius followed the liberal policy of Cornelius. St. Cyprian, who wrote a letter (now lost) of congratulation to Lucius on his elevation to the Roman see and on his banishment, sent a second letter (now extant as Letter 61 in the Cyprian collection) of congratulation to him and his companions in exile, as well as to the whole Roman Church.

3 St. Stephen I was consecrated on May 12, 254, and died August 2, 257, although great question is raised about these dates. The strife with regard to the lapsed continued under Stephen, but the most important controversy of his day was about the rebaptism of heretics. Great bitterness arose on this subject between the Church at Rome and that at Carthage. Stephen held, in accord with ancient usage and the uniform practice of the Roman Chuch, that baptism by heretics and schismatics is valid, and that those so baptized need not be rebaptized on entering the Catholic Church. Cyprian, however, supported by the Asiatic and African churches, insisted on the invalidity of such baptism and the necessity of rebaptism. But Stephen, and through him the Church of Rome, triumphed in this controversy. Stephen was buried in in the cemetery of St. Calixtus, whence his body was transferred by Paul I to a monastery which he founded in his honor. Two letters are extant from Cyprian (68 and 72) to Stephen, and a number of references to Stephen occur in Cyprian's other letters.

4 Eusebius mentions six epistles by Dionysius on baptism (cf. 7.5 n. 5). From Eusebius' words here and Dionysius' words in 7.5, it is clear that Dionysius followed the entire Eastern and African church in refusing to admit the validity of heretical baptism and in insisting on the rebaptism of all converted heretics.

soever. Since a custom, old at any rate, prevailed with regard to such persons of using only prayer with the laying on of the hands,

Chapter 3

Cyprian,[1] the shepherd of the parish at Carthage, considered it necessary that they be admitted after they had first been purged of their error. But Stephen, thinking that no innovation should be made contrary to the tradition which has prevailed from the beginning, was full of indignation at this.

Chapter 4

Therefore Dionysius, who had communicated at great length with him on this subject by letter,[1] at its conclusion shows that, when the persecution[2] abated, the churches everywhere rejected the innovation of Novatian and resumed peace among themselves. He writes as follows.

Chapter 5

But 'know now, brother, that all the churches in the East and still farther away, which had formerly been separated, have been united, all those in charge of these churches are

---

1 Cyprian of Carthage (Thascius Caecilius Cyprianus), saint, bishop (247 or 248 to 258), and martyr.

---

1 From the context we judge this to be a single letter or epistle, the Greek plural, *grammata*, being often used like its Latin counterpart, *litterae*, in a singular sense.
2 I.e., the persecution of Decius.

of one mind, rejoicing exceedingly at the peace which has come unexpectedly: Demetrian[1] in Antioch, Theoctistus in Caesarea, Mazabanes in Aelia, Marinus at Tyre (Alexander having fallen asleep), Heliodorus in Laodicea (Thelymidres having died), Helenus in Tarsus, and all the churches of Cilicia, Firmilian and all Cappadocia. I have named only the more illustrious of the bishops, that I may add neither length to my letter nor tediousness to my speech. However, all the Syrias and Arabia which you help on every occasion,[2] and to which you have written,[3] and Mesopotamia and Pontus and Bithynia, and, to put it briefly, all everywhere are rejoicing in this harmony and brotherly love, glorifying God.'

Such are the words of Dionysius. Stephen, after fulfilling the duties of his office for two years, was succeeded by Xystus.[4] Dionysius drew up a second letter[5] *On Baptism* for him, and points out the opinion and decision both of Stephen and of the other bishops, speaking as follows about

1 On Demetrian, Thelymidres, and Helenus, cf. 6.46. On Theoctistus, Firmilian, and Mazabanes, cf. 6.19,26.39.
2 The Church at Rome from an early date was always ready to help the needy everywhere. Cf. the epistle of Dionysius of Corinth to Soter, Bishop of Rome, quoted in 4.23.
3 In all probability, this epistle dealt in some measure with the heresy of Novatian, about which Dionysius is now writing. We know nothing more about it than what is said here.
4 Xystus II (Sixtus), Bishop of Rome after Stephen for about one year, was martyred under Valerian, August 6, 258. This date is given in the Liberian catalogue, and is confirmed by a contemporary letter (Ep. 80) of Cyprian. Stephen had been at odds with Cyprian over the rebaptism of heretics. While Xystus followed his predecessor in this matter, he was more conciliatory, and under him peace was restored. Cf. Pontius' *Life of Cyprian* 14.
5 Dionysius' first epistle on baptism was addressed to Stephen of Rome (7.2); a second, to Philemon, a Roman presbyter (7.7); a third, to Dionysius of Rome (7.6); a fourth, to Xystus of Rome (7.9); a fifth, to Xystus and the Church of Rome (7.6).

Stephen: 'He had written before regarding Helenus and Firmilianus and all those from Cilicia and Cappadocia and evidently Galatia and all the bordering peoples in order, as if he would not hold communion even with them for this same reason, since, he says, they rebaptize heretics. And consider the magnitude of the matter. Actually, decrees on this subject have been passed in the largest synods of the bishops, as I learn, so that those who come over from heresies after first being instructed are then washed and purged of the filth of the old and impure leaven.[6] And I wrote entreating him on all these matters.

After other remarks he says: 'And also to our beloved fellow presbyters Dionysius[7] and Philemon,[8] who formerly held the same opinion as Stephen and who wrote to me concerning the same matters, I wrote first briefly and now in greater detail.'

But let this suffice regarding the question which is being presented.

Chapter 6

And referring in the same letter also to the heretical teachings of Sabellius,[1] on the ground that they were be-

---

6 Cf. 1 Cor. 5.7; 6.11.
7 Later became Xystus' successor as Bishop of Rome; cf. 7.27.
8 We know only that this Philemon was a presbyter of Rome at this time. Cf. 7.7, where a fragment from Dionysius' epistle to him is quoted.

---

1 Little is known of the life of Sabellius. All fourth-century writers follow St. Basil in saying that he was born in Africa. The scene of his activity, however, was Rome, where he appears during the episcopate of Pope Zephyrinus (198-217). In *Refut.* 9.6, Hippolytus says that Callistus perverted Sabellius to Monarchian views. Hippolytus argued

coming prominent in his day, he says the following: 'Regarding the doctrine now agitated in Ptolemais of Pentapolis, which is an impious thing and contains much blasphemy about Almighty God, Father of our Lord Jesus Christ, and much disbelief as to His only-begotten Son, the first-born of every creature,[2] the Word who was made man, and a lack of perception of the Holy Spirit, when the documents and the brethren ready to discuss them came to me from both sides, I wrote some things, as I was able with the help of God, giving instruction in a rather formal manner, the copies of which I am now sending you.

Chapter 7

And in the third of the letters *On Baptism*, which the same Dionysius wrote to Philemon[1] the presbyter at Rome, he presents the following: 'I on my part have read the compositions and traditions of the heretics, defiling my soul for a little while with their abominable thoughts, but then

with him and with Noetus and his followers (*Refut.* 9.3). Sabellius was convinced for a time, but was again led astray by Callistus. Indeed, during the episcopate of Zephyrinus, Callistus, Sabellius, and the Pope appeared to have united in constantly opposing Hippolytus. Callistus, soon after his accession (217), excommunicated Sabellius, according to Hippolytus, to acquire a reputation for orthodoxy and to shield himself against the attacks of his persistent foe. Sabellius then disappeared. Sabellianism is a general term for various forms of so-called Monarchianism, all tending in one direction—the denial of any distinction in the Godhead, and so the identification of Father and Son. All the works of Sabellius have disappeared, although some quotations appear in Epiphanius, *Haer.* 62, and in Athanasius, *Contra Arian. oratio* 4.

2 Col. 1.15.

1 Known only from what can be gathered from here.

receiving this profit from them: the ability to refute them by myself and to loath them much more. And when a brother, one of the presbyters, kept me off and frightened me away from being involved in the mire of their wickedness, for he said that I would injure my own soul, and he said truly, as I perceived, a God-sent vision came and strengthened me, and a message which was for me bade me, saying distinctly: "Read all things that you may receive in your hands, for you are able to set right and prove all things, and this has been for you from the beginning the cause of your faith." I accepted the vision as agreeing with the apostolic expression, which says to the stronger: "Be skilful money-changers." '[2]

Then, after making some remarks about all the heresies, he adds, saying: 'This rule and ordinance I received from our holy father[3] Heraclas.[4] For, those who came over from the heresies—rather, did not come over, but, while seeming to meet with the others, were charged with associating with some one of the false teachers—he drove from the Church, and did not admit them, though they besought it, until they publicly related all that they had heard from those who resist the truth,[5] and then he admitted them without requiring a second baptism[6] upon them; for they had received the Holy Spirit from him.' Then, after belaboring the question at length, he adds this: 'I have learned this also, that those in

---

2 Cf. 1 Thess. 5.21. This saying is quoted by many earlier writers, and usually as a saying of Christ.
3 The Greek word *papa*, 'pope', the earliest known use of the word for an Alexandrian bishop, although a little later several instances appear. In 1075, Gregory VII forbade the use of the word for anyone other than the Pope himself.
4 On Heraclas, cf. 6.3.
5 2 Tim. 2.25.
6 They, like Cyprian, repudiate the term rebaptism, on the ground that those baptized by heretics were not baptized at all.

Africa have not introduced this practice[7] now for the first time, but long before this in the days of the bishops before us in the most populous churches and the synods of the brethren. In Iconium[8] and Synnada[9] and in many places this was decided upon, and I do not dare by overturning their counsels to throw them into strife. "For thou shalt not remove," he says, "thy neighbor's landmarks which thy fathers placed." '[10]

The fourth of his letters *On Baptism*[11] was written to Dionysius[12] of Rome, who was then deemed worthy of the presbyterate, and not long afterwards received the episcopate over those there. From this it is possible to see how this man also was born witness by Dionysius of Alexandria as a learned and honorable person. And among other things he writes to him in the following words, when speaking of the affair of Novatian.

Chapter 8

'With good reason do we feel hatred for Novatian,[1] who split the Church, and dragged some of the brethren into

---

7 I.e., rebaptism, or, as they would say, the *baptism,* of those who had received baptism at the hands of heretics not in communion with the Church.

8 Iconium, the chief city of Lycaonia. The synod mentioned here is also spoken of in Firmilian's letter to Cyprian (*Ep. Cypriani* 75). Bishops from Phrygia, Cilicia, Galatia, and other countries attended it, and completely rejected the baptism of heretics. It was held between 230 and 240.

9 A city of Phrygia. Nothing is known about the synod held here, except that it probably took place at the same time.

10 Deut. 19.14 (Septuagint).

11 Cf. 7.2, for Dionysius' other epistles on baptism.

12 Cf. 7.5, for Dionysius of Rome.

---

1 On Novatian and his schism, cf. 6.43.

impieties and blasphemies, and introduced most unholy teaching about God, and falsely accused our most compassionate Lord Jesus Christ as unmerciful. Besides all this, he rejects holy baptism[2] as spurious, and overturns the faith and confession which precedes it,[3] and entirely banishes the Holy Spirit from them, if, indeed, there was any hope of his remaining with or returning to them.'

Chapter 9

And his fifth letter[1] was written to Xystus,[2] Bishop of Rome. In it, after saying much against the heretics, he sets forth something that happened in his time, saying 'Truly, brother, I am in need of counsel, and I ask an opinion of you on a certain matter that has come before me, for I fear lest possibly I am mistaken. For of the brethren who are brought together for worship, one long considered a believer, a member of the congregation before my ordination, and I think also before the establishment of the blessed

2 Novatian rebaptized all who went over to him from the Church. Cf. Cyprian's Epistle to Jubaianus (73.2). His principle was that baptism was valid only when performed by priests of true and approved Christian character.

3 As early as the beginning of the second century (cf. *Didache*) it was customary for the candidate for baptism to go through a period of special training. This included a confession of faith or baptismal creed which formed the basis of the Apostles' Creed. Dionysius probably means here that, since Novatian did not accept the Church baptism, he overturned and perverted the instruction that preceded it.

1 I.e., the fifth epistle on baptism (cf. 7.5). The sixth, which is also addressed to Xystus, is mentioned in 7.9.

2 Xystus II of Rome; cf. 7.5.

Heraclas,[3] having been present with those who were recently baptized, and having heard the questions and answers, came to me weeping and lamenting himself and falling before my feet, confessing and swearing that the baptism with which he had been baptized by the heretics was not this nor did it have anything at all in common with this, for it was full of impiety and blasphemies, and saying that he had great compunction in his heart,[4] and did not have the courage to lift up his eyes toward God,[5] setting out from those unholy words and deeds for this reason, and begging to obtain this most pure cleansing and reception and grace. This very thing I did not dare to do, saying that his long-standing communion had been sufficient for this. For, him who had heard the Thanksgiving, and had joined in saying the Amen, and had stood beside the Table, and had stretched forth his hands to receive the holy food, and had received it, and had shared in the Body and Blood of our Lord for a long time, I would not dare to build up again from the beginning. But I kept urging him to take courage, and with strong faith and good hope to approach for the participation in holy things. And he never ceases lamenting this, and he shudders to approach the Table, and with difficulty, though invited, does he endure to be present at the prayers.'

In addition to the Letters mentioned above, still another of the same author is extant *On Baptism*, addressed by him and the parish over which he ruled to Xystus and the Church at Rome, in which by a long proof he extends the discussion over the question under consideration. And still

3 Heraclas is mentioned in 6.3.
4 Cf. Acts 2.37.
5 Cf. Luke 18.13.

another of his besides these is extant, to Dionysius at Rome, regarding Lucian.[6] Let this suffice about these.

Chapter 10

Now, Gallus and those with him,[1] after holding power for less than two whole years, were put out of the way, and Valerian with his son Gallienus succeeded to the sovereignty. Now, again, what Dionysius relates about this man, also, it is possible to learn from his letter to Hermammon,[2] in which he gives an account as follows: 'And also to John it is likewise revealed: "For there was given him," he says, "a mouth speaking great things and blasphemy, and power was given to him and forty and two months."'[3] It is possible to wonder at both of these things[4] under Valerian, and to note especially the first of these, that he was so disposed as to be mild and friendly toward the men of God. No one else of the emperors before him was so graciously and rightly disposed toward them, not even those who were said to have been openly Christian,[5] as that one evidently was when he received them

---

6 The identity of this Lucian is uncertain. It has been suggested that the well-known Carthaginian confessor is meant. He caused much trouble by issuing letters of pardon indiscriminately to the lapsed, contrary to custom and to Cyprian's authority (cf. Cyprian's *Letters* 21, 22, 23, 26, 27). This may well have been the subject of this letter.

1 The reference is undoubtedly to Gallus, Volusian, his son and co-regent, and Aemilian, his enemy and successor.
2 Cf. 7.2.
3 Cf. Apoc. 13.5.
4 Dionysius had probably quoted another passage of Scripture in the preceding context, which predicted Valerian and was favorable to the Church. 'Both' refers to it and Apoc. 13.5.
5 Eusebius may be referring to Philip, the only emperor before this time openly proclaimed to have been a Christian (cf. 6.34), and to Alexander Severus, who was very favorable to the Christians.

in the beginning most intimately and most friendly, and his entire house was filled with God-fearing men, and was a church of God. But the master and ruler of the synagogue of the Magi[6] from Egypt persuaded him to make away with them, bidding him to kill and persecute the pure and holy men[7] as being rivals and interferers with the abominable and disgusting incantations (for they are and were able, by being present and being seen, by merely breathing and speaking,

6 I.e., Macrianus, one of Valerian's ablest generals; cf. 7.5.
7 Before the end of 253 Valerian (C. Publius Licinius Valerianus) was proclaimed emperor by the legions of Rhaetia and Noricum, and he declared his son Gallienus as emperor with himself. Their reign was the most disastrous period in the history of Rome until that of Honorius. The Empire apeared on the verge of destruction; every frontier was threatened by barbarian attacks, and even the interior provinces were invaded and ravaged, Besides all this, the most terrible persecution the Church had yet experienced was introduced. In the beginning of his reign Valerian was very favorable to the Christians, and his court was full of them. But in 257 a terrible change took place. Valerian came more and more under the influence of the pretorian prefect, Macrianus, an Egyptian, chief of the Magi of that country. Through his influence, Valerian ordered those not of the religion of Rome at least to conform externally or be exiled. By the same edict, Christians were forbidden under pain of death to assemble for worship or enter their cemeteries. This edict was followed in 258 by a rescript of still greater severity. The punishment for the clergy was death. Other persons of high station, both men and women, were punished with degradation and confiscation of property, and even with death if they would not recant. The first victim of this rescript was Pope Xystus, who was put to death on August 6 as he sat in his episcopal chair. Four of his deacons were martyred with him. This was the beginning of a violent persecution (cf. Cyprian, *Ep.* 82) in which four days later St. Lawrence followed his master. Cyprian was beheaded on September 14. Both in Rome and in Africa a great number of Christians suffered. Some notion of the severity of the persecution may be gained from the fact that the sees of Rome and Carthage were vacant for about eleven months. Eusebius tells us something here of the ravages of the persecution in Palestine. Thus it continued until Valerian's captivity, probably late in 260; Dionysius says for forty-two months, from late in 257 to 261, when it was brought to an end by Gallienus. In Egypt and the Orient it seems to have continued for a few months longer.

to scatter the plots of the baneful demons), having persuaded
him to practice impure initiations and abominable juggleries
and ill-omened sacrifices: cutting the throats of wretched
boys and sacrificing children of unhappy fathers and dividing
the entrails of the new-born and cutting up and mutilating
the creatures of God, as if as a result of this they will attain
happiness.'

And he adds to this, saying: 'Splendid, indeed, were the
thank-offerings which Macrianus made to them for the
Empire, the object of his hopes.[8] When, formerly, he was
regarded as the emperor's minister of general finance, he
showed no reasonable or catholic mind, but he fell under
the prophetic curse which says: "Woe to those who prophesy
from their heart, and see not the whole."[9] For he did not
perceive the general providence, nor did he suspect the judgment of Him "who is above all, and through all, and in us
all."[10] Therefore, he became an enemy of His Catholic
Church, and he alienated and estranged himself from the
compassion of God, and went into banishment as far away
as possible from his own salvation, thus proving the truth of
his name.[11]

And again, after other remarks, he says: 'Valerian, led on
to this action by this man, was given over to insults and
reproaches according to the words spoken to Isaias: "And
these have chosen their own ways and their own abomi-
nations; their soul is delighted, and I will choose their

---

8 The meaning is not very clear, probably that Macrianus propitiated
   the demons to gain his ambitious ends. Since the evil spirits had
   promised him power, Marianus showed his gratitude by causing
   Valerian to persecute the Christians.
9 Cf. Ezech. 13.3.
10 Eph. 4.6; Col. 1.17.
11 Macrianus means 'far off,' 'at a distance.'

mockeries and render to them their sins."[12] This man,[13] being mad for the imperial power of which he was unworthy, and being unable to put the imperial garment on his crippled body, set forward his two sons who took over their father's sins.[14] In these the prophecy which God spoke was clear: "Visiting the iniquity of the fathers upon the children, unto the third and fourth generation of them that hate me."[15] He heaped his own evil desires, in which he failed, upon the heads of his sons, and upon them he wiped off his own wickedness and hatred for God.'

So much does Dionysius relate about Valerian.

Chapter 11

But regarding the persecution of his time which raged most fiercely, what the same Dionysius together with others endured for the sake of their piety toward the God of all will be disclosed by his words which he wrote to Germanus,[1] one of the bishops of his time, who was trying to slander him. He makes his statement as follows: 'I run the risk, truly, of

12 Cf. Isa. 66.3,4.
13 I.e., Macrianus; he was lame.
14 Dionysius, quoted in 7.23, states that Valerian was betrayed by Macrianus (the view commonly held), and fell into the hands of the Persians (late in 260). Macrianus was then proclaimed emperor by the troops. He associated with himself his two sons, Quietus and Macrianus. After a few months, he left his son Quietus in command of Syria, and with his son Macrianus marched against Gallienus to capture the West. However, he was met in Illyrium by the pretender Auriolus (262), and both he and his son were slain. Meanwhile, his son Quietus was slain by the pretender Odenathus.
15 Exod. 20.5.

1 Cf. 6.40.

falling into great foolishness and stupidity,[2] being forced into a necessity of relating the wonderful dispensation of God with regard to us. But, since, he says, "it is good to hide the secret of a king: but honorable to reveal and confess the works of God,"[3] I will join issue with the violence of Germanus. I went before Aemilianus,[4] not alone, but my fellow-presbyter, Maximus,[5] and deacons Faustus,[6] Eusebius,[7] and Chaeremon[8] followed me, and one of the brothers on hand from Rome went in with us. Aemilianus did not begin by saying: "Do not hold assemblies." This was superfluous for him, and the last thing for him [to say] who was retracing his steps to the first. For his words were not about not bringing others into assembly, but about ourselves not being Christians, and he ordered me to cease from this, thinking that, if I should change, the others also would follow me. And I answered in no unfitting manner, and not far from "We ought to obey God, rather than man";[9] moreover, I testified outright that I worship God, who is the only God, and none other, nor would I change or ever cease to be a Christian.

---

2 Cf. 2 Cor. 11.1,17.

3 Tob. 12.7.

4 Aemilianus, deputy-prefect of Egypt in 258, in the reign of Gallienus. He was forced by the troops of Alexandria to revolt against Gallienus, and assume the purple. But he was defeated by Theodotus, Gallienus' general, and put to death in prison at a time unknown.

5 Maximus succeeded Dionysius as Bishop of Alexandria. We know little or nothing about him. Cf. 7.28,30,32.

6 On Faustus, cf. 6.40.

7 This Eusebius later became Bishop of Laodicea. All we know about him is contained here and in 7.32.

8 Chaeremon is known only from this chapter.

9 Acts 5.29.

After this he ordered us to go off to a village near the so-called desert of Cephro.[10]

'But hear the very things that were spoken by both sides, as they were recorded. When Dionysius and Faustus and Maximus and Marcellus[11] and Chaeremon were arraigned, the prefect said: "I have discussed with you verbally the kindness of our lords,[12] which they have employed toward you; for they have given you an opportunity for safety, if you should be willing to turn to what is according to nature, and worship the gods that preserve the Empire, and forget what is contrary to nature. What, then, do you say to this? For I do not expect that you will be ungrateful for their kindness, since they urge you to the better things."

'Dionysius answered: "Not all men worship all gods, but each one certain gods whom he considers such. We, then, worship and adore the one God and Maker of all things, who entrusted the Empire to Valerian and Gallienus, most beloved of God, and to Him we pray unceasingly for their Empire, that it may remain unshaken."

'Aemilianus, the prefect of the government, said to them: "Who prevents you from worshiping this one, also, if he is a god, along with the gods according to nature? For you have been bidden to worship gods, and gods whom all know."

'Dionysius replied: "We worship no other god."

'Aemilianus, the prefect of the government, said to them: "I see that you are at once ungrateful and insensible to the kindness of our Augusti; therefore, you will not be in this city, but will depart for parts of Libya, and [remain] in a

10 In Libya.
11 Otherwise unknown.
12 Valerian and Gallienus.

place called Cephro. I have selected this place according to the order of our Augusti. And never will it be permitted either to you or to any others either to hold assemblies or to enter the so-called cemeteries.[13] If anyone be shown not to have gone to this place which I have ordered, or should be discovered in any assembly, he will bring danger upon himself, for the necessary supervision will not be lacking. So, be gone where you have been commanded."

'Although I was sick, he rushed me off without giving me a respite of one day. What leisure, then, did I have for holding an assembly or not holding one?'

Then, a little farther on, he says: 'But we were absent not even from the visible assembling with the Lord, but the more zealously did we call together those in the city, as if being with them, "absent in body," as he[14] said, "but present in spirit,"[15] and in Cephro a large church was associated with us, some brethren following us from the city, others joining us from Egypt. And there God opened a door of speech.[16] At first we were persecuted, we were stoned, but later some, not a few, of the pagans abandoned their idols and turned to God. Then for the first time was the word spread through us among those who had not received it before, and, as if for this purpose, did God lead us to them, and, when we had fulfilled this ministry,[17] led us away again.

---

13 Greek, *koimētēria* (literally, 'sleeping-places') , so called by the Christians who looked upon death only as sleep. The pagan officials felt it to be dangerous to allow Christians to gather at the graves of martyrs; cf. 9.2.

14 St. Paul.

15 1 Cor. 5.3.

16 Col. 4.3.

17 Cf. Acts 12.25.

'For Aemilianus wished to transport us to rougher, as he thought, and more Libyan-like places,[18] and he ordered those scattered in every direction to assemble in the Mareotian district,[19] assigning villages throughout the country to each party, but placed us more on the road and so the first to be captured. For it is clear that he arranged and prepared things so that, whenever he wished, he could capture all of us easily. But, when I was ordered to go off to Cephro, and I did not know where in the world this place was, having scarcely heard the name before, I nevertheless departed with good grace and quietly. But when it was told me that I was to remove to the regions of Colluthion,[20] those who were present know how I was disposed (for here I shall accuse myself); at first I was vexed and extremely angry, for, even if the places were really rather well known and familiar to us, report was that the place was destitute of brethren and men of character, and exposed to the annoyances of travelers and the raids of robbers. But I gained some solace when the brethren reminded me that it was nearer the city,[21] and that Cephro used to bring us frequent contact with the brethren from Egypt, so that we were able to gather a congregation from a wider area, but here, since the city is closer, we will enjoy more frequently the sight of our truly loved ones, most intimate and dear. For they will come, and

18 'Libyan' became a synonym for the dreaded unknown, just as Libyan referred to the Great Desert of Africa and all the unknown country west and south of it.
19 Just south of Alexandria, but not including it.
20 Possibly a section of the district of Maerotis; nothing more definite is known of it.
21 Alexandria.

stay the night, and, as in the more remote suburbs, sectional assemblies[22] will be held. And so it happened.'

And after other remarks about what happened to him, he again writes as follows: 'On many confessions, indeed, does Germanus exalt himself; many things can be mentioned that happened to him, as many inventories as he can enumerate about us: sentences, confiscations, proscriptions, plundering of possessions, loss of dignities, contempt of worldly glory, disregard for the commendation and the reverse of governors and councilors,[23] endurance of threats and outcries and perils and persecutions and wandering and distress and all kinds of tribulation, such as happened to me under Decius and Sabinus,[24] and such as continued up to the present time under Aemilianus. But, where did Germanus appear? What was the report about him? I desist from the great folly into which I fall on account of Germanus, for which reason, too, I desist giving a detailed description of what took place to the brethren who already know.'

The same Dionysius, in the letter to Domitius and Didymus,[25] again recalls the events of the persecution in these words: 'But it is superfluous to list our people by name, who are numerous and unknown to you; rest assured that men and women, both young men and old, both girls and aged women, both soldiers and civilians, both every race and every age, some by scourging and fire, others by the sword, con-

---

22 It appears clear that those living in the suburbs were permitted to hold services in their homes or elsewhere, and were not obliged to attend the church in the city, which might be far away.
23 Cf. Heb. 10.34.
24 Already mentioned in 6.40.2. Here we gather that Sabinus held the same post under Decius that Aemilianus held under Valerian.
25 Otherwise unknown.

quered in the contest and have received their crowns; in the case of some, a very long time was not enough to reveal them acceptable to the law, as, indeed, until now it would seem not even so for me. Therefore, until such time as He knows to be proper He has put me off who says: "On an accepted time I heard thee, and in the day of salvation have I helped thee."[26] Since you inquire of our affairs and wish to be shown how we fare, you have heard, without doubt, how as we were being led away prisoners by a centurion and magistrates and the soldiers and servants with them, certain persons from Mareotis came up and against our will and in spite of our refusal to follow, dragged us by force and carried us away—Gaius and Faustus and Peter and Paul and me.[27] Now Gaius and Peter and I alone, bereft of the other brethren, have been shut in a deserted and dry place in Libya, a three-day journey distant from Paraetonium.'[28]

And farther on he says: 'But in the city the presbyters, Maximus,[29] Dioscorus,[30] Demetrius, and Lucius[31] have concealed themselves, and secretly visit the brethren. Faustinus and Aquila,[32] who are better known in the world, are wandering in Egypt. But the deacons who survived those who died on the island are Faustus, Eusebius, Chaeremon. Eusebius is the one whom God strengthened from the beginning, and prepared to fulfill energetically the services to the confessors who were in prison, and at no little risk to perform

---

26 Isa. 49.8; 2 Cor. 6.2.
27 Cf. 6.40.
28 An important town and harbor, about 150 miles west of Alexandria.
29 Cf. above, n. 5.
30 Not to be identified with the Dioscorus of 6.41.19. Nothing more is known of this Dioscorus.
31 Nothing more is known of these last two men.
32 Nothing more is known of these.

the laying out of the corpses of the perfect and blessed martyrs. For even to the present day the governor does not cease to put to a cruel death, as I said above, some of those who are brought to trial, mutilating others by tortures, allowing still others to waste away in prison and bonds, and giving orders that no one approach these, and investigating whether anyone has been seen so doing; yet God gives relief to those who are hard pressed, by the zeal and the perseverance of the brethren.'

Such does Dionysius say. But it should be known that Eusebius, whom he saluted as deacon, was a little later established as Bishop of Laodicea in Syria,[33] and Maximus, whom he then mentioned as presbyter, succeeded Dionysius himself in the service of the brethren in Alexandria,[34] and Faustus, who was pre-eminent at that time with him in confession was preserved until the persecution of our own time[35] and, while a very old man and full of days, in our own time was perfected for martyrdom and was beheaded.

Such are the things that happened to Dionysius at that time.[36]

Chapter 12

During the persecution of Valerian, which is being con-

33 Cf. 7.32.5.
34 Cf. 7.28.
35 Until the persecution of Diocletian (303).
36 According to Eusebius, in the time of Valerian. But this is true only of the events mentioned in the early part of the chapter. The affairs mentioned in the epistle to Domitius and Didymus belong to the time of Decius.

sidered, three persons who were conspicuous in Caesarea of Palestine for the confession of Christ were adorned by holy martyrdom, becoming food for wild beasts. Of these, one was called Priscus; another, Malchus; and the third had the name Alexander.[1] It is said that these men, who lived in the country, at first reproached themselves for being careless and lazy, because, although the present opportunity bestowed prizes upon those who clung to a heavenly desire [for martyrdom], they themselves belittled them and did not rush forward to seize the crown of martyrdom; but that, after they had deliberated on this matter, they set out for Caesarea and met with the judge and obtained the end mentioned above. Besides this, they relate that a certain woman endured a similar conflict during the same persecution in the same city; but report holds that she belonged to the sect of Marcion.[2]

Chapter 13

But after a little while, when Valerian had undergone slavery at the hands of the barbarians,[1] his son became sole ruler[2] and administered government more prudently. Through

1 Nothing more is known of these men.
2 It was not customary among the orthodox Christians to recognize heretics as Christians, even when they were martyred together. In the eyes of the state, however, they were all Christians and subject to the same persecution and punishment.

1 Valerian, taken captive by Sapor, king of Persia, late in 260 (?), died in captivity.
2 Gallienus, already associated with his father, Valerian, in the Empire since 253, became sole emperor in 260 or 261, when Valerian fell into the hands of the Persians.

edicts[3] he straightway brought to a close the persecution against us, ordering those who presided over the word to fulfill their customary duties freely, by a rescript[4] which runs as follows: 'The Emperor Caesar Publius Licinius Gallienus Pius Felix Augustus to Dionysius and Pinnas and Demetrius[5] and the other bishops. I have ordered that the benefit of my bounty be declared throughout the whole world, that they may depart from places of religious worship,[6] and thus you also can make use of the copy of my ordinance that no one may molest you. And this matter which you now may fulfill I long since conceded,[7] and for this reason Aurelius Cyrenius,[8] the supreme finance minister, will observe the ordinance given by me.'

Let this, which for the sake of clarity was translated from the Latin, be inserted. And another ordinance of the same is extant, which he composed for other bishops, granting permission to recover the sites of the so-called cemeteries.[9]

---

3 These edicts, not preserved by Eusebius, were public proclamations; they differed from rescripts, which were private instructions. The rescript quoted by Eusebius here shows that the edicts not only put an end to the persecution but made Christianity a lawfully recognized religion for the first time. This rescript, moreover, acknowledged the right of Christians to hold property, and, since they were addressed to the bishops, by implication at least recognized the organization of the Church.

4 The Greek *antigraphé*, the technical term for rescript as described in note 3. Although its exact date is uncertain, it was probably written late in 261 or early in 262, soon after the downfall of the usurper Macrianus.

5 Pinnas and Demetrius mentioned here cannot be identified with certainty.

6 This is commoly taken to mean that the *heathen* should depart from the places of worship which they had taken from the Christians, and should return them to the Christians.

7 A reference to the edicts mentioned above, which had been issued on his accession but had not been enforced in Egypt because of Macrianus.

8 Known only from this passage.

9 Valerian had denied the Christians any use of their cemeteries, either as burial places or places of worship. Cf., also, 7.11 n. 13.

Chapter 14

At that time Xystus[1] was still directing the Church at Rome, Demetrian[2] the Church at Antioch after Fabius,[3] and Firmilian[4] at Caesarea in Cappadocia, and, besides these, Gregory[5] and his brother Athenodore,[6] pupils of Origen, the churches in the Pontus; when Theoctistus[7] passed away, Domnus[8] succeeded to the episcopate of Caesarea in Palestine, but, after he had continued as bishop for a short time, Theotecnus,[9] a contemporary of ours, was established as his successor. This one also was of the school of Origen. But at Jerusalem, when Mazabanes[10] went to his rest, Hymenaeus[11] succeeded to the throne, the same one, indeed, who was distinguished in our day for a great many years.

---

1 Xystus II. Cf. 7.5 n. 4.
2 Cf. 6.46.
3 Cf. 6.39.
4 Cf. 6.26.
5 Cf. 6.30 n. 1.
6 Cf. 6.30 n. 2.
7 Cf. 6.19.
8 Nothing further is known of Domnus.
9 The dates of Theotecnus are quite uncertain. Cf. 7.27,30, and 32. He was evidently a very prominent man, being present at the two Antiochian synods convened to consider the heresy of Paul of Samosata.
10 Cf. 6.39.
11 Hymenaeus was Bishop of Jerusalem from 265 to 298. Cf. Eusebius, *Chron.*; also, below, 7.27,30.

Chapter 15

In the time of these persons, when there was peace among the churches everywhere, Marinus,[1] one of those honored by high rank in the army and a man famous for his family and wealth, because of his testimony to Christ was beheaded in Caesarea of Palestine for the following reason. The vine-switch[2] is a kind of mark of honor among Romans, and those who obtain this, it is said, become centurions. When a post became vacant, the order of succession called Marinus to this advancement, and, when now he was on the point of receiving the honor, another came before the tribunal and charged that according to the ancient laws it was not possible for Marinus to share in a rank that belonged to Romans, since he was a Christian and not accustomed to sacrifice to emperors, but that the office fell to himself. The judge (his name was Achaeus),[3] it is said, was disturbed at this, and at first asked of what opinion Marinus was; when he saw that the man steadfastly confessed himself to be a Christian, he gave him an interval of three hours for consideration.

When now he came out of the courthouse, Theotecnus,[4] the bishop of that place, took him aside, engaging him in conversation, and taking him by the hand led him forward to the church, and when within he made him stand near the

---

1 Knowledge of the martyrdom of Marinus is confined to the information contained in this chapter. It is dated after the slaying of Macrianus (262), who continued the persecution of Christians even after the promulgation of the edict of toleration by Gallienus.

2 The vine-switch or vine-branch was the badge of office of the centurion. It was called *vitis* by the Romans.

3 Otherwise unknown; it has been assumed with little or no support that he was governor of Palestine.

4 Cf. 7.14 n. 9.

altar[5] itself, and drawing his cloak aside a little he pointed to the sword which girded him, and at the same time he brought and placed before him the Scripture of the divine Gospels, and he ordered him to make his deliberate choice of the two.

And when without hesitation he stretched forth his right hand and took the divine Scripture Theotecnus said to him, 'Hold fast, then, hold fast to God, and made strong by Him may you obtain what you have chosen, and go in peace.' Immediately when he returned thence the herald shouted, calling him before the court of justice, for the conditions of the appointed time had already been fulfilled. And now, standing near the judge, he displayed even greater zeal for the faith, and immediately, just as he was, was led away to death and so was perfected.

Chapter 16

There, too, Astyrius[1] is commemorated for his God-beloved boldness. He was one of the senators at Rome, a favorite with emperors and known to all for his noble birth and wealth. He was present with the martyr as he was being perfected, and taking the corpse[2] upon his shoulder he placed it upon a splendid and costly garment, and laying it out with great opulence gave it over to a fitting burial.

---

5 Greek, *tò hagiásma,* 'altar' or 'sanctuary.'

1 Nothing more is known of Astyrius. Rufinus (*H. E.* 7.23), probably misinterpreting Eusebius, says that he suffered martyrdom at about this time.
2 The Greek word is *skênos,* 'tabernacle.'

The friends of this man who survived to our time relate countless other things, including the following marvelous event.

Chapter 17

At Caesarea Philippi,[1] which the Phoeniceans call Paneas, it is said that on a certain festival a victim is cast down among the springs pointed out there on the slopes of the mountain called Paneion, from which the Jordan flows forth, and that this in some marvelous manner disappears by the power of the demon, and what takes place is a much talked of wonder among those present. Now Astyrius, being present on one occasion at what was being done, and seeing the multitude struck with amazement at the affair, pited their error, and then, looking up to heaven, besought through Christ the God who is over all things[2] to confound the demon who was leading the people astray, and to put an end to the deception of these men. And it is said that, after he had prayed this, the sacrifice suddenly floated on the surface of the springs, and thus their miracle departed, no marvel ever taking place again about the place.

---

1 To be distinguished from the Caesarea mentioned before, the chief city of Palestine. It was originally called Paneas by the Greeks also. Philip the Tetrach enlarged and beautified it, and changed the name to Caesarea Philippi. It is now a small village, called Banias by the Arabs.

2 Rom. 9.5.

Chapter 18

Since I have come to mention this city, I do not think it right to pass over a story also worthy of being recorded for our posterity. For it is said that the woman 'troubled with an issue of blood,'[1] who we learned from the divine Gospels found relief from her suffering at the hands of our Saviour, came from here, and her home is pointed out in the city, and wonderful memorials of the Saviour's benefaction to her still remain. For [it is said] that a brazen figure in relief of a woman, bending on a knee and with outstretched hands like a suppliant, stood on a high stone at the gates of her house, and opposite this there was another of the same material, an upright figure of a man, clothed modestly in a double cloak and extending his hand to the woman, and at his feet upon the monument itself grew a strange kind of plant, which climbed up to the hem of the brazen cloak and acted as an antidote for all kinds of diseases. They said that this statue bore the likeness of Jesus, and it survived even to our own time, so that we ourselves saw it with our own eyes when staying in the city. And it is not at all strange that those of the pagans who were benefitted by our Saviour made these objects, since we have observed that likenesses of His Apostles, Peter and Paul, and, indeed, of Christ Himself are preserved in pictures made with colors,[2] since,

1 Matt. 9.20. The story of the statue erected by the woman 'troubled with an issue of blood' is told by many later writers, cf. Sozomen (*H. E.*, 5.21) and Philostorgus (*H. E.* 7.3). There is strong suspicion that Eusebius was mistaken by this statue, and that it commemorated something else.
2 Eusebius has been regarded from passages such as this as being opposed to the use of images in the worship of the Church, and his orthodoxy was fiercely attacked on this ground by the later defenders of this practice. However, it cannot be said that we have a full description of Eusebius' stand on this question.

as is probable, the ancients were accustomed without restraint to honor them, according to a pagan practice, as saviors, in this fashion.

Chapter 19

The throne of James,[1] who was the first to receive the episcopacy of the Church at Jerusalem from the Saviour and the Apostles, whom the sacred Books persist in calling a brother of Christ,[2] has been preserved until this day. By treating this with respect the brethren in succession there clearly show to all what respect the men of old and those of our day held and do hold for those holy men because of their piety. So much for these matters.

Chapter 20

Dionysius,[1] besides the letters of his mentioned, also composed at that time festal letters[2] which are still extant, employing words in them more in the nature of a panegyric with reference to the festival of the Pasch. One of these he addressed to Flavius,[3] another to Domitius and Didymus,[4]

1 It was universal tradition that Christ himself appointed James as Bishop of Jerusalem. Cf. 2.1.
2 Cf. Gal. 1.19.

1 On Dionysius of Alexandria, cf. 6.40.
2 The bishops of Alexandria annually before Easter wrote a kind of homily or epistle announcing the time of the festival. These were called festal or festival epistles or homilies. Eusebius mentions such in 7:21,22 as written by Dionysius. A number by Athanasius in a Syriac version, a few by Theophilus in Latin, and thirty by Cyril in Greek are extant.
3 This epistle is no longer extant, and Flavius is otherwise unknown.
4 On Domitius and Didymus and the epistle in question, cf. 7.11.

in which also he sets forth a canon based on an eight-year cycle, holding that it is not proper to observe the festival of the Pasch at any other time than after the vernal equinox. Besides these, he also wrote another letter to his fellow presbyters at Alexandria, and to others at the same time in different places, and these he wrote while the persecution was still going on.[5]

Chapter 21

When peace had all but arrived, he returned to Alexandria,[1] but, when insurrection and war again broke out there, so that it was impossible for him to oversee all the brethren in the city, being separated into one or the other part of the insurrection, he again at the festival of the Pasch addressed them by letter,[2] as if he were an exile from Alexandria itself. And writing another festal letter after this, to Hierax,[3] a bishop of those in Egypt, he mentions the insurrection of the Alexandrians in his time in the following words:

'But as for me, what wonder is it, if it is difficult to communicate by letter with those who live far away, when it has become impossible to converse with my very self and to take counsel with my own soul? Surely I need to write letters to those who are "as my own bowels,"[4] brethren of the same household and of the same mind with myself, and citizens of the same Church; and it seems impossible to send this

---

5 All these epistles have disappeared, and we know nothing more about them.

1 Probably in 261 or early in 262, after the fall of Macrianus; cf. 6.13.
2 No longer extant.
3 Otherwise unknown.
4 Philem. 12.

correspondence through. For it would be easier for one to go, not to a foreign country, but even from east to west, than to Alexandria from Alexandria itself. The road through the very middle of the city is harder to traverse and more difficult to pass than that great and trackless desert which Israel traveled over for two generations. The smooth and waveless harbors have become an image of the sea, which, divided and walled up on either side, they had as a carriage road, and in the highway the Egyptians were drowned; and from the murders among them they often appeared like a Red Sea. And the river that flows by the city seemed drier at one time than the waterless desert and more parched than that through which Israel passed when it became so thirsty that Moses cried out,[5] and there flowed to them drink out of a rock of flint, from Him who alone does wonders.[6] And on one occasion it overflowed so much that it inundated the entire surrounding country, both the roads and the fields, and brought on a threat of the rush of water which took place in the time of Noe. And it ever flows on polluted by blood and murders and drownings, such as it was for Pharao at the hands of Moses, when it was turned into blood and stank.[7] And what other water could be the purifier of water that purifies all? How could the ocean, great and impassable for men, when poured out, cleanse this bitter sea? Or how could the great river that comes out of Eden, after diverting its four heads into which it is divided into the one of Geton,[8] wash away the gore? Or when could the air poisoned by the

5 Deut. 8.15; Ps. 78.20.
6 Cf. Ps. 136.4; Wisd. 11.4.
7 Cf. Exod. 7.20,21.
8 Cf. Gen. 2.10,13.

noxious exhalations from all sides become pure? For, such are the vapors from the land and winds from the sea, and breezes from the rivers, and mists from the harbors that dews are discharged from the dead bodies, putrefying in all their underlying elements. Yet men wonder and are at a loss whence the continuous pestilence,[9] whence the severe diseases, whence the different forms of death, whence the widespread and varied destruction of human beings, why this great city no longer contains within itself so great a multitude of inhabitants, from tender infants up to those of extreme old age, as it used to support those whom it called hearty old men. But those from forty years of age to seventy were so much more numerous at that time that their number is not to be matched today, even when those of fourteen to eighty years have been registered and reckoned together for the public allowance of food;[10] and the youngest in appearance have become, as it were, of equal age with the oldest[11] of long ago. Thus, although they see the race of men on earth being diminished and wasted away, they do not tremble, as their complete destruction is increasing and advancing.'

Chapter 22

After these events, when war succeeded pestilential disease, and the feast was drawing near, he again addressed the

---

9 Alexandria was probably the first city visited by the pestilence which began in 250 and visited the Empire at various intervals.
10 This passage is the sole evidence for this public rationing of food.
11 The young by sharing in the dole, were classed with the old.

brethren in writing, pointing out the sufferings of the calamity[1] in these words:

'To other men[2] the present would not seem to be a proper time for a festival, nor for them is this or any other time such; I do not have reference to times of mourning nor to any joyful time which one might especially consider so.[3] Now all is lamentations, and all are mourning, and wailings re-echo daily throughout the city because of the multitude of the dead and the dying. As it was written of the first born of the Egyptians, so is it now: "There arose a great cry; for there was not a house wherein there lay not one dead,"[4] and would, indeed, that it were only one.

'Many and terrible also were the things that happened before this. First they drove us out, and alone we kept the festival even then when being pursued and put to death by all, and every spot of each individual affliction became for us a place of festival—field, desert, ship, inn, prison—but the perfect martyrs kept the most brilliant festival of all, when they feasted in heaven. And after this, war and famine took hold of us, which we endured along with the heathen, we alone enduring such injuries as they inflicted upon us, but reaping the benefit also of what they inflicted on one another and what they suffered, and again we rejoiced in the peace of Christ, which He gave to us alone. But when both we and they obtained a very brief respite, this disease descended upon us, something more fearful to them than any fear, and more

---

1 The festal letter to Hierax quoted above was written while the war was going on, in 262; the present letter after its close, in 263, and before Easter of that year.
2 The pagans.
3 The pagans can rightly rejoice at no time.
4 Exod. 12.30.

perverse than any calamity whatsoever, and, as one of their own writers has declared, "the only thing of all that was worse than they expected"[5]; to us it was not such, but, no less than any of the other things, a means of disciplining and testing. For it did not keep away even from us, but it came out against the heathen in force.'

To this, in turn, he adds the following: 'At any rate, most of our brethren, through their surpassing love and brotherly kindness being unsparing of themselves and clinging to one another, fearlessly visiting the sick and continually ministering to them, serving them in Christ, most cheerfully departed this life with them, becoming infected with the affliction of others, and drawing the sickness from their neighbors upon themselves, and willingly taking over their pains. And many, after they had cared for the sickness of others and restored them to health, themselves died, transferring their death to themselves, and actually fulfilling then the popular saying, which always seems to be merely a courtesty, "departing as their humble servants."[6] The best, at any rate, of the brethren among us departed from life in this manner, some presbyters and deacons and some of the laity who were praised exceedingly, so that this form of death, which had its origin in much piety and strong faith, seemed to be little short of martyrdom. And taking up the bodies of the saints with open hands at the bosom, and closing their eyes, and shutting their mouths, and bearing them away on their shoulders, and

5 Cf. Thucydides 2.64.1.
6 Cf. 1 Cor. 4.13. The Greek *perípsēma* was used in classical times for the offscouring among the population, who in time of trouble were thrown into the sea to wipe away the guilt of the nation. However, by the third century of our era the expression, *perípsemá sou,* took on the complimentary meaning of 'Your humble servant.'

laying them out, clinging to them, embracing them, adorning them by washings and garments, after a little they obtained like services, those who were left behind always following upon those who went before. But the action of the pagans was entirely the opposite. They would thrust away those who were just beginning to fall sick, and they fled their dearest; they would cast them upon the roads half-dead, and would treat the unburied bodies as vile refuse, shunning the communication and contagion of the death, which it was not easy by many schemes to avoid.'

And after this letter,[7] also, when the affairs of the city had become peaceful, he again sent a festal writing to the brethren in Egypt, and after this he again composed others. A certain letter of his *On the Sabbath* is extant, and another *On Exercise*.[8]

And again communicating by letter with Hermammon[9] and the brethren in Egypt, and recounting many other things about the wickedness of Decius and of those after him, he mentions the peace under Gallienus.

Chapter 23

There is nothing like hearing the nature of those events as follows.

'Now that one,[1] after inciting one of his emperors and

---

7 Probably Dionysius' festal letter for the year 263.
8 We know nothing about these two sermons.
9 Cf. 7.1 n. 3. A quotation from this letter is given in 7.1,10.

---

1 Macrianus; cf. 7.10. He incited Valerian to persecute, and tried to dethrone Gallienus. Later, both he and his son were defeated in battle and killed.

attacking another, quickly disappeared with all his family, root and branch, and Gallienus was proclaimed and acknowledged by all as at once an old and a new emperor, being before them and coming after them. For, according to what was said to the Prophet Isaias: "The things that are first, behold they are come, and new things which shall now spring forth."[2] Just as a cloud, which ran under the rays of the sun and obscured it, for a little while darkened it and appeared in its place, then, when the cloud passed and dissolved, the sun that shone before and shone again appeared, so Macrianus who came forward and obtained access for himself to the Empire which belonged to Gallienus is no more, since he never was, while the other [Gallienus] is like he was; and the Empire, having, as it were, put aside old age and cleansed itself of its former wickedness, blooms forth more luxuriantly, and is seen and heard more widely, and extends everywhere.'[3]

Then, in turn, he also indicates the time at which he wrote this, in the following words: 'And it occurs to me again to observe the days of the imperial years. For I note that those very impious men, though named with honor, have not long since become nameless, but the holier and more God-loving one,[4] having passed the period of seven years, is now completing the ninth, in which let us feast.'[5]

2 Cf. Isa. 42.9; 43.19.
3 Dionysius is prejudiced by the favor shown by Gallienus to the Christians. In reality, the reign of Gallienus was one of the most disastrous in the history of the Roman Empire, as we learn from the pagan historians. Numerous calamities fell upon the Roman people at that time.
4 Again Dionysius is influenced by Gallienus' kindly disposition toward the Christians. As a matter of fact, although possessed of ability and courage, he was one of the most abandoned and profligate of emperors.
5 Cf. 1 Cor. 5.8. The seventh year of Gallienus came to a close toward the end of 260, shortly before the capture of Valerian. From then until the capture of the two Macriani in his ninth year he was, as Dionysius says, 'under a cloud.'

Chapter 24

Besides all these, he also carefully prepared the two works *On Promises*,[1] and his occasion for this was Nepos,[2] a bishop of those in Egypt, who taught that the promises made to the saints in holy Scripture should be interpreted in a more Jewish way, and who assumed that there would be a kind of millenium of bodily luxury on this earth. Thinking, then, to establish his private opinion from the Apocalypse of John, he composed a book on this subject and he entitled it *Refutation of the Allegorists*.[3] Dionysius opposed him in the books *On Promises*, in the first of which he sets forth the opinion which he himself held regarding the doctrine, and in the second he treats of the Apocalypse of John. There in the beginning he makes mention of Nepos and writes the following about him: 'But since they bring forward a certain work of Nepos, on which they especially rely as irrefutably proving that the kingdom of Christ will be on earth, [permit me to say] I approve of him in many other matters, and I love Nepos for his faith and his industry and his study of the Scriptures and his extensive psalmody,[4] by which many of the brethren up to this day have been cheered, and I am moved by great respect for the man, the more so because he

---

1 In Book 1 Dionysius presents his own views on the subject under discussion, and in Book 2 he gives a detailed treatment of the Apocalypse on which Nepos draws to support his Chiliastic views. Of this work we have only the extracts given by Eusebius in this and the next chapter, and three fragments preserved in a Vatican manuscript.

2 All our information on Nepos is to be found here. On Chiliasm in the early Church, cf. 3.39.

3 This work of Nepos has entirely disappeared. It was directed against persons who, like Origen and Dionysius, rejected a literal interpretation of the Apocalypse in favor of the allegorical; cf. 7.25.

4 On eary Christian hymnody, cf. 5.28.

has already gone to his rest. But the truth is dear and most honored of all things,[5] and we should praise and approve ungrudgingly whatever is rightly said, but examine and correct whatever appears to be unsoundly composed. And if he were present and teaching by mere words, unwritten conversation would be sufficient, persuading and instructing by question and answer "them that resist."[6] But when a book is published which seems most convincing to some, and when some teachers think the Law and the Prophets of no account and disregard the following of the Gospels and depreciate the Epistles of the Apostles, but make promises as to the teaching of this work as if some great and hidden mystery, and do not allow our simpler brethren to have high and noble thoughts, either regarding the glorious and truly divine coming of our Lord[7] or our resurrection from the dead or our gathering together unto Him[8] and being like to Him,[9] but persuade them to hope for the small and mortal and such as are of the present in the Kingdom of God—then it is necessary that we, too, argue with our brother Nepos as if he were present.'

After other remarks he adds to this, saying: 'Now when I was in the district of Arsinoë,[10] where, as you know, this doctrine was popular for a long time, so that schisms and apostasies of entire churches took place, after summoning together the presbyters and teachers of brethren in the villages, the brethren who wished also being present, I urged them to

---

5 Cf. Aristotle, *Eth. Nic.* 1.1096A.
6 2 Tim. 2.25.
7 Cf. 1 Tim. 6.14.
8 Cf. 2 Thess. 2.1.
9 Cf. 1 John 3.2.
10 The district of Arsinoë was on the western bank of the Nile, between the river and Lake Moeris, southwest of Memphis.

make an examination of the question publicly, and, when they brought me this book as if it were some invincible weapon and rampart, I sat with them for three consecutive days from morning until night, and I tried to set right what had been written. At that time, also, I was exceedingly pleased with the steadfastness and the love of truth and the ability to follow an argument and the intelligence of the brethren, as we considered in order and with justice the questions and the newly raised difficulties and points of agreement: on the one hand, refusing to cling by every means and contentiously to opinions once formed unless they were manifestly right; on the other, not evading counter-arguments, but, in so far as possible, attempting to face the problems that lay before us and to conquer them, nor, if reason decided, being ashamed to change our opinions and give assent, but conscientiously and without dissimulation and with hearts laid open to God accepting whatever was established by the proofs and teachings of the holy Scriptures. Finally, the leader and introducer of this teaching, called Coracion,[11] within the hearing of all the brethren present, confessed and bore witness to us that he would no longer adhere to this, nor discuss it, nor mention nor teach it, inasmuch as he had been sufficiently convinced by the arguments against it. And of the rest of the brethren, some rejoiced at the joint conference and at the spirit of conciliation and harmony on the part of all.'

11 Nothing more is known of him.

Chapter 25

Then, passing on in order, he says the following about the Apocalypse of John:[1] 'Some of those before us have rejected and entirely discredited the book, examining it chapter by chapter, declaring it unintelligible and illogical, and that its title was false. They say that it is not John's, that, moreover, it is not even an unveiling [apocalypse] since it is veiled by an exceedingly thick curtain of obscurity, and that none of the Apostles or even any one at all of the saints or of the members of the Church was the author of the book, but Cerinthus, the one who established the heresy called "Cerinthian" after him, for he wished to affix a name worthy of trust to his forgery. This was the doctrine of his teaching, that the kingdom of Christ would be on earth, and he dreamed that it would be made up of those things which he himself desired —since he was a lover of the body and quite carnal—the full satisfaction of the belly and of things below the belly, that is, feasts and drinking bouts and marriages, and, as a means of providing these under a better name, festivals and sacrifices and slaying of victims.[2] As for me, I would not dare to reject the book, since many brethren hold it in high esteem; but, assuming my understanding inadequate to form an opinion of it, I hold that there is some concealed and more hidden interpretation[3] in each passage. For, even if I do not understand it, I suspect that some deeper meaning underlies the words. I do not measure and judge these things by my own

---

1 On the Apocalypse in the early Church and its treatment of Dionysius, cf. 3.24.
2 Part of this quotation has already been given by Eusebius in 3.28.
3 Apoc. 22.7,8.

reason, but assigning more importance to faith, I have thought them too high to be understood by me, and I do not reject that which I have not comprehended, but I rather wonder that I did not really see them.'

After this, when he had closely examined the whole work of the Apocalypse and had demonstrated that it cannot be understood according to the literal sense, he adds, saying: 'Having finished all, so to speak, of his prophecy, the Prophets proclaim those blessed who keep it, and indeed even himself. For he says: "Blessed is he that keepeth the words of the prophecy of this book, and I, John, who have heard and seen these things."[4] Therefore, that he is called John and that this work belongs to John I do not deny, for I agree that it belongs to someone holy and inspired. However, I could not readily agree that this person is the Apostle, the son of Zebedee, the brother of James, to whom belong the Gospel entitled "According to John" and the Catholic Epistle.[5] I base my judgment on the character of each and the forms of expression and the so-called arrangement of the book that the author is not the same. For the Evangelist nowhere gives his name, nor announces himself throughout either the Gospel or the Epistle.'

Then, passing on, he again speaks, thus: 'John nowhere, either in the first or the third person.[6] But he who wrote the Apocalypse proclaims himself immediately at the beginning: "The Apocalypse of Jesus Christ, which he gave to show his servants quickly; and he sent and signified it by his angel to his servant John, who bore witness to the word of God and His testimony of as much as he saw."[7] Then he also

---

4 I.e., than appears at first reading.
5 Cf. 3.24 and notes.
6 He never speaks of himself as 'I, John,' or as 'his servant, John.'
7 Cf. Apoc. 1.1,2.

writes an Epistle: "John to the seven churches in Asia, grace to you, and peace."[8] But the Evangelist did not even write his name at the head of the Catholic Epistle, but without affection began with the mystery itself of the divine revelation: "That which was from the beginning, which we have heard, which we have seen with our eyes."[9] For with respect to this revelation, also, the Lord called Peter blessed, saying: "Blessed art thou, Simon Bar-Jona: because flesh and blood hath not revealed it to thee, but my Father who is in heaven."[10] But not even in the second and third extant Epistles of John, although they are short is John placed at the beginning by name,[11] but "the ancient" has been written without mentioning a name. But this man did not even think it enough, after mentioning his name once, to narrate succeeding events, but he takes his name up again: "I John, your brother and your partner in tribulation, and in the kingdom, and patience in Christ Jesus, was in the island, which is called Patmos, for the word of God, and for the testimony of Jesus."[12] And now, also, toward the close, he spoke as follows: "Blessed is he that keepeth the words of the prophecy of this book. And I, John, who have heard and seen these things."[13]

'Accordingly, that he who wrote these words was John we must believe, since he says so. But what person this is, is not clear. For, he did not say, as in many places in the Gospel, that he was the disciple loved by the Lord[14] or he who

8 Cf. Apoc. 1.4.
9 1 John 1.1.
10 Matt. 16.17.
11 2 John 1; 3 John 1.
12 Apoc. 1.9.
13 Apoc. 22.7,8.
14 Cf. John 13.23; 19.26; 20.2; 21.7,20.

leaned on His breast,[15] or the brother of James, or he who
was the eyewitness and hearer of the Lord. For he would
have said some of these afore-mentioned things if he had
wished to make himself clearly known. Yet, he has mentioned
none of these, but speaks of himself our brother and partner,[16]
and a witness of Jesus, and blessed in the seeing and hearing
of the revelations.[17] But I believe that there have been many
of the same name as John the Apostle, who because of their
love for him, and for their admiration and esteem for him and
their desire to be loved as he was by the Lord,[18] gladly also
took over the same name after him, just as Paul, and, indeed,
Peter, is commonly used among the boys of the faithful.
There is also, for example, another John in the Acts of the
Apostles, who was surnamed Mark, whom Barnabas and Paul
took with them,[19] about whom also it is said: "And they
had John also in the ministry."[20] But if this one is the writer,
I would say No. For it is written that he did not come to
Asia with them, but it is said: "Now when Paul and they
that were with him had sailed from Paphos, they came to
Perge in Pamphylia, and John departing from them, returned
to Jerusalem."[21] But I think that there was a certain other
[John] among those who were in Asia, since they say that
there were two tombs in Ephesus and each is said to be
John's.[22]

'And from their ideas, also, and from their vocabulary and

15 Cf. John 13.23,25.
16 Apoc. 1.9.
17 Apoc. 22.7,8.
18 Cf. John 21.20ff.
19 Acts 12.25.
20 Acts 13.5.
21 Acts 13.13.
22 Cf. 3.39 and notes.

from their sentence structure, this writer will naturally be assumed to be different from the other.[23] For the Gospel and Epistle are in agreement, and begin in the same way. The one says: "In the beginning was the Word";[24] the other: "That which was from the beginning."[25] The one says: "And the Word was made flesh, and dwelt among us, (and we saw his glory, the glory as it were of the only begotten of the Father)";[26] the other, the same words slightly changed: "That which we have heard, which we have seen with our eyes, which we have looked upon, and our hands have handled, of the word of life; and the life was manifested."[27] For he introduced these words by way of a prelude, aiming, as he shows in what follows, at those who deny that the Lord is come in the flesh.[28] Therefore, he also carefully added: "And that which we have seen, we bear witness, and declare to you the eternal life which was with the Father, and was manifested to us; that which we have seen and heard, we declare unto you also."[29] He clings to his purpose and does not stray from it, but discusses everything under the same heads and names, some of which we will mention briefly. He who reads attentively will discover frequently in each "the life," "the light," "turning from darkness," continually "the truth," "the grace," "the joy," "the flesh and blood of the Lord," "the judgment," "the forgiveness of sins," "the love of God toward us," "the commandment of love for one another," that we should "keep

23 I.e., the writer of the Apocalypse and the author of the Gospel and the Epistles are different.
24 John 1.1.
25 1 John 1.1.
26 John 1.14.
27 Cf. 1 John 1.1,2.
28 Cf. 1 John 4.2.
29 1 John 1.2,3.

all the commandments," "the conviction of the world, of the Devil, of Anti-Christ," "the promise of the Holy Spirit," "the adoption of God," "the faith always demanded of us," "the Father" and "the Son"—these are everywhere. It is clear that those who note the characteristics everywhere throughout see at a glance that the Gospel and the Epistle have the same complexion. But the Apocalypse is very different from and foreign to these writings, neither touching nor bordering upon either of them, having almost, so to speak, not a single syllable in common with them. Moreover, the Epistle has neither a mention nor a thought of the Apocalypse (for we pass over the Gospel), nor does the Apocalypse of the Epistle, although Paul in his Epistles gives some little indication also of his revelations, which he did not write separately.[30]

'Furthermore, it also is possible to judge by the style the difference between the Gospel and the Epistle with reference to the Apocalypse. For the former have not only been written flawlessly in the language of the Greeks, but also most skilfully in the expresions, the reasonings, and constructions of the commentary. It is, moreover, far from possible to discover any barbarous word or solecism or any vulgarism at all in them. For, as it seems, the author had each kind of word— the Lord having bestowed both upon him—the word of knowledge[31] and the word of speech.[32] I will not deny to the other writer the seeing of visions and possession of knowledge and prophecy; yet I note that his speech and language are not accurate Greek, but make use of barbarous idioms

30 Cf. 2 Cor. 12.1,2; Gal. 2.2.
31 1 Cor. 12.8.
32 Cf. 1 Cor. 14.6.

and in some places even of solecisms, which it is not necessary to pick out now. I have not mentioned these matters to mock (lest anyone think this), but only to set forth clearly the difference between these writings.'

Chapter 26

Besides these letters of Dionysius there are extant many others, also, such as those against Sabellius[1] to Ammon,[2] bishop of the church at Bernice,[3] and that to Telesphorus, and that to Euphranor, and to Ammon again, and to Euporus. And he also composed four other works on the same subject, which he addressed to his namesake, Dionysius in Rome. Besides these, we have many of his letters, and also extensive works written in epistolary form, for example, those *On Nature*,[4] addressed to the boy Timothy, and one *On Temptations*,[5] which he also dedicated to Euphranor. Besides these, when writing to Basilides,[6] bishop of the parishes in the Pentapolis, he also says that he has written an interpretation

1 On Sabellius and Dionysius' attitude toward Sabellianism, cf. 7.6.
2 Nothing is known of the works addressed to Ammon, Telesphorus, Euphranor, and Euporus; cf. 7.6.
3 The usual form is Berenice. Of the several cities of this name in North Africa, this is probably the one in Libya Pentapolis, or Cyrenaica, on the Mediterranean, about 600 miles west of Alexandria.
4 The date and occasion of this work are not known. It was probably a refutation of the teachings of various pagan philosophers on the origin of the universe.
5 This work is now lost, and nothing is known of the time and occasion of its composition.
6 All our information about this Basilides is contained in this passage. A canonical epistle by Dionysius addressed to him is still extant; cf. 6.40. We are told by Eusebius that Dionysius wrote various epistles to him, but no others are known.

of the beginning of Ecclesiastes,[7] and he has left us different letters also addressed to this person.

So much for Dionysius. But come now, after the story of these events, let us hand down to posterity the story of our time, that they may know the nature of this generation.

Chapter 27

Xystus, after being at the head of the Church at Rome for eleven years,[1] was succeeded by Dionysius,[2] namesake of him at Alexandria. And at this time also, when Demetrian[3] departed life at Antioch, Paul of Samosata[4] took over the

---

7 A few very questionable fragments of this work are extant.

1 Xystus II. Eusebius is very much confused about the chronology of the bishops of this time. Here he should have said 'eleven months' (from August or September 257 to August 258), not 'eleven years.'

2 After Xystus II was martyred, because of the harsh persecution by Valerian, the bishopric of Rome remained vacant for nearly a year. According to the Liberian catalogue, Dionysius became bishop on July 22, 259. He is believed to have continued as bishop until December 27, 268.

3 On Demetrian, cf. 6.46.

4 Paul of Samosata, one of the most famous heretics of the early Church, Bishop of Antioch from 259 or 260 to 265. Several synods, probably three, were held to try him about 264-266. St. Dionysius of Alexandria failed to attend the first of these because of illness. Firmilian of Caesarea, St. Gregory Thaumaturgus, his brother Athenodorus, and many others were on hand. Paul also held the civil office of *Procurator ducenarius*, and thus was protected by the famous Queen of Palmyra, Zenobia. He was a wealthy man, and had many slavish followers even among the neighboring bishops. These defended his doctrine and he declared himself orthodox. In the first of the meetings the bishops were satisfied. At another he was condemned, but promised to retract his errors, which he never did. A final council was called. Firmilian died while traveling to it. Malchion, a priest of Antioch, an accomplished man of letters, took the principal part. In the disputation with Paul, he thoroughly refuted him and brought about his deposition. Malchion was the author of a letter written in

episcopacy. Since the latter held mean and low views contrary to the teaching of the Church, about Christ—for example, that He was an ordinary man in His nature—Dionysius of Alexandria was invited to come to the synod. Giving both old age and physical weakness as an excuse, he put off his arrival, although presenting by letter[5] the opinion which he held on the subject in question. But the rest of the pastors of the Church gathered from all directions, as against a despoiler of the flock of Christ, all hastening to Antioch.

Chapter 28

Of those who were especially distinguished among these, Firmilian[1] was Bishop of Caesarea in Cappadocia, and

---

the name of the synod to Pope Dionysius of Rome, Maximus of Alexandria, and all the bishops and clergy throughout the world. This has been preserved in part, as well as a few fragments of the shorthand report of the disputation, in 7.30. Of his doctrine we may present the following points: 'The Father, Son, and Holy Ghost are but a single Person. The Son or Logos is without hypostasis, being merely the wisdom and science of God, which is in Him as reason is in a man. Before all worlds He was born as Son without a virgin; He is without shape and cannot be made visible to men. He worked in the Prophets, especially in Moses . . . , and in a far higher way in the Son of David who was born by the Holy Ghost of a virgin. The Christ, the Saviour, is essentially a man, but the Holy Ghost inspired Him from above. The Father and the Son are one God, whereas Christ is from the earth with a personality of His own. Thus there are two Persons in Christ.' Cf. *Catholic Encyclopedia*, art, 'Paul of Samosata.'

5 This epistle is no longer extant. A copy of it was originally appended to the encyclical of the Antiochian synod (cf. 7.30.) , and so was extant at the time of Eusebius and also of Jerome.

---

1 On Firmilian, cf. 6.26.

Gregory[2] and Athenodore, brothers, pastors of the parishes in the Pontus; and besides these Helenus,[3] [bishop] of the parish in Tarsus, and Nicomas[4] of the parish in Iconium; also, Hymenaeus, of the church in Jerusalem, and Theotecnus,[5] of this neighboring church of Caesarea; also, in addition to these, Maximus;[6] this one also was presiding with distinction over the brethren in Bostro; and one would not be at a loss to count up countless others, including presbyters and deacons who were gathered together for the same cause in the city[7] mentioned above. But these were the most illustrious among these. Now, when all came together frequently on different occasion, arguments and questions were stirred up at each meeting, the Samosatene and his group trying to conceal and cover over the facts of his heterodoxy, others zealously working to lay bare and to bring his heresy and blasphemy against Christ into the open.

At this time, Dionysius died in the twelfth year of the reign of Gallienus,[8] having held the episcopate at Alexandria for seventeen years, and Maximus[9] succeeded him.

---

2 On Gregory Thaumaturgus and his brother, Athenodorus, cf. 6.30 and notes.

3 Helenus presided at the final council which deposed Paul of Samosta; cf. 6.30,46.

4 Of this Nicomas, Bishop of Iconium in Lycaonia, nothing is known.

5 Cf. 7.14 and note.

6 Nothing is known of this Maximus, Bishop of Bostra, in Arabia.

7 Antioch.

8 August 264 to August 265. On the dates of the accession and death of Gallienus, cf. 6.40.

9 A presbyter, while Dionysius was Bishop of Alexandria, a fellow sufferer with him during the persecutions of Decius and Valerian. Cf. 7.11,32.

After Gallienus had held the power for fifteen entire years,[10] Claudius[11] was established as his successor.

The latter, after completing two years, passed on the government to Aurelian.

Chapter 29

In Aurelian's time, when a final synod[1] of a very large number of bishops was organized, the leader of the heresy[2] at Antioch, on being detected and now clearly condemned of heterodoxy by all, was excommunicated from the Catholic Church under heaven. And especially was he set straight and refuted, as he sought concealment, by Malchion,[3] a learned man in every respect and the head of a school of

---

10 Eusebius here reckons the reign of Gallienus from August, 253, the date of his association with his father as emperor.
11 Claudius II (M. Aurelius Claudius, surnamed Gothicus), emperor from 268 to 270, rose to distinction by his military talents under Decius, Valerian, and Gallienus. He succeeded to the Empire in 268 on the death of Gallienus. He ded at Sirmium in 270, and was succeeded by Aurelian.

---

1 Eusebius is regarded as in error when putting this synod in the reign of Aurelian (270-275). In all probability it was held as early as 265 and no later than 268. It could not have been held earlier than 264, because it was not until that year that Dionysius of Alexandria was succeeded by Maximus.
2 I.e., Paul of Samosata.
3 Cf. Jerome, *De vir. ill.* 71, where Malchion is called author of an epistle sent to the bishops of Alexandria and Rome, probably the one mentioned in the next chapter. This statement has been generally accepted, although Jerome is the only authority for it. Both Eusebius and Jerome state that the report of Malchion's discussion with Paul was extant in their day, and fragments of it have been preserved by Leontius (*De sectis* III).

rhetoric, one of the Greek educational institutions at Antioch, but also thought worthy, because of the surpassing sincerity of his faith in Christ, of the presbyterate in the parish there. This man conducted a cross examination of Paul, in the presence of stenographers who recorded it, which we know is still extant even in our time, and he alone of all was able to detect the man who was so crafty and deceitful.

Chapter 30

Now, the pastors, who had been assembled together, by unanimous consent composed a single letter addressed personally to Dionysius,[1] Bishop of Rome, and Maximus,[2] Bishop of Alexandria, and dispatched it to all the provinces, thereby making their own zeal manifest to all, and also the perverse heterodoxy of Paul, together with the arguments and questions which they had addressed to him, and in addition describing the entire life and character of the man. It might be well for the sake of a memorial on the present occasion to give the following quotation from all this.

'To Dionysius and Maximus and to all our fellow ministers throughout the world, bishops, presbyters, and deacons, and to the whole Catholic Church under heaven, Helenus[3] and Hymenaeus and Theophilus and Theotecnus and Maximus, Proclus, Nicomas and Aelianus and Paul and Bolanus and Protogenes and Hierax and Eutychius and Theodore[4] and

---

1 Cf. 7.27.
2 Cf. 7.28.
3 Cf. 6.46.
4 Some suggest that the Theodore here is really Gregory Thaumaturgus who was also known by that name, but this is unlikely. This Theodore does not seem to be a very prominent person. Cf. 6.30,31.

Malchion and Lucius and all the rest who with us inhabit the neighboring cities and provinces, bishops and presbyters and deacons and the churches of God, greeting to the beloved brethren in the Lord.'

After a little, they add the following to this: 'And we wrote and at the same time invited many even of the bishops at a distance to come and heal us of this deadly doctrine, as for example, both Dionysius at Alexandria[5] and Firmilian[6] of Cappadocia, blessed men. The former of these also wrote to Antioch, not considering the leader of the error worthy of being addressed, and not writing to him personally, but to the whole parish, of which also we have attached a copy. But Firmilian even came twice and condemned the innovations effected by him, as we who were present know and bear witness, and many others know, also, but when he promised that he would change, trusting and hoping that he would restore the matter fittingly without any reproach to the Word, he adjourned [the meeting], being deceived by him who denied both his God and his Lord, and did not keep the faith which he himself formerly had. Firmilian now was about to cross over into Antioch and had come as far as Tarsus, for he had experienced the wickedness of this denier of God, but, when we had come together and were calling him and waiting until he should come, in the midst of all this he reached the end of his life.'[7]

Further, after other matters, they describe his life, the kind of existence he[8] led, in these words: 'But whereas, after

5 Cf. 7.27.
6 Cf. 6.26.
7 On the date of Firmilian's death, cf. 6.26.
8 Paul of Samosata.

departing from the canon [of faith], he has turned to false and spurious doctrines, we do not have to judge the actions of him who is without,[9] not even because, although he was formerly poor and a beggar and had received no means of livelihood from his fathers and had not gotten it from a trade or occupation, he now had come into an abundant wealth through his lawless and sacrilegious acts and through what he demanded and extorted of his brethren, for he deprives the injured of their rights, and promises to help them for a bribe, and deceives these also, and at random makes gain from the readiness of those engaged in lawsuits to give that they may be freed of the troubles that beset them, supposing godliness to be a means of gain.[10] Nor [do we judge him] because he minds high things[11] and is puffed up, clothing himself in worldly dignities, and preferring to be called *ducenarius*[12] rather than bishop, and strutting in the market places,[13] and reading and dictating letters while walking in public, and being attended by a bodyguard, some going ahead and others following after, many in number, so that the faith is both ill thought of and hated because of his pride and the haughtiness of his heart. Neither [do we judge] the trickery in ecclesiastical synods which he devises, courting popularity and deceiving with appearances and astounding the minds of the more simple by such things, preparing for

9 Cf. 1 Cor. 5.12.

10 Cf. 1 Tim. 6.5.

11 Cf. Rom. 12.16; 1 Tim. 6.17.

12 A procurator of high rank in the service of Zenobia, Queen of Palmyra, so called because his salary was 200 sestertia. He was permitted to hold his bishopric, although deposed by the synod, because of Zenobia. She was, however, a person of high character, and her friendship toward Paul is usually regarded as in his favor.

13 Cf. Demosthenes, *Katà Mediou* 158.

himself a tribunal and lofty throne,[14] not like a disciple of
Christ, and possessing a *secretum*,[15] like wordly rulers, and
calling it such, and striking his thigh with his hand, and
stamping the tribunal with his feet; and rebuking and insulting those who do not applaud and wave their hand-
kerchiefs as in a theatre and do not shout out and do not
jump up just as the men and women do who belong to his
group and who do not give heed to him in so disorderly a
manner, but who listen, as in a house of God, in an orderly
and reverent manner; and acting insolently and vulgarly in
public toward the expounders of the Word who have gone
from this life and bragging about himself as if he were not a
bishop but a sophist and a charlatan; putting an end to the
psalms addressed to our Lord, Jesus Christ, on the theory that
they are modern and the compositions of modern men, but
in the middle of the church, on the great day of the Pasch,
training women to sing psalms to himself, which one would
shudder to listen to. Such ideas he also permits the bishops
of the bordering country and cities, who fawn upon him, and
the presbyters to dwell upon in their sermons to the people.
For he does not wish to confess with the rest that the Son of
God came down from heaven (to anticipate something of
what we shall presently write, and this will not be stated
with mere words, but is proved from many sources among
the documents which we have sent, not the least where he
says that Jesus Christ is from below[16]), but those who sing
psalms to him and praise him among the people declare that

---

14 Paul is condemned not because he had a throne, but because he
  erected a tribunal in the church and placed his throne upon it.
15 The place where a judge or magistrate sat to decide cases.
16 According to Paul, Christ had no divine origin from above, but was
  'from below.'

their impious teacher is an angel come down from heaven.
He does not prevent this—the arrogant fellow is even present
while they say these things. And his women, the *subintroductae*,[17] as the Antiochenes call them, and those of the
presbyters and deacons among his followers, with whom he
co-operates in concealing this and the other incurable sins,
though he is cognizant of them and has convicted them of
those acts, that he may hold them under obligation to him,
and keep them from daring because of fear for themselves to
accuse him of the wrong he does by word and deed,[18] but
he has even made them rich, for which cause he is loved
and admired by those who covet such things—why should
we write about all this? Moreover, we know, beloved, that
the bishop and all the clergy should be an example to the
multitude of all good works,[19] and we are not even ignorant
of this: How many have fallen by procuring *subintroductae*
for themselves, so that, even if one should grant him that
nothing licentious is committed, he should at least have been
on his guard against the suspicion that arises from such action,
lest he scandalize someone, and induce others to imitate him.
For, how could he rebuke another or admonish him to
associate with a woman on familiar terms no longer, remaining on guard lest he slip,[20] as it is written, when he has already
sent one away, but has two with him blooming with youth
and beautiful to behold, and if he goes away anywhere, he
brings them around with him, all this while living in luxury
and surfeiting himself? Because of this all groan and lament

17 I.e., spiritual 'sisters.'
18 It is difficult, because of the lack of evidence otherwise, to believe
   entirely the black picture given of Paul here.
19 Cf. Titus 2.7.
20 Cf. Eccli. 9.8,9.

by themselves, but they so fear his tyranny and power as not to dare to accuse him. Yet, as we have said above,[21] one might have called to account a man who at least has a Catholic mind and is also numbered with us,[22] but one who has disgraced the mystery,[23] and has strutted about in the abominable heresy of Artemas[24] (for why should we not make his father entirely known?), of such a man we do not think that we should demand an accounting for these things.'

Then, at the end of the letter, they add the following: 'So we have been forced to excommunicate him, since he sets himself up against God and does not yield, and to establish in his place another bishop for the Catholic Church, by the providence of God, as we are persuaded, Domnus,[25] the son of the blessed Demetrian,[26] who formerly presided notably over this same parish and is adorned by all the noble qualities befitting a bishop, and we have made this clear to

21 Cf. 7.6.
22 It is interesting to note that had Paul been orthodox some effort would have been made to reform his character, but as a heretic this was not worth while. He is condemned because he is heretical.
23 Cf. 1 Tim. 3.16.
24 In 5.28 he is called Artemon. As noted in 7.27, Paul's heresy was like that of Artemas.
25 Domnus was appointed Bishop of Antioch in 269, on the deposition of Paul of Samosata. This was done on the sole authority of the council of bishops, without any reference to the clergy and the people, since they feared that the latter would re-elect Paul. Paul, through the support of Zenobia, retained the episcopal residence and the church for two years. The orthodox group appealed to Aurelian after he had conquered Zenobia and had taken Antioch in 272. The emperor decided that the right of occupation belonged to the party in communion with the bishops of Italy and the Church of Rome. This decision was backed by the civil power, and Paul was forced to leave the palace in disgrace (cf. 7.30). Domnus died in 274, and was succeeded by Timaeus.
26 Cf. 6.46.

you, that you may write to this man and receive letters of communion[27] from him. But let him write to Artemas, and let those who think as Artemas does have communion with him.'

Now, when Paul had fallen from the episcopacy and also from the orthodoxy of the faith, Domnus, as has been said, succeeded to the service of the Church at Antioch. When Paul refused to stay out of the church building, the Emperor Aurelian was importuned and he gave out a very just decision as to what had to be done, ordering to assign the building to those to whom the bishops of the faith[28] in Italy and in the city of Rome should enjoin. Thus, then, was the aforesaid man driven out of the Church with extreme disgrace by the worldly power.

Such truly was the attitude of Aurelian toward us at that time, but, as his reign proceeded, he thought differently about us, and he was now moved by certain counsels to stir up a persecution against us,[29] and widespread was the discussion among all about this. But now, as he was about to do this and, so to speak, was undersigning the decrees against us, divine justice came upon him, all but keeping him from his undertaking by holding his arms, and clearly presenting for all to see the fact that never would it be easy

---

27 In Greek, *tà koinōnikà grámmata*; in Latin *litterae communicatoriae*; also, *formatae* (cf. Augustine, *Epistle* 163). The use of such letters is very old in the Church. They were of two kinds: those given to the clergy and laity about to travel so as to be admitted to communion by foreign bishops; those sent by bishops to other bishops to declare their communion with them. The latter are mentioned here.

28 I.e., the Christian religion, probably a translation of the exact words of Aurelian. The Bishop of Rome here referred to was Felix.

29 Eusebius here probably gives the correct account of a much disputed subject. Auerlian never actually instituted hostile action.

for the rulers of the world to proceed against the churches of Christ, unless the hand that defends them in divine and heavenly judgment permits this to be done for the sake of discipline and correction, at whatever times it should approve. At any rate, after Aurelian had ruled for six years,[30] Probus succeeded him, and he, after holding the power for about the same number of years, was succeeded by Carus together with his sons Carinus and Numerianus, and again, when these in turn had continued in office for less than three years, the affairs of government fell upon Diocletian and those who were brought in after him,[31] and under these the persecution against us was accomplished and the destruction of the churches which was a part of it.

But a short time before this Dionysius,[32] Bishop of Rome, after having completed nine years, was succeeded in the service by Felix.[33]

---

30 Aurelian ruled from 270 to 275. His successors were, in order: Tacitus, who ruled for only six months; Probus 276-282; Carus and his sons Carinus and Numerian; and Diocletian in 284. Eusebius does not mention Tacitus here, but he does in *Chron*.

31 In 284. After associating Maximian with himself in the government in 286, he gave him the title of Augustus and placed him in command of the West. In 293 he gave Constantius Chlorus and Galerius the title of Caesar, and assigned the government of Gaul and Britain to Constantius Chlorus, and the power over the provinces between the Adriatic and Euxine to Galerius, while Maximian held Africa and Italy, and Diocletian himself held the provinces of Asia. As Eusebius tells us in Book 8, he published his edict, opening his famous persecution against the Christians, on February 23, 303.

32 Cf. 7.27.

33 Felix I, Bishop of Rome from January 5, 269, to December 30, 274, in the reigns of Claudius and Aurelian. The account of his martyrdom is probably an error, due to confusing him with Felix II, Bishop of Rome in the fourth century. Nothing is known with certainty about his acts, except the part he played in the deposition of Paul of Samosata from the see of Antioch.

Chapter 31

At this time, also, the madman,[1] named after his demoniacal heresy, armed himself with the perversion of his reason, when the Devil, namely, Satan himself, the enemy of God, put the man forward for the destruction of many. Certainly a barbarian in life by his very speech and manner of living, and being by nature demoniacal and mad, attempting things consistent with these traits, he tried to fashion himself as Christ; sometimes he himself proclaiming himself the Paraclete[2] and the Holy Spirit Itself,[3] and, puffed up in his madness, at other times choosing, like Christ, twelve disciples as partners in his doctrinal innovation.[4] Indeed, having sewed together false and atheistic doctrines gathered from countless atheistic heresies long since extinct, he swept them like a deadly poison from the land of the Persians to our part of the world, and from him the impious name of the Manichaeans has been on the lips of many even down to our own time. Such, then, was the basis for this knowledge falsely so called,[5] which sprang up in the times mentioned above.

---

1 The name Manes or Mani is, of course, of Persian or Semitic origin. The Greek is *Mánēs* or *Manichaîos*. Eusebius makes a play upon the word by calling him *ho maneìs tàs phrénas* (deranged of mind). Eusebius, as all the Fathers did, thought it significant that the Persian name which he adopted should in the Greek be so appropriate. Eusebius' brief account here is the earliest authentic description of Manes and Manichaeism, For a good brief account, cf. *Catholic Encyclopedia*, art. 'Manichaeism.'

2 While the Fathers in general agree with Eusebius, some modern scholars declare that Manes pretended to be only a mere man, the messenger of the Paraclete.

3 Cf. John 14.16.

4 Cf. Matt. 10.1ff.

5 Cf. 1 Tim. 6.20.

Chapter 32

At this time, Felix[1] who had been in charge of the Church at Rome for five years, was succeeded by Eutychianus.[2] The latter, after having survived for not even ten months, left the office to Gaius,[3] who was of our time. And when he had been in charge for about fifteen years, Marcellinus[4] was established as his successor, the very one whom the persecution has overtaken.

During the time of these bishops, Timaeus[5] guided the episcopacy of Antioch after Domnus,[6] and he was succeeded by our contemporary Cyril.[7] During his episcopate we became acquainted with Dorotheus,[8] who was thought worthy of

1 Cf. 7.30.
2 Eutychianus, Bishop of Rome from January 275 to December 283, for a period of eight years, eleven months, and three days, was buried in the Catacombs of St. Callistus, as has been confirmed by the discovery of De Rossi of an inscribed slab in the papal crypt. He was not a martyr.
3 Gaius, Pope from December 17, 283 (9 or 10 days after the death of his predecessor Eutychianus) to April 22, 296, i.e., for twelve years four months and one week. Eusebius is wrong here. The story of his martyrdom is erroneous.
4 Marcellinus, Bishop of Rome after Gaius, from June 30, 296, to October 25, 304, elected after a vancancy of about two months. These dates are those of the Liberian Catalogue, and seem to be correct. Eusebius is in error here. The eleven bishops preceding, from Pontianus to Gaius, were buried in the Catacombs of St. Callistus, but Marcellinus was buried in those of Priscilla.
5 Nothing is known with certainty about Timaeus.
6 Cf. 7.30.
7 Cyril became bishop in the fourth year of Probus, i.e., 279-280, according to Jerome's *Chron.*, which places the accession of his successor, Tyrannus, in the eighteenth year of Diocletian, i.e., 301-302. Nothing of certainty is known about this Cyril.
8 Dorotheus and Lucius (8.13) are the earliest representatives of the school at Antioch and its sound method of Biblical exegesis in contrast to the school at Alexandria and its allegorical method. Dorotheus suffered martyrdom by hanging (8.6) early in the Diocletian persecution. He must accordingly have received his appointment from Diocletian and not from Constantine.

the presbyterate at Antioch, a learned man. He was very zealous about the beautiful in divine things, and devoted himself so carefully to the Hebrew language that he read intelligently the Hebrew Scriptures in the original tongue.[9] He was not unacquainted with the most liberal studies and with primary education among the Greeks. Besides this, he was a eunuch[10] by nature, having been such from birth itself, so that even the emperor,[11] on this account, as if it were a kind of miracle, considered him his friend and honored him with the charge over the purple dye works at Tyre. We have heard him expound the holy Scriptures temperately.

And after Cyril, Tyrannus[12] succeeded to the episcopacy of the parish of the Antiochenes, in whose time the attack upon the churches reached its height.

After Socrates,[13] Eusebius,[14] who had come from the city

---

9 A knowledge of Hebrew was uncommon in the early Church, and so was worthy of note.

10 Dorotheus, since he was a eunuch by birth, was not subject to Canon 1 of Nicaea which prohibted those who made themselves eunuchs of their own volition or for no special cause from becoming priests.

11 Diocletian.

12 Nothing certain is known of the character of Tyrannus or of the dates of his episcopate. He became bishop in the eighteenth year of Diocletian (301-302) according to Jerome's *Chron.* His successor Vitalis, according to Theodoret (*H. E.* 1.3), became bishop after peace had been restored to the Church. From this we may conjecture that Tyrannus lived until that time, i.e., 311.

13 Nothing is known of this Socrates.

14 All that is known of this Eusebius is contained in 7.11,32. He was a native and deacon of Alexandria. During the persecution under Valerian (257), when Dionysius had been banished from Alexandria, Eusebius remained to minister to those in prison and to bury the martyrs. During the civil war at the death of Valerian, when Alexandria was in revolt (262), Eusebius also did noble service ministering to the sick and the dying. Dionysius, Bishop of Alexandria, sent him as his representative to the synod of Antioch (264), which had been summoned to deal with Paul of Samosata. The see of Laodicea was

of Alexandria, was in charge of the parish in Laodicea. The affair of Paul was the underlying cause for his migration. When, on this account, he went to Syria he was prevented from returning home by those zealous there in divine things, for he was a beloved example of piety among people of our time, as it is easy to recognize even from the statements of Dionysius quoted above.[15] Anatolius[16] was appointed his successor, a good man, as it is said, following a good man, by birth also an Alexandrian, who for his learning and general education and Greek philosophy had carried off first place among the most illustrious of the men of our time, since in arithmetic and geometry and astronomy and the rest, whether logic or physics, as well as in speculation and in arts of rhetoric, he had reached the top. Because of these accomplishments report has it that he was deemed worthy by the citizens there to establish a school at Alexandria in

---

vacant at that time, and the Laodiceans insisted on Eusebius becoming their bishop. As Bishop of Laodicea he sat at the synod when Paul of Samosata was deposed in 270. He was succeeded by his old friend Anatolius.

15 In 11.3.24.

16 Bishop of Laodicea in Syria Prima, as we learn here. He had been famous at Alexandria for his knowledge of the liberal arts, and his reputation for practical wisdom was so great that, when the suburb of Brucheium was besieged by the Romans during the revolt of Aemilianus in 262, the command of the place was given to him. Having passed over to Palestine, he was ordained by Theotecnus, Bishop of Caesarea, as coadjutor bishop with the right of succession. But when in 269 he went to Antioch to attend the synod against Paul of Samosata, on his way through Laodicea, which had just lost its bishop, his old friend Eusebius, he was halted and made bishop in his room. Eusebius speaks of him as not having written much, but sufficient to show his eloquence and broad learning. He makes special mention of a work on the Paschal question. Some fragments of his mathematical works were published in Paris in 1543. The Ante-Nicene Library (Vol. 6) contains an English translation of his extant works.

the Aristotelian tradition.[17] Now, they also relate countless
other deeds of prowess at the siege of the Pirucheum[18] at
Alexandria, for he was considered by all those in authority
to be worthy of special privilege, but I shall mention only
the following as an example. It is said that, when wheat
failed the besieged, so that hunger now became more unbearable to them than the enemy without, this man being
present made some such arrangement as this. As the other
part of the city was in alliance with the Roman army and so
was not under siege, Anatolius sent for Eusebius (he was
still there at that time before his migration to Syria), who
was among those not besieged and had won such great fame
and widespread reputation that it reached even the general
of the Romans, and informed him of those who were perishing of hunger in the siege. When he learned it, he asked
the general of the Romans as a very great favor to grant
safety to the deserters from the enemy, and, on obtaining
his request, made it known to Anatolius. As soon as Anatolius
received the promise, he summoned a council of the Alexandrians, and at first asked that all give a friendly right hand
to the Romans, but, when he noticed that they were getting
angry at the proposal, he said: 'I do not think that you will
ever oppose me if I should advise permitting the superfluous people and in no way useful to us ourselves, old women
and children and old men, to go outside the gates wherever
they wish. Why do we keep with us to no purpose persons
who are all but ready to die? Why do we exhaust with hunger

---

17 Lit., 'succession.'
18 Pyrucheum or Brucheium, as other ancient writers called it, was one
   of the three districts of Alexandria. Here the royal family and the
   Greeks lived. It also contained the most important and the most
   beautiful buildings.

the crippled and maimed in body, when we ought to sustain men and youths alone and husband the necessary wheat for those required for the defense of the city?' Having persuaded the assembly with some such arguments, he was the first to rise and cast a vote that the entire class, whether of men or of women, not required for the army be released from the city, since even if they remained and continued in the city to no avail they would have no hope of safety, for they would perish from hunger. When all the rest of those in the senate agreed with this plan, he saved almost all of those who were being besieged, providing first of all for those belonging to the Church and all the rest of those in the city of every age to escape, not only those who were covered by the terms of the vote but countless others, also, under pretext of belonging to these, who secretly clothed themselves in women's garb, and according to his plan went out of the gates of the city during the night and hastened to the Roman army. There Eusebius, like a father and a physician, received all of them wasted away by the long siege, and revived them with all prudence and care. Of two such pastors in succession was the church of Laodicea deemed worthy, who in the providence of God came there from the Alexandrians after the aforesaid war. To be sure, Anatolius was not the author of a great many works, but enough have come down to us to enable us through them to become acquainted with both his eloquence and great learning. In these works he especially sets forth his opinions on the Pasch, from which I might be obliged to quote the following on the present occasion.

From the Canons of Anatolius on the Pasch.

'It has, then, in the first year the new moon of the first

month, which is the beginning of all the nineteen-year cycle,[19] according to the Egyptians on the twenty-sixth of Phamenoth, but according to the months of the Macedonians the twenty-second of Dystrus,[20] but, as the Romans would say, the eleventh before the Kalends of April. The sun is found on the aforesaid twenty-sixth of Phamenoth not only to have arrived at the first sign of the zodiac, but to be already passing through the fourth day in it. This sign is customarily called the first of the twelve signs of the zodiac, and the equinox and the beginning of months, and the head of the cycle, and the starting point of the planetary course, but the last of the months preceding this is the twelfth and the last of the twelve signs and the end of the planetary circuit. Therefore we say that those who place the first month in it, and determine by it the fourteenth day of the Pasch, commit no small or ordinary mistake. And this statement is not ours, but it was known to the Jews of old even before Christ, and it was especially observed by them. It is possible to learn this also from what is said by Philo, Josephus, and Musaeus,[21] and not only by these but also by the still more ancient writers, the two Agathobuli,[22] surnamed the Masters of Aristobulus[23]

19 Anatolius appears to have been the first Christian to employ the old Metonic nineteen-year cycle.

20 Phamenoth was the seventh month of the Alexandrian year, and began on August 29. It was introduced in the reign of Augustus, 25 B.C. Dystrus was the seventh month of the Macedonian year, and corresponded exactly with our March.

21 Known only from this reference of Anatolius.

22 Quite unknown.

23 A well-known Hellenistic philosopher of Alexandria, who lived in the second century B.C., in the time of Ptolemy Philometor. He was deeply versed in Greek philosophy, and is regarded by some scholars as the forerunner of Philo. All that is left of his works are two fragments from *On the Mosaic Law*, quoted by Eusebius in his *Praep. Evang.* 7.14 and 8.10.

the Famous; the latter was reckoned among the Seventy who translated the holy and divine Scriptures of the Hebrews[24] for Ptolemy Philadelphus and his father, and he dedicated the exegetical books on the Law of Moses to the same kings. These authors, resolving the problems in regard to Exodus, say that all equally ought to sacrifice the Passover after vernal equinox, in the middle of the first month; and that this is found while the sun is passing through the first sign of the solar, or, as some of them have named it, the zodiacal circle. And Aristobulus adds that it is necessary for the feast of the Passover that not only the sun be passing through an equinoctial sign, but the moon, also. For as there are two equinoctial signs, the vernal, the other autumnal, directly opposite each other, and as the day of the Passover was set on the fourteenth of the month, in the evening, the moon will hold a position diametrically opposite the sun, as can be seen in full moons; and the one, the sun, will be in the sign of the vernal equinox, and the other, the moon, will of necessity be in that of the autumnal. I know a great many other things also that they say, some of them probable, and others approaching absolute demonstrations, by which they try to establish that the feast of the Passover and of unleavened bread ought to be celebrated absolutely after the equinox. But I overlook demanding proofs for such matters from those for whom the veil upon the Mosaic Law has been taken away, and for whom it now remains with uncovered face to behold as in a mirror Christ and the teachings and

---

24 The Septuagint was clearly in existence before the time of Aristobulus, as is evident from the latter's words, quoted by Eusebius in *Praep. Evang.* 13.12,1-2. On the beginnings of the Septuagint, cf. 5.8.

sufferings of Christ.[25] But that the first month with the
Hebrews is around the equinox the teachings of the Book of
Henoch[26] also make clear.'

The same writer has left us an *Introduction to Arithmetic*
in ten complete books and other examples of his study and
wide knowledge of divine subjects. Theotecnus,[27] Bishop of
Caesarea in Palestine, first ordained him as bishop, endeavor-
ing to provide a successor for himself after death, and, indeed,
for a short time both were in charge of the same church.
But when the synod regarding Paul called him to Antioch,
as he was passing by the city of the Laodiceans he was
retained by the brethren there, Eusebius having gone to rest.

And after Anatolius also departed this life, Stephen[28] was
placed over the parish there, the last of the bishops before
the persecution, admired by the populace for his knowledge
of philosophy and other Greek learning. But he was not
equally disposed toward the divine faith, as the progress of
the persecution definitely proved, for it disclosed him to be
more of a dissembler and a craven and a coward than a
true philosopher. However, the affairs of the Church were
not to suffer on his account, but Theodotus,[29] proclaimed

25 Cf. 2 Cor. 15,16,18; also, Heb. 5.8.
26 Cf. Enoch (Henoch) 72.6,9,31,32. One of the apocrypha of the Old
Testament, widely used in the early Church, and quoted in the
Epistle of Jude 14f. Cf. *Catholic Encyclopedia*, art. 'Apocrypha.'
27 Cf. 7.14.
28 Nothing further is known of this Stephen, Bishop of Laodicea.
29 Theodotus, Bishop of Laodicea in Syria Prima, one of the most
zealous supporters of the Arian cause. Eusebius here speaks of his
great skill as a physician of both body and soul, declares him remarkable for kindness, sympathy, sincerity, and zeal in helping all
who needed aid, and praises him for reinstating the Church in its
prosperity which had suffered much through the cowardice of its
last bishop, Stephen, who apparently renounced his faith during the
persecution of Diocletian. The date of his accession is no later than
311, and of his death about 340.

bishop of that parish by God himself, the Saviour of all, set them right, a man who by his very deeds proved true to his own name and that of bishop. He held first rank in the science of healing bodies, but in that of caring for souls he was such as was no other man in kindness, sincerity, sympathy, and zeal for aiding those who need his help; and his training in matters pertaining to God was also great. Such, then, was this man.

But in Caesarea of Palestine, Theotecnus, after he had carried on his episcopacy most zealously, was succeeded by Agapius.[30] And we know that this man also labored much, displaying a most genuine concern for the protection of the people and caring with a liberal hand especially for all the poor. In his day we became acquainted with Pamphilus,[31] a very eloquent man and a true philosopher in life itself, who was thought worthy of the presbyterate of the parish there. It would be the part of no small undertaking to show what kind of a man he was, and whence he came. Moreover, the details of his life, and of the school which he established, and his struggles in the various confessions during the persecution, and the crown of martyrdom with which after all he was bound, we have described in a special work about him. But his man was the most admirable of those in that city; yet among those especially connected with our time we know the rarest of men: Pierius, one of the presbyters of Alexandria, and Meletius, bishop of the churches in Pontus.[32]

---

30 Known only from this passage. Since Eusebius speaks of him in the past tense, he was probably dead at this time.
31 Eusebius' teacher and closet friend.
32 Pierius (Hierius), called the 'younger Origen' for his theology as well as his literary character, was an eminent presbyter of Alexandria, famous for voluntary poverty, philosophical knowledge, and public expositions of Scripture. He ruled the catechetical school of Alexandria

Moreover, the former was famous for his life of extreme poverty and for his knowledge of philosophy, for he was exceedingly well trained in the contemplation and exposition of the things of God and in discoursing publicly in church. Melitius (people of education used to call him the honey of Attica) was such a person as one would describe as most accomplished in all fields of learning. It is not possible to admire adequately his rhetorical skill, but this one might say to be his by nature; but who would surpass the excellence of the rest of his great experience and, also, of his great erudition, because, after making only a trial of him, you would have called him the most skillful and learned in all fields of literature? Of equal excellence, also, were the qualities of his virtuous life. We observed him well during the period of the persecution as he was in exile in the regions of Palestine for seven whole years.

The service of the Church in Jerusalem, after Hymenaeus the bishop mentioned a little above,[33] was taken over by Zabdas.[34] And not long after, when he went to his rest, Hermo,[35] the last of the bishops up to the persecution of our

under Bishop Theonas in 265. Cf. Jerome, *De vir. ill.* 76. This Meletius is to be identified with the orthodox Meletius referred to with praise by Athanasius in his *Ep. ad Episc. Aeg.* 8, and by Basil in his *De Spiritu Sancto* 29.74. 'The honey [*meli*] of Attica' is a pun on his name.

33 7.14.

34 In the *Chron.*, Zabdas is called the thirty-eighth bishop, and is said to have come into office on the fifteenth year of Diocletian, i.e., in 298. This and what Eusebius tells about him here are all that is known about him.

35 Hermo became bishop probably in 301, and was succeeded by Macharius in 312. Nothing more is known about him.

time, succeeded to the apostolic throne which has been preserved even to our own day.

And at Alexandria also, Maximus,[36] who had served as bishop for eighteen years after the death of Dionysius,[37] was succeeded by Theonas.[38] In his time at Alexandria, Achillas,[39] who was considered worthy of the presbyterate together with Pierius, became famous, having been entrusted with the school of the sacred faith,[40] and having displayed a very rare activity in philosophy, inferior to none and a true manner of life according to the Gospel. After Theonas, who had rendered his utmost service for nineteen years, Peter[41] succeeded to the episcopate over those in Alexandria, being himself also especially prominent for twelve entire years. Of this

36 Cf. 7.28.
37 Cf. 6.40.
38 Bishop of Alexandria from about 283 to 301, according to the *Chron.* The celebrated letter of Theonas to Lucianus, chamberlian to Diocletian, often quoted as giving such a lifelike description of the position of a Christian in the imperial court has been pronounced by the leading Catholic and some Protestant patristic scholars as spurious. Theonas is commemorated in the Roman Martyrology on August 27.
39 Athanasius, in his *Epistle to the Bishops of Egypt* 23, refers to him as 'the great Achilles.' He succeeded Peter as Bishop of Alexandria, but the date of his accession and the length of his episcopate are very uncertain.
40 The famous catechetical school of Alexandria.
41 Archbishop of Alexandria, who succeeded Theonas in 300. He had three years of tranquil administration, which he so carried on as to acquire this high praise from Eusebius, both in 8.13 and in 9.6. Then came the Diocletian persecution, and early in 306 Peter found it necessary to draw up conditions of reconciliation to the Church, and of readmission to her privileges, for those who through weakness had compromised their fidelity. These are still extant, and, together with fragments of his other work, may be found in English translation in the Ante-Nicene Fathers 6.269-283. Peter, judging from the extant fragments of his works, was in the main an Origenist, although he parted from Origen in some important respects, especially on the subject of anthropology.

time he governed the church for less than three entire years before the persecution. For the remaining period of his life he guided himself to a severer discipline, and in no secret manner cared for the common good of the churches. For this reason, then, he was beheaded, in the ninth year of the persecution, and was decorated with the crown of martyrdom.

Having described in these Books the subject of the successions, which extends from the birth of our Saviour for 305 years[42] to the destruction of the houses of prayer, come, let us leave behind in writing, for those who come after us also to learn, the conflicts of those in our time who fought manfully for piety, what their number and nature were.

42 Diocletian's edict calling for the demolition of churches was issued in February 303; cf. 5.2.

BOOK EIGHT

HAVING DESCRIBED THE SUCCESSION of the Apostles in seven complete Books, we think in this eighth unit, as one of our most necessary duties, we should hand down for the knowledge of those who come after us those events of our time which are worthy of no casual record, and our account will begin from this point.

Chapter 1

It is beyond our ability to describe worthily the extent and the nature of the glory, before the persecution of our time, as well as the freedom of which the word of piety toward the God of the universe proclaimed to the world through Christ was thought worthy by all men, both Greeks and barbarians. As proofs there might be the favors of those in power to our people, to whom they were accustomed to entrust even the government of the provinces, relieving them of the mental agony with regard to offering sacrifice because of the great friendliness which they preserved toward their doctrine. Why should one speak of those in the imperial households and of the all-powerful rulers, who permitted the members of their households to speak freely in their presence on the divine word and life—wives,[1] children, and servants—almost allowing them to boast of the freedom accorded the faith? And these they regarded with high esteem and as even more acceptable than their fellow servants, as, for example, was that Dorotheus,[2] the most devoted and faithful of all to them, and for this reason especially honored along with men in the positions of rulers and governors; and with him was the celebrated Gorgonius[3] and as many as, like these, were thought worthy of the same honor because of the word of God. And it was possible to see of what favor the rulers in each church were thought worthy by all the procurators and governors. And how could anyone describe those assemblies attended by thousands, and the multitudes of the gatherings in every city, and the glorious concourses in the houses of prayer, because of which, not being satisfied any longer with the ancient buildings, they built, from the foundations up, spacious churches throughout all the cities? And as these projects advanced with the times, and day by day increased in dimension and magnitude, no envy held them back, nor was any evil demon able to disparage or hinder them by human

1 Prisca, the wife of Diocletian, and Valeria, their daughter and wife of Galerius, were not only friendly to the Christians, but were, if not Christians, at least catechumens (cf. Lactantius, *De mort. pers.* 15). Eusebius is probably referring here not only to these, but also to all the women and children of the imperial household.
2 This Dorotheus is not to be identified with the Dorotheus of 7.32. All that we know of this Dorotheus is contained in this passage and in 8.6, where we are told that he was put to death by strangulation.
3 Gorgonius is mentioned also in 8.6. He was one of the imperial household, and together with Dorotheus and others was strangled because of the fires in the Nicomedian Palace.

plotting, so long as the divine and heavenly hand sheltered and guarded its own people, as being worthy.

But when, because of greater freedom, our affairs went over to conceit and sloth, as we envied and reviled one another, and all but went to war among ourselves with weapons, if it should happen, and with spears made of words, rulers attacking rulers, and laity forming factions against laity, and unspeakable hypocrisy and pretence advancing to the highest possible degree of wickedness, the divine judgment with forbearance, as is its custom, since the assemblies were still crowded, gently and moderately began to practice its oversight, the persecution beginning with the brethren in armies. But when, being insensible, we took no care to make the Deity well disposed and propitious, but, like some kind of atheists, thinking that our affairs were unheeded and without supervision, we continued to add one wickedness upon another, and those seemingly our shepherds, thrusting aside the bond of piety, were inflamed with mutual contentions, doing nothing else but to heap up strifes and threats and jealousy and enmity and hatred against one another, and claiming vehemently their ambitious ends like a tyrant's spoils, then, indeed, then, according to the spoken word of Jeremias, 'the Lord covered with obscurity the daughter of Sion in his wrath and hath cast down from heaven the glory of Israel; he hath not remembered his footstool in the day of his anger; but the Lord hath also swallowed up all that was beautiful in Israel, and hath destroyed all his strongholds,'[4] and according to what was foretold in the Psalms, He has overthrown the covenant of his servant, and

---

4 Cf. Lam. 2.12, with variations from the Septuagint.

has profaned his sanctuary on the earth, through the destruction of the churches, and He has broken down all his hedges, He has made his strongholds cowardice.[5] All that pass by the way have plundered the multitudes of the people, and now, besides this, he has become a reproach to his neighbors. For he has exalted the right hand of his enemies, and has turned back the help of his sword, and has not taken his part in the war. But has also deprived him of purification, and has cast his throne to the ground, and has shortened the days of his time, and, besides all these, he has poured shame upon him.

Chapter 2

All things, indeed, have been fulfilled in our time, when we saw with our own eyes the houses of prayer cast down to the very foundations from top to bottom, and the inspired and sacred Scriptures given over to flames in the midst of the market places, and the pastors of the churches shamefully hiding here and there, some being captured ignominiously and made a mockery by their enemies, when, too, according to another prophetic word, 'contempt was poured forth upon [their] princes, and he caused them to wander where there was no passing, and out of the way.'[1] But it is not our task to describe the melancholy misfortunes of these men at the end, as it is not proper for us to hand down to memory their dissensions and unnatural conduct toward one another before the persecution. Therefore, we have decided to relate

5 Cf. Ps. 88.39-45.

1 Ps. 6.40.

nothing more about them than what would justify the judgement of God. Therefore, we have been moved to make mention not even of these tried by the persecution or of those who have made complete shipwreck of their salvation,[2] and by their own will have been plunged into the depths of the flood, but we shall add to the general history only those which may be of profit first to us, and then to those who come after us.[3] Let us proceed, therefore, at this point to describe briefly the sacred conflicts of the witnesses of the divine Word.

This was the nineteenth year of the reign of Diocletian,[4] the month Dystrus, which would be called March among the Romans, in which, as the festival of the Saviour's Passion was approaching,[5] an imperial letter was promulgated everywhere, ordering the churches to be razed to their foundations, and the Scriptures to be put out of existence by fire, and proclaiming that those who held positions of honor be disenfranchised, and that household servants,[6] if they clung to the profession of Christianity, be deprived of their freedom.[7]

2 Cf. 1 Tim. 1.19.
3 On the basis of this passage, Gibbon (Ch. 16) makes a vicious attack on the honesty of Eusebius. He does him a grave injustice.
4 Diocletian became emperor on September 17, 284. Thus his nineteenth year was from September 17, 301, to September 16, 302.
5 This Easter fell on April 18, 303.
6 Not necessarily slaves.
7 The notorious First Edict of Diocletian, described in a general way by Lactantius, but presented with detail, even reproducing the same language, by Eusebius here. It provided, first, that the churches should be leveled to the ground. This was in accord with the old principle that it was unlawful for Christians to hold assemblies. Its second provision, an attack on sacred books, was a shrewd move and entirely new, recognizing the important place of sacred Scriptures in the Church. The third provision was clearly and deliberately based on a part of the edict of Valerian. It is to be noticed that all forms of punishment consisted not of torture or death but of some kind of civil degradation.

The first written pronouncement against us was of such a nature. But not long afterwards, as other letters continued to circulate, he ordered that all the bishops of the churches in every place be first committed to prison,[8] then, later, be forced by every device to offer sacrifice.[9]

Chapter 3

Then, truly, then very many of those in control of the churches eagerly contended with terrible torments, and exhibited examples of mighty conflicts; but countless others, growing numb of soul beforehand because of cowardice, thus readily proved weak at the first attack, and of the rest each endured various forms of torture, one having his body

---

8 There had been popular uprisings in Mitelene and in Syria, for which the Christians were in some way held responsible. Diocletian commanded that the church officers be seized and committed to prison. From these local incidents a general religious persecution developed, the Christians by reason of their close ties and allegiance to the Church authorities being regarded as a menace to the State. The decrees or letters mentioned in this paragraph constitute one decree and is known to us as the Second Edict of Diocletian.

9 Under the terms of the Second Edict the officers of the Church were summarily cast into prison, and, as in the case of Valerian's edict, were given no condition on which they might escape. Later, they were asked to sacrifice, and, as is seen in the next chapter, many did and were consequently released. The decree commanding the release of church officers on the condition of sacrificing is known as the Third Edict of Diocletian. While death was not decreed in the case of refusals to do so, every means was taken to make them do so which resulted in extreme tortures. Thus, the Third Edict is regarded as more severe than any that preceded it. In a desire to empty the prisons some governors released their prisoners even if they did not sacrifice. Some, on the other hand, did so by finding some excuse to put them to death. The edict itself, however, did not permit death as a penalty for being a Christian. This penalty was not decreed until the Fourth Edict.

scourged with rods, another being punished by the rack and by unbearable scrapings, because of which some presently obtained an inauspicious end to life. But others again passed through the struggle in other ways: one, as others pushed against him with force and brought him to the abominable and impure sacrifices, was dismissed as if he had sacrificed, even though he had not; another, although he had by no means approached or touched any accursed thing, when others stated that he had sacrificed, departed enduring the calumny in silence; another, being taken up half-dead, was cast aside as if already a corpse; and again, a certain person who was lying on the ground was dragged a long way by the feet, reckoned among those who had sacrificed of their own accord. And one cried out and testified with a loud voice to his refusal to sacrifice, and another that he was a Christian, glorying in the confession of the saving name; another maintained firmly that he had never sacrificed and never would sacrifice. However, they were struck on the mouth and silenced by the many hands of a detachment of soldiers drawn up for this purpose, and being beaten on the face and cheeks they were driven away by force. So important did the enemies of religion regard it to seem by all means to have accomplished their purpose.

But these means also did not avail them against the holy martyrs, for an accurate description of whom what word would be adequate for us?

Chapter 4

One might relate the story of countless who displayed a
marvelous zeal for the religion of the God of the universe,
not only from the time when the general persecution was
stirred up, but long before that when the affairs of peace
were still well established. For, at the very moment when he
who had received the power[1] was awakening as from a deep
torpor,[2] and while he was still, even secretly and unseen
during the time after Decius and Valerian, making attempts
against the churches, and was not getting himself in readiness
for war all at once, but as yet was making trial of those only
in the camps (for he thought that in this way the rest also
were easily taken, if first he should overcome these in conflict),
it was possible to see a great many of those in the army
most gladly embracing private life, that they might not be
deniers of the religion of the Creator of all things. For, when
the military commander,[3] whoever he was, was just making
his first attempt at persecuting the armies, separating into
classes and purging those serving in the camps, and giving
a choice either by obeying to enjoy the honor which they
held or on the other hand to be deprived of it, if they were
opposed to the command, a great many soldiers of the
kingdom of Christ, without delay, preferred unquestionably
to confess Him to the apparent glory and prosperity which
they had. But presently, in rare instances, one or two of them
perhaps not only were receiving loss of honor but also death

---

1 Galerius; some suggest the Devil.
2 The time intervening between the persecution of Valerian and
  Diocletian, the forty years' peace.
3 In the *Chronicle* Eusebius calls him Veturius, probably an insignificant
  official, as he now shows by his contemptous 'whoever he was'.

in return for pious opposition, for at that time the instigator of the plot dared to proceed only with moderation and unto blood only in some instances,[4] since, as it seems, the multitude of the faithful still frightened him, and caused him to hesitate to bring war against all at once. But when he stripped for battle still further, it is impossible to describe with words the number and the nature of the martyrs of God it was made possible for those dwelling in all the cities and lands to see with their own eyes.[5]

Chapter 5

Then, straightway, a man[1] among those not undistinguished but even most highly honored according to the prominence recognized in life, as soon as the decree against the churches was published in Nicomedia,[2] roused by his zeal for God and driven on by a burning faith, seized the decree, when it was posted openly and publicly, as something unholy and most profane, and tore it to pieces,[3] while the two emperors were present in the same city, the senior[4] of them all and he who controlled the fourth place in the government after him.[5]

---

4 Cf. Heb. 12.4.
5 A reference to the general persecution which did not begin until some time later.

---

1 Probably Euethius, martyred in Nicomedia on February 24, the day on which the edict was published.
2 The capital city of Bithynia, Diocletian's chief place of residence and the Eastern capital of the Empire. The great church of this city was destroyed on February 23, 303, the day before the First Edict was published.
3 Cf., also, Lactantius, *De mort. pers.* 13, where the same incident is described. In the old martyrologies the man is called John.
4 Diocletian.
5 Galerius.

But this man, first in that place who distinguished himself in this way, and who endured such experiences as was natural in the case of such daring, kept himself cheerful and undisturbed to his very last breath.

Chapter 6

Of all, as many as have ever been sung, most worthy of admiration and celebrated for courage, either among Greeks or among barbarians, the period produced those divine and outstanding martyrs Dorotheus[1] and his followers, the servants of the emperor. These men were considered worthy of the highest honor by their masters, and did not fall short of their master's children in the affection received; they esteemed the reproaches and labors for religion and the many forms of death newly devised against them as truly greater riches than the glory and luxury of this life.[2] After we have recalled the end of life which one of these experienced, we shall leave it to our readers to gather from his case what also happened to the others.

A certain man was brought forward in the afore-mentioned city under the rulers of whom we have spoken.[3] Now, then, when commanded to sacrifice, since he refused, he was ordered to be hung in midair naked, and to be scourged over his whole body until, overcome, even though unwilling, he should do what was bidden him. But when, even though undergoing these sufferings, he was unmoved, they then

1 Cf. 8.1.
2 Cf. Heb. 11.26.
3 In Nicomedia, before the time of Diocletian and Galerius.

mixed vinegar with salt, and poured them where the bones were already showing into the mangled parts of his body. And when he despised these pains also, a gridiron and fire were then brought forward, and, even as flesh for eating, the remnants of his body were consumed by fire, not all at once, that he might not be relieved [of life] quickly, but little by little, while those who placed him on the pyre were not permitted to desist until after such sufferings he assented to what was ordered. But clinging grimly to his purpose, he triumphantly gave up the ghost at the very climax of his tortures. Such was the martyrdom of one of the royal servants, truly worthy of his name, for he was called Peter.[4]

Having regard for the proportions of this book, we shall pass over the martyrdom of the rest, though they were not inferior, placing only so much on record that Dorotheus and Gorgonius,[5] together with many others of the imperial household, after struggles of various kinds departed this life through strangulation and carried off the trophies of God-given victory.

At this time, Anthimus,[6] who at that time presided over the church at Nicomedia, was beheaded because of his witness to Christ. A continuous number of martyrs was added to this man, for in some way or other in the palace at

---

4 Greek *petros* ('rock'). It must be recalled that the Christians at this time were being tortured and martyred, not so much because they were Christians as because of their apparent deliberate breaking of the laws of the State. There was no desire on the part of the authorities to punish Christians as such.

5 Cf. 8.1.

6 Anthimus probably suffered martyrdom under Maximinus in 311 or 312, and not under Diocletian, as Eusebius thinks. This is based chiefly on the preserved fragment of the *Chron. Paschale,* assuming that it is genuine. Doubt also is cast on the chronology of the other martyrdoms of this paragraph. They probably belong after the Fourth Edict or still later.

Nicomedia a fire broke out in those very days, which through
a false suspicion, as rumor went around, was charged our
people,[7] and some of the pious there, by whole families and
in piles, were by an imperial decree slaughtered with the
sword; others reached perfection through fire, when, a report
has it, men and women with a divine and indescribable eagerness leaped upon the pyre; and the executioners bound a multitude of others and placed them on boats and hurled them
into the depths of the sea.[8] And as for the imperial servants
committed to the earth after death with fitting honors, those
regarded as their masters thought it necessary, starting afresh,
to exhume them and to throw them also into the sea, that
some, regarding them, indeed, as gods (as at any rate they
actually thought), might not worship them as they lay in their
tombs.[9]

Such were the deeds accomplished in Nicomedia at the
beginning of the persecution. Not long after this, when some
in the so-called country of Melitene[10] and, in turn, others
about Syria attempted to attack the Empire,[11] an imperial
command went forth that those in charge of the churches
everywhere be confined to prison and bonds. And the spectacle of what took place thereafter surpasses all description,

7 Lactantius (14) speaks of two fires, fifteen days apart, and accuses
  Galerius of starting them. Constantine (*Orat. ad Sanct. Coet.* 25.2)
  refers to one fire only and says that it was caused by lightning.
  Common belief places the guilt on the Christians.
8 Drowning was also regarded as the most disgraceful of all punishments,
  since it implied that the criminals were not worthy of burial.
9 Cf. 4.15.41; and Lactantius, *Div. Inst.* 5.11. That the Christians
  gathered about the tombs of martyrs for religious ceremonies was well
  known. In this case the emperor was not concerned so much with the
  religious ceremonies as with fear lest such gatherings would foster a
  spirit of rebellion.
10 The province and its capital in Armenia Minor.
11 This rebellion cannot be identified definitely. From the words of
  Eusebius he may be referring not to a single rebellion but to several.

when a countless throng was imprisoned in every place, and the prisons everywhere, long ago prepared for murderers and robbers of graves, were then filled by bishops and presbyters and deacons and readers and exorcists, so that there was no longer any place left here for those condemned for wrong-doing.

And when in turn the first edict was followed by others, in which it had been ordered to permit the imprisoned to walk to freedom if they sacrificed, but to tear them to pieces with countless tortures[12] if they refused, how, then, could anyone here number the multitude of the martyrs in each province, and especially of those in Africa and Mauritania[13] and Thebais and Egypt? From this last country, also, going forth now into other cities and provinces they became distinguished by their martyrdoms.

Chapter 7

We know surely those who became conspicuous in Palestine, and we know also those at Tyre in Phoenicia.[1] Who on seeing these was not struck with amazement at the numberless lashes and at the resistance in these on the part of the truly wonderful athletes of religion, and at the struggle with man-eating wild beasts that followed immediately upon the lashes, and at the attacks at this time from leopards and

---

12 The Third Edict of Diocletian.
13 *tò Maúrōn éthnos*, lit., 'the province of the Moors.'

1 Cf. *Martyrs of Palestine* 8f. Here we learn that in the sixth and subsequent years of the persecution many of the Christians of Egypt were sent to labor in the mines of Palestine, and suffered extreme tortures there.

different kinds of bears and of wild boars and of bulls goaded by fire and hot iron, and at the marvelous feats of endurance on the part of the noble people against each of the wild animals? We ourselves also were present as these things happened, when we recorded the divine power of our Saviour who was borne witness, Jesus Christ Himself, as it became present and manifested itself distinctly to the martyrs; for the man-devouring beasts for a long time did not dare to touch nor even to approach the bodies of the dear to God, but rushed upon the others, as many as from the outside were presumably urging them on by irritations, but the holy athletes alone, although they stood naked and waved their hands to draw them to themselves (for they were ordered to do this), were not touched at all, but sometimes, as they rushed upon them, they were held back, as it were, by some divine power and again went to the rear. And since this went on for a long time, it occasioned no small wonder to the spectators, so that, as the first beast did nothing, a second and a third were let loose against one and the same martyr.

One could be astonished at the undaunted endurance of those holy men and at the firm and unbending resistance in young bodies in the face of these troubles. Thus, you would have seen a youth, not fully twenty years old, standing without fetters and spreading his hands in the form of a cross, and, with a mind undaunted and unmoved, most leisurely engaged in earnest prayer to the Deity, and not at all changing his stand or retreating from the place where he had taken his post, while bears and leopards breathing anger and death almost touched his very flesh, but somehow by a divine and mysterious power just checking their mouths and running back again to the rear. Such a one was this young man. And again you might have seen others (for they were five in all) thrown to an enraged bull who tossed the others of those who approached from the outside into the air with his horns and dismembered them, leaving them to be picked up half-dead, but only when he rushed with threatening anger against the holy martyrs was he unable even to approach them, and although he pawed with his hoofs and made use of his horns in this direction and that, and although he breathed threatening rage because of the irritations of the hot irons, he was dragged away backwards by Divine Providence, so that, since this animal did not do them any harm at all, other wild beasts were let loose against them. Then, finally, after the various frightful attacks of these beasts, they were all butchered with the sword and, instead of receiving burial, were given over to the waves of the sea.

Chapter 8

Such was the struggle of the Egyptians[1] who displayed their conflicts for religion at Tyre.

One would admire, also, those among them who were martyred in their own land, where countless numbers, men together with women and children, in behalf of the teaching of our Saviour, despising this transient life, endured various forms of death; some of them, after scrapings and tortures and most terrible scourgings and countless other torments various and frightful to hear, were given over to fire; some

1 The tyrant C. Julius Verus Maximinus became Caesar in 305, and ruled in Egypt and Syria, where the Christians suffered more than anywhere else in these years.

were engulfed by the sea; and others courageously offered
their heads to those who cut them off; some, too, died in the
midst of their tortures, and others perished from hunger, and
others again were impaled, some in the customary manner
accorded malefactors, others even more cruelly were nailed
upside down, head downwards, and were kept alive until they
would perish from hunger even on the gibbet.

Chapter 9

The outrages and sufferings which the martyrs in the
Thebais[1] endured surpass all description, their whole bodies
being torn to pieces by shells instead of claws even until life
was gone; and women were tied by one foot and were raised
on high through the air, head downwards, by certain machines, with their bodies completely naked and without even
a covering, and they furnished this most shameful and cruel
and inhuman sight of all to all the onlookers. And others
again died on being fastened to tree trunks and stumps; for
having brought together the very strongest of the branches
by certain machines, and stretching the legs of the martyrs
one by one on each of these, they released the branches to
be carried back to their natural position, planning a sudden
separation of the limbs of those against whom they devised
this. And all these things, indeed, were carried out not for a
few days or a short time, but for a long interval of entire years,

---

1 From 8.9.4 we learn that Eusebius himself witnessed some of the
martyrdoms to which he refers in this chapter. Thebais or Upper
Egypt, of which the chief town was Ptolemais, was one of the three
great divisions of Egypt.

sometimes of more than ten, sometimes more than twenty in number being destroyed, sometimes not less than thirty and then again nearly sixty; and again at other times one hundred men in a single day together with very young children and women were slain, being condemned to various alternating punishments.

And we ourselves also observed, being present at the places, many all at once in a single day, some suffering decapitation, others punishment by fire, so that the murdering axe was blunted, and, becoming worn out, was broken into pieces, and the executioners themselves, becoming quite weary, relieved one another in turns. On these occasions we observed a most wonderful zeal, and a truly divine power and eagerness on the part of those who believed in the Christ of God. For example, as soon as the decision was made against the first, one after another they jumped up to the tribunal before the judge, confessing themselves Christians, being completely unconcerned about the terrors and the various forms of torture, but speaking boldly without dismay about their religion for the God of the universe, and with joy and laughter and gladness accepting the last judgment of death, so that they sang and sent hymns and thanksgivings up to the God of the universe until the very last breath. Marvelous indeed were these, but exceptionally marvelous were those distinguished for wealth and birth and reputation and learning and philosophy, who put all things second to true religion and faith in our Lord and Saviour Jesus Christ, as was Philoromus,[2] who had been entrusted with an office of no ordinary

---

2 Nothing more is known of Philoromus than is told here. There is no good ground for saying, as some do, that he was 'the general finance minister of Egypt.'

importance in the imperial administration at Alexandria, and who administered justice every day attended by a bodyguard of soldiers in connection with his dignity and Roman rank, and Phileas,[3] bishop of the church of the Thumites, a man distinguished for his services to his country and patriotism and for his philosophical learning. These men, although a great many relatives and other friends entreated them, besides men of high rank, and although, furthermore, the judge himself called upon them to have pity on themselves and mercy on their children and wives, were by no means induced by such actions to choose the love of life, and to despise the ordinances of our Saviour about confessing and denying,[4] but with a noble and philosophic determination, or, rather, with pious and God-loving souls they resisted all the threats and insults of the judge, and were both beheaded.

Chapter 10

Since we have said[1] that Phileas was worthy of a high reputation for secular learning also, let him come forward as his own witness, both to show the world who he was, and

---

3 Bishop of Thumis in lower Egypt, one of the important martyrs under Diocletian. A large part of his letter to his people is quoted in 8.10 and he is also quoted in 8.13. Jerome, *De vir. ill.* 78, merely follows Eusebius. A Latin version of a letter supposedly written in prison by Bishops Hesychius, Pachymius, Theodorus, and Phileas to the author of the Meletian schism is also ascribed to Phileas. His *Acts* are also extant, in which he is acclaimed for his scholarship and learning. His erudition is proclaimed by both Eusebius and Jerome. He was martyred probably sometime in 306.

4 Cf. Matt. 10.32,33; Luke 12.8,9.

1 Cf. Phil. 2.6-8.

also to describe in the following words, more accurately than we can, the martyrdoms that took place in his time in Alexandria.

From the writings of Phileas to the Thumites.

'Since all these examples and models and noble tokens lie before us in the divine and sacred Scriptures, the blessed martyrs with us, without hesitation directing the eye of the soul clearly toward the God over all and keeping in their minds death for religion, clung tightly to their calling, having discovered that our Lord Jesus Christ became man for our sakes, that He might cut off all sin, and that He might establish ways and means for our entering eternal life. "For he thought it not robbery to be equal with God, but emptied himself, taking the form of a servant; and being found in fashion as a man, he humbled himself unto death, even to the death of the cross."[1] Therefore, also being zealous for the better gifts,[2] the Christ-bearing martyrs endured every suffering and all kinds of devices for torture, not once but some even a second time; and although the guards strove with one another in all manner of insult against them, not only by words but also by deeds, they did not give up their resolution, "because perfect charity casteth out fear."[3] What words would suffice to recount their virtue and their courage in the face of every torture? For, when all who wished to insult them had complete freedom to do so, some struck them with clubs, others with rods, others with scourges, others, again, with straps, and others with ropes. And the sight of their tortures was varied and possessed of much malice within it. Thus, some, with their hands bound behind them, were hung

2 Cf. 1 Cor. 12.31.
3 1 John 4.18.

upon the gibbet, and they were stretched in every limb by certain machines; then, while in this position, the torturers set upon them over their whole bodies, not as with murderers on their sides alone, but they punished with their instruments their bellies and legs and cheeks also. Others were raised on high and hung from the porch by one hand, suffering the most terrible of all pain through the stretching of their joints and limbs. Others were bound with their faces toward pillars, with their feet failing to touch the ground, their bonds, forced by the weight of their bodies, being drawn tight. And this they endured, not as long as the governor talked or was at leisure with them, but almost throughout the entire day. For, when he passed on to others, he left behind to watch over the first those who served his authority, if perchance anyone being overcome by the tortures seemed to be giving in; and he commanded them to approach also with bonds mercilessly, and, when after this they were at the last gasp, to arrange them upon the ground and drag them off. For [he said] that they should not have a particle of regard for us, but should so be minded and act, as if we no longer existed, our enemies having devised this second torture in addition to the stripes. And there were those who even after the tortures were placed in stocks, with both feet stretched out to the fourth hole, so that of necessity they lay on their backs on the stocks, since they were unable [to sit up] because of the fresh wounds they had from the scourgings over the whole body. Others, on being thrown to the ground, lay there by reason of the continuous application of tortures, offering to the spectators a sight more frightful than the actual punishments, for they bore on their bodies varied and diverse signs of the tortures which had been devised. While this was going on, some died because of the tortures, having shamed the adversary by their endurance; others, being shut up in prison half-dead, after not many days being afflicted by pain were made perfect; and the remainder, obtaining recovery under treatment with time and by their stay in prison, became more confident. Thus, then, when the choice lay before them and the order was given either to touch the abominable sacrifice and be undisturbed, receiving from them the accursed freedom, or not to sacrifice and to receive the death penalty, without hesitation they gladly went to their death; for they knew what had been determined for us beforehand by the sacred Scriptures. For he says: "He that sacrificeth to other gods shall be put to death," and "Thou shalt not have strange gods before me." [4]

Such are the words of the truly philosophical and also God-loving martyr, which, before the final sentence, while still in the state of imprisonment, he sent to the brethren in his parish, at the same time presenting the circumstances in which he lived and urging them to hold closely, even after his death as he was about to be perfected, to the religion of Christ. But why need we speak at length and present one fresh instance after another of the conflicts of the divine martyrs throughout the world, especially since they were assailed no longer by the common law, but as if they were enemies?

Chapter 11

At this time, for example, soldiers surrounded a little town inhabited entirely by Christians, and throwing fire in it they

---

4 Cf. Exod. 22.20; 20.3.

burned them up, to a man—including children and women—
as they were calling upon the God who is over all.[1] They did
this because all the inhabitants of the town in a body, the
curator himself and the duumvirs together with all who held
office and the entire citizenry, confessed themselves Christians,
and would not give the slightest heed to those who ordered
them to worship idols.

And there was a certain other person who had attained
high office among the Romans, Adauctus[2] by name, of noble
Italian birth, who had advanced through every honor under
the emperors, so that he had blamelessly passed through even
the general offices of what they call the magistrary and the
ministry of finance, and besides all this had distinguished
himself by noble deeds of religion and by confessions of the
Christ of God, and was adorned with the crown of martyrdom,
having undergone the conflict in behalf of religion while
actually fulfilling the office of finance minister.

Chapter 12

Why should I now make mention by name of the rest or
number the multitude of the men or picture the various
sufferings of the wonderful martyrs, sometimes slaughtered
with the axe, as happened to those in Arabia, sometimes having their legs broken, as fell to the lot of those in Cappadocia,
and on some occasions being raised on high by the feet with

---

1 Lactantius, in *Div. inst.* 5.11, where he says, 'Some were quick to
slaughter, as someone in Phrygia who burned an entire people together with their meeting place,' may be referring to this incident.
2 Nothing more is known of him; Eusebius does not seem to connect
him with the town in Phrygia, as Rufinus does.

heads down and, when a slow fire was lit underneath them, choking to death by the smoke sent out from the burning wood, as was visited upon them in Mesopotamia, sometimes having their noses and ears and hands mutilated, and the other limbs and parts of the body cut to pieces, as took place in Alexandria?[1]

Why should we rekindle the memory of those in Antioch who were roasted on hot grates, not unto death but with a view to a lingering punishment, and of others who let their right hand down into the very fire sooner than touch the abominable sacrifice? Some of these [martyrs], avoiding their trial, before they were captured and had come into the hands of the plotters, threw themselves down from high buildings, considering death as booty taken from the wickedness of evil men.

And a certain holy and marvelous person in virtue of soul, but a woman in body, and otherwise celebrated among all those at Antioch for wealth and birth and good repute, who had brought up two unmarried daughters in the precepts of religion, pre-eminent for beauty and bloom of body, when the great envy that was stirred up over them endeavored in every way to track them to where they were concealed, then on learning that they were staying in a foreign country deliberately called them to Antioch and they presently fell within the trap of the soldiers, on seeing herself and her daughters in difficulty, and giving consideration to the terrible things that will arise from human beings, and the most

1 These mutilations began in the sixth year (308) of the persecution (cf. *Martyrs of Palestine* 8f.) and were carried on throughout the territory of Maximin. He apparently became alarmed at the number of deaths caused by the persecution, and resorted to this atrocious means to curb them.

terrible and unbearable of all, threat of fornication, exhorting both herself and her girls that they should not submit to listening to this even with the tips of their ears, but saying that the surrendering of their souls to the slavery of demons was worse than all deaths and very destruction, submitted that taking refuge with the Lord was the one release from all these troubles, and then when they had agreed with her opinion and had arranged their garments suitably about their bodies, as they came to the very middle of their journey, they requested of the guards a little time for retirement, and cast themselves in a river that was flowing by.[2]

Thus did they destroy themselves.[3] But another pair of maidens at Antioch itself, in every respect religious and true sisters, famous by birth, illustrious in their manner of living, youthful in years, blooming in body, holy of soul, pious in deportment, marvelous in zeal, as if the earth could not endure such virtue, the worshipers of demons ordered to be cast into the sea.

Such, then, was experienced by these martyrs. And in the Pontus others suffered in a manner frightful to hear: the fingers of both hands were pierced through by sharp reeds under the tips of the nails; in the case of others, after melting lead down by fire, they poured the boiling and burning stuff down their backs, roasting the most essential parts of the

2 This treatment of Christian women was not in accord with the principles of Diocletian's government, but rather was characteristic of the policies of Maximian and Maximin.

3 Eusebius seems to approve suicide under these circumstances. Suicide to avoid violation of chastity was much discussed by the Fathers, and usually approved. St. Augustine was the first Father to speak out definitely against it in a famous passage of his *City of God* (1.22-27). He denounces such action as sinful at all times, and as a crime against the law of God. This view has prevailed ever since.

body; and others in their privy parts and bowels endured
sufferings that were shameful and inhuman and quite un-
mentionable, which the noble and law-abiding judges devised
with more than ordinary eagerness, displaying their cruelty as
a kind of wise virtue, always striving to surpass one another
with their more recently invented tortures, as if prizes in a
contest were involved.

Now, the last of the misfortunes came when, by now worn
out by their excessive evil deeds, and completely weary with
killing, and having attained a surfeit and satiety of shedding
blood, they turned to what they considered merciful and
humane, so that they seemed no longer to be doing anything
excessively terible against us. They said that it was not proper
to pollute the cities with the blood of their own peoples, nor
to cause the lofty government of the rulers to be slandered
for being cruel, when it was well disposed and gentle to all,
but rather that the beneficence of the humane and imperial
authority should be extended to all, who are no longer being
punished by death; for [it was declared] that because of the
humanity of the rulers this punishment of theirs against us
had been stopped. Then orders were given to gouge out our
eyes and to maim one of our legs. They considered these
actions humane and the mildest of punishments against us,
so that now, because of this humaneness exhibited by the
impious, it was no longer possible to tell the great number,
which was beyond all reckoning, of those whose right eye
was first cut out by the sword and then cauterized by fire,
and whose left foot was made useless by continued application
of branding irons at the joints, and after this were condemned
to the copper mines in the province, not so much for service
as for mistreatment and hardship. Besides all this, others fell

in with other trials which it is impossible even to relate, for their brave and noble deeds surpass all relating.

In these struggles over the whole world the magnificent martyrs of Christ shone forth and naturally astounded everywhere the eye-witnesses of their bravery, and they gave proof through themselves of the truly divine and inexpressible power of our Saviour. To mention each by name would be a long task, not to say something impossible.

Chapter 13

Among the rulers of the Church who suffered martyrdom in renowned cities, the first to be recorded on our monuments to pious men, as a martyr of Christ's kingdom, shall be Anthimus,[1] bishop of the city of the Nicomedians, who was beheaded; but among the martyrs at Antioch there was a presbyter, excellent throughout his whole life, in the parish there in Nicomedia, Lucian,[2] and he himself in the presence of the emperor proclaimed first the heavenly kingdom of Christ by the spoken word in an *Apology,* and then also by deeds. Of the martyrs in Phoenicia the most distinguished in all respects were the God-beloved pastors of the spiritual flocks of Christ: Tyrannion, bishop of the church at Tyre, and a presbyter of the church at Sidon, Zenobius,[3] and, besides, Silvanus,[4] bishop of the churches around Emesa.

---

1 Cf. 8.6.
2 Cf. 9.6.
3 Nothing more is known of these two. All the martyrs mentioned here are presented in the martyrologies. Many of them are assigned *Acts,* but unfortunately most of these are spurious.
4 Cf., also, 9.6; all our information about him comes from these passages. In extreme old age, after forty years as bishop, he was thrown to the wild beasts in Diocletian's persecution, probably in the year 312.

The last of these, together with others at Emesa itself, became food for wild beasts and were taken up into the choirs of martyrs; the other two glorified the word of God[5] at Antioch by their endurance under death; one, the bishop,[6] being consigned to the depths of the sea, the other, the most noble of physicians, Zenobius, dying bravely from the tortures applied to his sides. Of the martyrs at Palestine, Silvanus,[7] bishop of the churches about Gaza, was beheaded at the copper mines in Phaeno,[8] together with thirty-nine others; and the Egyptians there, Bishops Peleus and Nilus,[9] together with others, suffered death by fire. And among these the great glory of the parish of Caesarea must be mentioned by us, Pamphilus, a presbyter, a most wonderful man of our time, the virtue of whose manly and good deeds we shall record at the proper time.[10] And of those who were perfected eminently at Alexandria and in all Egypt and the Thebais, Peter,[11] Bishop of Alexandria itself, a divine example of the teachers of the religion of Christ, must be recorded first, and of the presbyters with him Faustus[12] and Dius and Am-

---

5 Cf. Acts 13.48.

6 Tyrannion.

7 Cf., also, *Mart. Pal.* 7 and 13. From these passages we learn that he was a martyr (*c.* 305) in the persecution of Maximin. He was a presbyter at its outbreak, and from the very beginning endured many varied sufferings with the greatest courage. He obtained the episcopate not long before his martyrdom.

8 A village of Arabia Petraea, in which were the celebrated copper mines where condemned criminals worked.

9 Cf., also, *Mart. Pal.* These, like Silvanus, died in the seventh year of the persecution.

10 Cf. 7.32. The reference here is to Eusebius' *Life of Pamphilus*.

11 Cf. 7.32.

12 Probably the same as the deacon of the same name mentioned in 6.40 and 7.11. He lived to an advanced age and died during Diocletian's persecution.

monius,[13] perfect martyrs of Christ, and Phileas[14] and Hesychius and Pachymius and Theodore,[15] bishops of the
churches about Egypt, and countless other distinguished persons besides these, who are held in memory by the parishes
in their country and locality. To hand down in writing the
conflicts of those who struggled throughout the whole world
for worship of the Deity and to describe in detail everything
that happened to them is not our task, but would be the
special task of those who took these events in by sight. At
any rate, those with whom I myself associated I shall make
known to posterity through another work.[16] In the present
book I shall append to what has been said the recantation
of what was done to us and of what happened since the
persecution, for they are most profitable for those who will
read them.

Now, what language would suffice to describe the condition of the government of the Romans before the war
against us, during the periods in which the actions of rulers
were friendly toward us and peaceful, and the abundance
and plenty of blessings of which it was thought worthy; when,
also, those who held the highest places in the government of
the whole Empire, having completed ten and twenty years
in office,[17] were passing their days in festivals and public
games and in the most joyous feasts and merriment with a

---

13 Nothing is known of Dius and Ammonius.
14 Cf. 8.9.
15 A Latin version of a letter supposedly written by these four bishops
   is still extant; cf. 8.9. Nothing more is known of Hesychius, Pachymius,
   and Theodore.
16 Eusebius is here referring to his *Martyrs of Palestine*. His *Life of
   Pamphilus* was already written.
17 The festivals held at the beginning of the tenth and of the twentieth
   year of a reign were called the decennalia and vicennalia respectively.

fully well-established peace? As their authority thus increased without hindrance and went on greater day by day, change from an attitude of peace toward us suddenly took place and stirred up an implacable war. The second year[18] of such a movement had not yet been fulfilled when a kind of revolution arose over the whole Empire and overturned all public life. For, when a fatal disease fell upon the foremost[19] of the above-mentioned leaders, as a result of which the functioning of his mind was brought into confusion, along with him[20] who had been honored with the second place, he took up the private life of an ordinary citizen.[21] All this had not yet taken place when the whole empire was torn asunder, a thing which has never been handed down in memory as ever having happened before.[22]

But, after no very long period of time had passed, the Emperor Constantius, who all during his life had been most kindly and well disposed toward his subjects, and most friendly toward the divine Word,[23] came to the end of his life[24] according to the general law of nature, leaving his legitimate son Constantine as emperor and Augustus in his place, and he was the first (of the then existing four rulers)

---

18 305.
19 Diocletian.
20 Maximinian.
21 The abdication of Diocletian and Maximian, the two Augusti, took place on May 1, 305, a little more than two years after the publication of Diocletian's First Edict. This abdication was probably according to plan, and not due to any immediate cause. Diocletian retired to carry on rural pursuits in his native Dalmatia, where he died in 313.
22 The meaning of this passage seems to be that the Empire was divided according to its treatment of Christians, i.e., the persecution continuing in the East, but ceasing in the West.
23 All sources agree with Eusebius' evaluation of Constantius' character. Although not a Christian, he was free from bigotry and cruelty.
24 In 306.

to be publicly proclaimed among the gods by them, being considered worthy after death of every honor that anyone could have paid an emperor, being the kindest and gentlest of emperors. In truth, he alone of those of our time passed the entire period of his rule in a manner worthy of his high authority, and in other respects conducted himself most favorably and beneficently toward all, never sharing in the war against us, but even preserving the religious under him from injury and mistreatment, and not tearing down the church buildings[25] or devising any other new plot against us. He received a happy and thrice-blessed end of life, alone in his rule having come to a gracious and glorious death, with his legitimate son, most prudent and pious in every respect, as his successor.

His son Constantine at the very beginning of his rule was proclaimed most perfect emperor and Augustus by the armies, and even long before them by God Himself, the all-powerful Emperor; and he established himself as an emulator of his father's reverence toward our doctrine.

Such a man was he. And after this Licinius was declared emperor and Augustus by a common vote of those in power.[26] This grieved Maximin terribly, who up to now had been styled only Caesar by all. Now he, being especially tyrannical, seized the honor for himself and became Augustus, he himself being appointed by himself.[27] And at this time he who has

---

25 Not strictly accurate. Constantius did destroy churches; cf. Lactantius, *De mort. pers.* 15, extant Acts, and others sources. Eusebius is apparently carried away by the well-known good character of Constantius and his general tolerance of Christians.

26 I.e., the Congress of Carnuntum in November 307, when Licinius, apparently already Caesar, received the title of Augustus.

27 Maximinus, the first Caesar, was hailed as Augustus in 308 by his troops, who were incensed at Licinius being appointed to a position above himself.

been shown to have taken up office again after his[28] abdication was caught devising a scheme for Constantine's death, and came upon a most shameful death. In the case of this [emperor], for the first time they tore down the inscriptions in his honor, and statues, and such things as have customarily been set up publicly, on the ground that they belonged to a most wicked and irreligious person.

Chapter 14

His son Maxentius,[1] who obtained for himself the tyranny at Rome, at first counterfeited our faith with a view to pleasing and fawning upon the Roman people, and so he ordered his subjects to cease their persecution of the Christians, pretending religion that he might appear favorable and very kind beyond his predecessors. However, he did not prove by his deeds to be such as it was hoped that he would be, but, rushing into all kinds of wickedness, he did not fail to indulge in any act of defilement and excuse, committing adulteries and all kinds of rape. In fact, he used to separate lawfully wedded wives from their husbands, insult them most disgracefully, and send them back again to their husbands; and he regularly practiced these deeds not on the insignificant and obscure, but he insulted especially the most eminent of those who had attained the highest places in the assembly of

---

28 Maximian's; cf. 8.11.

---

1 Eusebius gives an accurate picture of Maxentius. There is no ground to believe that he ever persecuted the Christians, but this policy was based rather on political reasons than on any love or respect for these subjects of his. He was cruel and oppressive to all, and they all hated him. Cf. 9.9, where Eusebius depicts his final defeat by Constantine and his death.

the Roman Senate. All bowed down before him, peoples and rulers, famous and obscure, and they were worn out by his terrible tyranny, and, although they were unmoved and endured the terrible servitude, there was no relief from the tyrant's murderous cruelty. On one occasion, for example, on a slight pretext, he gave the people to his bodyguard to be slaughtered, and countless numbers of the Roman people were killed in the middle of the city, not by the spears and arms of Scythians nor even of barbarians, but of their own fellow citizens. It is not possible to enumerate the number of senators who were killed through plots for their wealth, countless numbers being destroyed for one feigned reason or another. But, as the crown of the tyrant's evil deed, he proceeded into the field of magic, in his divinations sometimes ripping up pregnant women, sometimes examining the entrails of newborn babes, slaughtering lions, and concocting some abominable deeds to invoke the demons and to avert war. For by these means he had his entire hope that the fruits of victory would be obtained.

Now, it is impossible to tell the nature of this man's deeds, while he was a tyrant at Rome, to enslave his subjects, so that they were reduced to such as extreme lack and want of the necessary foods, as our contemporaries relate never arose at Rome or anywhere else.

But the tyrant in the East, Maximin, secretly forming a friendship with him at Rome, as with a brother in wickedness, contrived to conceal it for a very long time. At any rate, he was later detected,[2] and paid the just penalty.[3] One

2 After the battle of the Milvian Bridge, when Constantine entered Rome; cf. 9.9.
3 Eusebius describes the alliance of Maximinus with Maxentius, and his war with Licinius, and his death in 9.9,10, his accession to the throne and usurpation of the title of Augustus in 9.13. Maximinus,

could marvel at how this tyrant achieved kinship and brother-liness with the tyrant at Rome in wickedness, and even more, the first prize and the reward for victory over him in wicked-ness. The foremost of fakirs and magicians were considered worthy of the highest honor with him, for he became especially fearful of every noise and very superstitious, and he regarded as of great importance the error of idols and demons. For example, without divinations and oracles he was not able even to dare to move the breadth of a nail, so to speak. On this account he applied himself to our per-secution more vehemently and more constantly than his predecessors, giving orders to erect temples in every city, and speedily to restore the sacred groves which with a long lapse of time had been destroyed; and he appointed idol priests in every place and city, and over these as high priest in each province some one of those in politics who had clearly dis-tinguished himself in every brand of the service, with a military escort and bodyguard of soldiers, and without re-straint he bestowed on all fakirs governments and the greatest privileges, as if they were religious and beloved of the gods.

---

called Daza, and later Galerius Valerius Maximinus, was emperor from 305 to 314. He was a nephew of Galerius by a sister. In early life he was a shepherd in his native Illyria. He entered the army and rose to the highest rank in the service. On the abdication of Dio-cletian in 305, he was adopted by Galerius and received the title of Caesar, and in 308 the title of Augustus. On the death of Galerius in 311, Maximinus and Licinius divided the East between them. When Licinius went to Milan to marry the sister of Constantine, Maximinus attacked his territory. But he was defeated by Licinius near Heracles, and fled to Tarsus, where he soon after died. Maximinus surpassed all his contemporaries in the wretchedness of his private life, in the cruelty of his administration, and in the severity of his persecution of the Christians. The greater part of the martyrdoms described by Eusebius in his *Martyrs of Palestine* took place under him. On his treatment of the Christians after the death of Galerius, and his final edict of toleration, cf. 9.2,3,9,10.

From this time on, not a single city or country, but the provinces completely and fully under his control, he oppressed and downtrod by exactions of gold and silver and incalculable wealth and by the heaviest taxes and various fines. Moreover, from the wealthy he took the possessions which they had acquired from ancestors, and he bestowed upon the flatterers about him riches and piles of goods all at once. Furthermore, he was carried away to such an excess of mad drunkenness that in his cups he became deranged and driven out of his mind, and while drunk gave such orders as on the next day, when sober, he regretted. He alowed no one to surpass him in debauchery and profligacy, and he established himself as a teacher of wickedness to the rulers and ruled about him, inducing the army to enervate itself by every kind of wantonness and excess, and even urging governors and commanders to go against their subjects by plundering and extorting, all but becoming fellow tyrants with himself. Why should I recall the man's disgraceful deeds of passion or enumerate the multitude of those who were debauched by him? Indeed, it was impossible for him to pass by a city without habitually ravishing its women and abducting its virgins. And these actions went well for him with all except Christians, who, despising death, counted such tyranny on his part as nothing. The men, enduring fire and sword and nailings and wild beasts and the depths of the sea, and cutting off and burning of limbs, and piercing and gouging of eyes, and mutilation of the whole body, and besides this, hunger and mines and bonds, in all displayed their endurance in behalf of religion rather than give to idols the piety due to God. And women in turn, no less than the men, were inspired by the teaching of the divine Word: some, undergoing the same contests as the men, carried off equal prizes for virtue; others, being carried off for debauchery, gave over their souls to death sooner than their bodies to debauchery. For example, a Christian woman,[4] most famous and illustrious of those at Alexandria, alone of those who had been ravished by the tyrant, overcame the impassioned and unbridled soul of Maximin by her very strong courage. In every respect renowned for wealth and birth and education, she nevertheless counted all as second to chastity. After he had entreated her many times, he was unable to kill her although she was ready to die, since his desire overcame his anger, but he punished her with exile, and deprived her of all her property. And countless others, who were unable even to hear of the threat of fornication at the hands of the provincial governors, endured every form of torture, and rackings, and mortal punishment.

Now, these truly were wonderful, but most wonderful by far was that woman[5] at Rome, truly the most noble and the most chaste of all upon whom the tyrant there, Maxentius, acting as did Maximin, tried to force his attentions. For when she learned that those who performed such services for the tyrant had stopped at her house (she also was a Christian), and that her husband (who was a prefect of the Romans) through cowardice had given permission to take and lead her away, excusing herself for a brief period that she might adorn her body, she entered her chamber, and, while alone, plunged a sword into her body, and dying instantly she left her corpse for the procurers, and by deeds that themselves were louder than all words proclaimed to

4 According to Rufinus, her name was Dorothea.
5 According to Rufinus, she was called Sophronia.

all men, both those present and those to come, that among
Christian virtue was the only possession impossible of being
conquered or destroyed. So great an accumulation of wickedness, indeed, was brought together at one and the same time,
wrought by the two tyrants who had divided among themselves East and West. Who, when searching for the cause
of such evil, would hesitate to name the persecution against
us—especially when such great confusion did not come to
an end until the Christians received back their rights of
freedom?

Chapter 15

During the entire ten-year period[1] of the persecution there
was no cessation in their plotting and warring against each
other. The paths of the sea were unnavigable, nor were any,
regardless of whence they sailed, able to withdraw without
being tortured by every outrage and having their sides torn,
and, lest they came from the enemy of the opposite side,
being examined under all kinds of tortures, and finally being
subject to crucifixion or punishment by fire. Beside this, in
every place preparations of shields and breastplates, and of
missiles and spears, and the getting ready of other warlike
accoutrements, and of triremes and naval supplies were
going on, and no one at all could expect anything else than
an attack from the enemy any day. Among these people
subsequent famine and pestilence also broke out, concerning
which we shall relate what is necessary at the proper time.[2]

---

1 This is a general estimate. There were many cessations during that
  period, and in Maximin's territory in the East the persecution continued beyond that period.
2 Cf. 9.8.

Chapter 16

Such were the happenings that were extended throughout the entire persecution, when in the tenth year[1] by the grace of God it ceased completely, although it began to abate and to be certain after the eighth year.[2] When the divine and heavenly grace displayed its kindly and gentle watchfulness over us, then, indeed, the rulers over us also, those very persons by whom the acts of war had been carried on against us for a long time, most unexpectedly changed their minds and issued recantations, quenching the fire of persecution, which had been enkindled so greatly, by merciful proclamations and most kind ordinances regarding us. But nothing human, nor the pity, as one might say, nor the humanity of the rulers was responsible for this. Far from it. Daily, from the beginning and up to that time, more numerous and more difficult measures against us were being devised, while they, by more varied devices invented new outrages against us from time to time. But the evident visitation of Divine Providence itself was responsible, becoming reconciled to the people on the one hand, but at the same time attacking the author[3] of the evils, and becoming angry at him as the chief source of the wickedness of the entire persecution. For, even if it was necessary that these things take place, according to divine judgment, Scripture says: 'Woe to that man by whom the scandal cometh.'[4] Thus a punishment sent by God came

---

1 313.
2 Eusebius refers here to Galerius' edict of toleration issued after the close of the eighth year, in April 311, and presented in 8.17.
3 Galerius.
4 Matt. 18.7; cf., also, Luke 17.1.

upon him, beginning in his very flesh and proceeding to the soul.[5] For an abscess suddenly appeared in the center of his privy parts, then a deeply perforated ulcer, incurable and feeding into the very depth of his bowels. From these an innumerable multitude of worms burst forth and gave out a deathly stench, for the entire bulk of his limbs through gluttony, even before the disease, had been changed into an exessive amount of soft fat, which then becoming putrid furnished an unbearable and most horrible sight to those who approached. Some of the physicians were quite unable to endure the terribly excessive stench, and were slain; others, since the entire bulk had swollen and had fallen into a hopeless state as regards recovery, being unable to help him, were killed mercilessly.

Chapter 17

Wrestling with so many evils, he felt conscious-stricken for the deed which he had brazenly committed against the pious, and so reflecting within himself, he first openly confessed to the God of the universe; then, summoning those about him, he commanded them without delay to put an end to the persecution against the Christians, and by an imperial law and decree to urge them to build their churches and to perform their customary rites, offering prayers in behalf of the emperor. Action straightway followed upon his word; royal decrees were promulgated in the cities, one by

5 Galerius was struck by the terrible disease toward the end of the year 310, and died in May of the following year. Lactantius (*De mort. pers.* 33) describes his disease at even greater length.

one, containing the recantation of the edicts issued against us in the following manner:

'The Emperor Caesar Galerius Valerius Maximianus Invictus Augustus, Pontifex Maximus, Germanicus Maximus, Aegyptiacus Maximus, Thebaicus Maximus, Sarmaticus Maximus five times, Persicus Maximus twice, Carpicus Maximus six times, Armeniacus Maximus, Medicus Maximus, Adiabenicus Maximus, with tribunician power for the twentieth time, Emperor for the nineteenth time,[1] Consul for the eighth time, Father of his country, Proconsul; and the Emperor Caesar Flavius Valerius Constantinus Pius Felix Invictus Augustus, Pontifex Maximus, with tribunician power, Emperor for the fifth time, Consul, Father of his country, Proconsul:[2] [and the Emperor Caesar Valerius Licinianus Licinius Pius Felix Invictus Augustus, Pontifex Maximus, with tribunician power for the fourth time, Emperor for the third time, Consul, Father of his country, Proconsul, to the people of their provinces, greeting.]

'Among the other measures which we conceive for the good and profit of the people, we wished formerly to set all aright in accord with the ancient laws and public discipline[3] of the Romans, and to make provision for the following: that

---

1 When, after a great victory, he was hailed as *Imperator* by the army.
2 This edict was issued in April, 311. As given by Eusebius, Maximin's names and titles are here omitted, and much discussion has arisen as to why. But according to Lactantius (*De mort. pers.*), the edict was issued in the name of all four emperors. Accordingly, Maximin's names and titles must have appeared in the lacuna. Some Mss. omit all reference to Licinius, which we have placed here within brackets. The omission of all reference to these two emperors may be due to their intolerance and persecution of Christians.
3 Latin *publica disciplina* is regularly translated into Greek *tèn dēmosian epistémēn.*

the Christians, also, whoever had left the religion of their
ancestors, should return to a good attitude of mind, since
by some reasoning such arrogance had laid hold on them and
such folly seized them as to cause them not to follow what
had been introduced of old by their ancestors, which perhaps
their own forefathers had formerly established, but, according
to their own attitude of mind and as each one wished, thus
made laws for themselves and observed these and assembled
various multitudes in various places. Therefore, when an
order by us soon followed to the intent that they transfer
themselves to the institutions established by the ancients, a
great many gave in to danger, but a great many were harassed and suffered all kinds of death; and since, when the
majority persisted in the same attitude of mind we say that
they were not carrying on the worship due to the gods of
heaven nor attending to Him of the Christians, having regard
for our humanity and our invariable custom by which we
regularly extended pardon to all men, we thought that in this
case, also, we should most eagerly accord our indulgence, that
they may be Christians again and build the houses in which
they used to gather, provided that they do nothing contrary to
the discipline. In another letter we shall show the judges what
they shall have to observe. Therefore, according to this
indulgence of ours they should beseech their own God for
our safety and that of the people and that of themselves, in
order that in every way both the welfare of the people may
be secured and they may be able to live free from care at
their own homes.'

Such was the way this edict went in the Latin language,

translated as well as possible into the Greek tongue.[4] As for what happened after this it is now time to consider.

Appendix[1]

But the author of the edict, after such a confession, straightway and not for long, was relieved of his pains and departed this life. Record has it that this person was chiefly responsible for the misfortune of the persecution, for long before the movement of the other emperors he had forced the Christians in the armed forces and first of all those in his own household to turn away [from the faith], and demoted some from their military rank, and insulted others most shamefully, and presently threatened others even with death, and lastly stirred up his associates in the Empire to the general persecution. It is not worthy to give over the passing from life of these very emperors to silence. Four had divided the supreme authority among themselves. Those who were advanced in age and honor, and who had remained in office not two complete years after the persecution, retired from

---

4 Eusebius does not say whether or not he himself made the translation. In other instances, as in 4.9, the epistle of Hadrian to Minucius Fundanus, he definitely informs us.

---

1 Even though this paragraph is found only in Codices A, E, R, all the editors give it. Its existence implies that the work, in only eight Books, came into the hands of a scribe who added the appendix to round them out. He adds nothing which was not already told by Eusebius, except the notice of Diocletian's death and the manner of the death of Maximin. Since Diocletian died in 313, the addition must have been made as late as that year.

the government, as we have shown above,[2] and spent the remainder of their days in ordinary private life, and obtained an end of life as follows: he who was thought worthy of the highest place in honor and age[3] was destroyed by a long and most painful infirmity of body; he who held second place to him[4] ended his life by strangling, according to a certain demoniacal prediction suffering this for the great number of reckless crimes perpetrated by him. Of those after these, the last, whom we have said was even the originator of the entire persecution, suffered as we have already indicated above;[5] but he who preceded this one, the very merciful and kindly Constantius,[6] passed the entire period of his principate in a manner worthy of his office, and in all other respects displayed himself most kindly and beneficent to all; indeed, he even remained out of the war against us, and kept his subjects free from harm and harsh treatment, and he did not tear down church buildings, nor did he devise any other new device against us at all; a truly happy and thrice-blessed end of life did he have, for he alone while still emperor died graciously and gloriously with a lawful son as his successor, most prudent and pious in every respect. He immediately, when he took office, was declared most perfect emperor and Augustus by the armies; and he established himself as an

---

2 Cf. 8.13. The reference is to Diocletian and Maximinian.
3 Diocletian died in 313, at sixty-seven. The final collapse of his grand plans for the Empire, the misfortunes of his daughters, and treatment accorded him by Maximin, Licinius, and Constantine finally crushed him. Cf. Lactantuis, *De mort. pers.* 42.
4 Maximinian; cf. 8.13.
5 Galerius, the second Caesar and therefore the last of the four rulers; cf. 8.16,17.
6 The first Caesar, thus holding the third rank in the government. The following passage repeats a portion of 8.13.

imitator of his father's piety toward our doctrine. Such was the passing from life, which took place at different times, on the part of the four of whom we have written above. Of these emperors he alone, whom we have mentioned a little above,[7] still remained, and, together with those who after this were introduced into the principate,[8] made the above-mentioned confession clear to all through the written document set forth above.

---

7 Galerius.
8 Constantine, Licinius, and Maximin.

BOOK NINE

Chapter 1

HE IMPERIAL EDICT of recantation presented above[1] was promulgated everywhere in Asia and in all the neighboring provinces. When this had been done in this manner, Maximin, the tyrant of the East, a most impious man if there ever was one, who had been most hostile to the religion of the God of the universe, being by no means pleased with what had been written, instead of promulgating the document gave verbal orders to the officials under him to relax the war against us. Since it was not possible for him otherwise to oppose the decision of his superiors, placing in a corner the law which had been promulgated, and taking thought on how it might not be brought into sight within the districts under him, by an unwritten order he ordered the officials under him to relax the war against us. They pointed out the content of the order to each other in writing. For example, Sabinus,[2] whom they had honored

---

1 Galerius' edict of toleration; cf. 8.17.
2 All that is known of Sabinus is contained in this passage. He was probably Maximin's prime minister or praetorian prefect. Cf. 9.9, where a letter of Maximin addressed to him is quoted.

with the rank of most excellent prefect, made clear to the
provincial governors the mind of the emperor by means of a
letter in Latin. A translation of this original is as follows:

'With a most brilliant and a devoted zeal, the Divinity of
our most divine masters, the emperors,[3] has already for a
long time decided to guide the thoughts of all men into
holy and straight paths of life, so that those also who seem
to follow a way of life foreign to that of the Romans may
perform the acts of worship due to the immortal gods. But
the obstinacy and the most unyielding will of some reached
such a point that they could not withdraw from their own
purpose because of just reasoning of the command nor did
the impending punishment intimidate them. Since, therefore,
it has come to pass that many by such conduct cast themselves
in the face of danger, the Divinity of our masters, the most
powerful emperors, in accord with the noble piety which they
possess, considering it foreign to the purpose of their Divinity
to cast men into such danger for such a reason, have ordered
through my Devotedness to write to your Wisdom that, if
any of the Christians should be discovered following the
religion of his own people, you should set him free from the
annoyances directed against him and from danger, nor
should you think that anyone should be visited with punishment on this pretext, since with the passage of so long a
time it has been established that they cannot be persuaded
in any way to abandon such stubbornness. Therefore, your
Solicitude should write to the curators and duumvirs and
the magistrates of the district of every city, that they may

---

3 The epistle is equally stilted throughout. It was clearly dictated or
inspired by Maximin himself.

know that it is not proper for them to give any further consideration to this letter.'[4]

Thereupon, the rulers of the provinces, having come to the conclusion that they had substantiated the purpose of what had been written to them, made known by letter the imperial mind to the curators and duumvirs and those in charge of the rural districts; and these matters went forward not only through writing, but even much more by action, so that, as if they might bring the imperial will to accomplishment, as many as they held confined in prison for confession of the Deity, they brought into the open and freed, releasing some of those very persons who had been consigned to the mines for punishment, for they were deceived in supposing that the emperor had truly decided upon this. When these matters had thus been carried out, it was possible to see, like a light shining suddenly forth out of a dark night,[5] churches being put together in every city, and crowded assemblies, and rites being performed at these according to custom. And every one of the unbelieving heathen was struck not a little at these things, marveling at the wonder of so great a change, and proclaiming the God of the Christians as great and alone true. Those of our people who had faithfully and courageously endured the struggle of the persecutions again took on an air of confidence before all, and such as had become diseased of faith and storm-tossed in soul eagerly

---

4 The general meaning of the letter is clear. Maximin is making concessions very begrudgingly and under pressure. He plainly suppressed the edict of Galerius, and substituted explicit instruction of his own, wishing to do as little as possible for Christians, and to be left free to act when in a more advantageous position. He did not want to hamper himself by sanctioning the clear and complete toleration granted by the edict of Galerius .

5 Cf. 2 Cor. 4.6.

strove for their own cure, beseeching and begging the strong
for a right hand of safety, and supplicating God to be
merciful to them. Then, also, the noble athletes of piety,
being freed of their evil plight in the mines, returned to their
own homes, going through every city, exalting and beaming
with joy and filled with unspeakable happiness and confidence that one cannot describe with words. Populous throngs
in the midst of throughfares and market places went on their
way praising God with songs and psalms, and you would
have seen those who shortly before had been driven from
their fatherlands in bonds under a very harsh punishment
resuming their fireside with happy and joyous countenances,
so that even those who before were stained with our blood,
on seeing the marvel contrary to all expectation, rejoiced
with us at what had happened.

Chapter 2

But the tyrant, who was a hater of things noble and a
plotter against everything good, and who, as we have said,
ruled over the regions of the East, was unable to endure
this any longer, and did not suffer things to go on in this
manner even for six entire months.[1] As he schemed so many

---

1 The change in Maximin's policy toward the Christians recorded here
about October 311, the edict of Galerius having been issued in April
of that year. Cf. Lactantius, *De mort. pers.* 35, and, above, 8.17. The
reason for this renewal of the persecution was probably due to
irritation at the exaltation of the Church, and the rapid recovery of
the Christians as soon as the pressure was removed. That the persecution was not renewed earlier was caused by the fact that Maximin,
immediately after the death of Galerius, was occupied with the
division of the Eastern Empire between himself and Licinius. Cf.
Lactantius, *De mort. pers.* 36.

ways to overturn the peace, he first tried by a pretext to
prevent our meeting in the cemeteries, then through some
wicked men he sent embassies to himself against us,[2] stirring
up the citizens of Antioch to ask to obtain from him as a
very great favor that no Christian be permitted ever to
dwell in their country, and to cause others to make the same
suggestion. The orignator of all this in Antioch itself was
Theotecnus,[3] a clever fakir and a wicked man and quite
foreign to his name. But he seemed to have been the curator[4]
in the administration of the city.

Chapter 3

Now, this man, after he had conducted a great many
campaigns against us, and had eagerly resorted to every plan
to hunt our people out of their hiding places, as if they
were certain unholy thieves, and had devised every means
to slander and accuse us, and had been responsible for the
death of countless numbers, finally erected a statue of Zeus
Philius[1] by certain juggleries and sorceries, and inventing
unholy initiations for it, and ill-omened mysteries, and

---

2 Cf. 7.11. Lactantius, *De mort. pers.* 36, gives the same account. Whether
these embassies were genuine is entirely a matter of conjecture.
3 Knowledge of Theotecnus comes from the *Passion of St. Theodotus*
and from this passage of Eusebius. He was an apostate from Christianity, and, while chief magistrate of Galatia, was most cruel to
Christians. After the death of Maximin, he was executed at the
command of Licinius (9.11). In Greek, Theotecnus means 'child of
God.'
4 The chief finance officer of a municipality.

---

1 The god of friendship and good will, widely honored in the East.

abominable purifications,[2] even in the presence of the emperor he displayed his jugglery by such oracles as he pleased. Now, this fellow by a flattery to the liking of him who was ruling stirred up the demon against the Christians, and even said that the god ordered the expulsion of the Christians beyond the borders of the city and the country round about the city, on the ground that they were his enemies.

Chapter 4

When this individual of set purpose was the first to take action, the rest of those in office who inhabited the cities under the same rule rushed to make a similar decision, since the provincial governors saw at a glance that it was pleasing to the emperor, and they had suggested to their subjects that they do this very thing. And when the tyrant through a rescript now most gladly gave assent to their decisions, the persecution against us was again enkindled afresh.

Priests of the idols and, besides, high priests in every city were established by Maximin himself, those who had especially distinguished themselves in public office and had become pre-eminent in all offices, and by whom, also, a great zeal was introduced for the worship of those being served by them. Certainly, the extraordinary superstition of the rulers, to speak briefiy, was inducing all those under him, the governors and the governed, to do everything against us to please him, as they bestowed upon him this greatest of

---

2 The pagan ceremonies used in the erection and consecration of images were varied. Eusebius is here using certain phrases from Dion. Alex. (7.10.4).

favors in return for the benefits which they thought to obtain from him, namely, to thirst for our blood and to show some rather novel forms of viciousness toward us.[1]

Chapter 5

Having forged, of course, *Memoirs* of Pilate[1] and of our Saviour, full of every blasphemy against Christ, they disseminated them with the knowledge of their superior in every region under his power, urging by letter those in every place, country and city, to set them forth in full view for

---

1 Cf. Lactantius (*De mort. pers.* 36), who says: 'In compliance with those addresses, Maximin introduced a new kind of government in matters pertaining to religion. For each city he established a high priest, selected from among those of the highest distinction. Their duty was to perform daily sacrifices to all their gods, and, assisted by former priests, to keep the Christians from erecting churches, or from worshiping God, either publicly or in private. He also empowered them to force the Christians to sacrifice to idols, and, if they refused, to take them before the civil magistrate, and, as if this was not enough, he created in every province a superintendent priest, one of special eminence in the state. He furthermore commanded all these newly instituted priests to appear in white habits, this being the most honorable distinction of dress.' Thus, Maximin was the first to conceive the idea of opposing to Christianity a paganism equally as well organized and aggressive. A half-century later Julian attempted a similar plan.

---

1 These *Memoirs* or *Acts* are no longer extant, but they are well described in this chapter. They are, of course, not to be confused with the numerous Acts of Pilate that came from Christian sources. While filled with the worst calumnies, in particular, against Christ's moral and religious character, and being patently forgeries, they did much harm, spreading among the youth of the Empire a feeling of contempt and disgust for the founder of Christianity, the Christians' Saviour and Lord. Luckily, Maximin's reign lasted but a short time. Some would assign the dubious honor of this master stroke to Theotecnus. This, however, is purely conjecture.

all, and teachers of elementary schools to give these out to children instead of lessons to study and to commit to memory.

While these things were being accomplished in this manner, another military commander, whom the Romans call *dux*,[2] had certain wretched women in Damascus[3] of Phoenicia abducted from the maket place, and threatened to inflict tortures upon them, thus forcing them to state in writing that they truly were once Christians, and were conscious of their lawless deeds, and that even in the churches they performed lewd acts, and such other things as he wished them to say in defamation of our religion. Of these statements he also made written memoranda and communicated them to the emperor, and presently, at his command, he also made this letter public in every place and city.

Chapter 6

Not long afterwards, the military commander committed suicide and thus paid the penalty for his wickedness.

And, in turn, our banishments and harsh persecutions were again renewed, and in all provinces there were terrible uprisings against us on the part of the governors, so that some of those eminent in the divine Word were seized and received the sentence of death with no mercy.

---

2 The commander of the Roman frontier troops in Damascus.
3 Damascus from the time of Hadrian or that of Severus was the capital of the newly formed province of Syria-Phoenice or Syro-Phoenicia.

Of these, three in Emesa,[1] a city of Phoenicia, having confessed themselves Christians, were given over to beasts as food. There was among these a bishop, Silvanus,[2] far advanced in age, having fulfilled his service for forty complete years.

And at the same time, also, Peter,[3] who had presided most illustriously over the parishes of Alexandria, a divine example for bishops by reason of his virtuous life and his study of the holy Scriptures, having been seized for no cause at all, without receiving any inkling of it beforehand, was so suddenly and unaccountably beheaded that Maximin might have commanded it, and with him many others, also, of the bishops in Egypt underwent the same penalty.

Lucian,[4] an excellent man in every respect, temperate in living, and very learned in the sacred sciences, a presbyter of the parish at Nicomedia, was taken to the city of Nicomedia, where the emperor at that time happened to be staying, and on presenting his defence for the doctrine which he professed was committed to prison and killed.

Such things, then, were concocted against us by Maximin, the hater of the noble, in a brief period, so that he seemed to have stirred up this persecution against us to a much more difficult degree than the previous one.

---

1 Emesa, an important city in Northern Phoenicia, famous for its great Temple of the Sun.
2 Cf. 8.13.
3 Cf. 7.32. He suffered as early as April, 312.
4 One of the greatest scholars of the early Church, head of the famous theological school at Antioch; cf. 7.32 and 8.13. He was the author of several works, including a revised version of the Septuagint which had a wide circulation. Cf. Jerome, De vir. ill. 77. Except for several fragments, his writings have perished.

Chapter 7

Indeed, widespread through the cities, something which has never before happened, the petitions of the cities against us[1] and rescripts of the imperial commands in reply to these were set up engraved on brazen tablets,[2] and the children in the schools every day bore on their lips the names of Jesus and Pilate and the *Memoirs* forged to insult us.[3]

It seems to me to be necessary at this point to insert this very document of Maximin which was set up on tablets, in order that both the boastful and disdainful arrogance of this God-hating man and the sleepless hatred of wickedness on the part of the divine justice which followed close on his heels may be made clear. It was by this that he was smitten, and not long afterwards he reversed his policy toward us, and by written laws laid down his opinion.

Copy of a translation of the Rescript of Maximin in reply to the petitions against us, taken from the tablet in Tyre.

'Now, at last, the feeble boldness of the human mind has grown strong, shaking off and dispersing all the obscurity and the fog of error which hitherto enveloped and attacked with the baneful darkness of ignorance the senses of men not so much wicked as wretched; and it has grown strong enough to recognize that it is governed and established by the beneficent providence of the immortal gods. And this matter is beyond belief, to express how grateful and how very pleasing and dear it has been for us that you have given a very great proof of your pious purpose, since even

---

1 Cf. 9.2 and 4.
2 These decrees were so published in June, 312; cf. 9.8.
3 Cf. 9.5.

before this it was not unknown to anyone of what regard and piety for the immortal gods you really were possessed, in whom a faith not of bare and empty words but a faith continuous and wonderful in noble deeds is made known. Therefore, your city might worthily be called a temple and a dwelling place of the immortal gods. At any rate, it appears by many signs that she flourishes because of the sojourning there of the heavenly gods. Behold, your city, disregarding all private advantages to herself, and overlooking earlier petitions in behalf of her own affairs, when she perceived again that those who belonged to the accursed folly were beginning to spread, just as a neglected and smoldering fire, when its firebrands are rekindled, bursts forth into very large flames, immediately and without delay took refuge with our piety, as with the mother-city of all pieties, seeking some kind of healing and assistance. It is evident that the gods have placed this saving thought within you because of the faith of your piety. Therefore, that god, that highest and mightest Zeus, he who presides over your most illustrious city, he who guards your ancestral gods and wives and children and hearth and homes against every fatal destruction, inspired your spirits with this saving purpose, pointing out and making clear how remarkable and splendid and salutary a thing it is to approach the worship and the sacred rites of the immortal gods with due piety. For, who can be found so without reason or lacking all understanding as not to perceive that it is by the benevolent zeal of the gods that it happens that the earth does not refuse the seeds given over to it, thus foiling the hope of the husbandman with vain expectation; and, again, that the sight of impious war is not planted upon earth without hindrance and squalid bodies, as the wholesome air of heaven is polluted, are dragged off to death; that the sea does not swell and rise on high by the blasts of intemperate winds; that unexpected hurricanes do not break forth and stir up a destructful storm; still further, that the earth, the nourisher and mother of all, does not sink from its deepest hollows with a terrible tremor and the mountains resting upon it do not disappear as chasms open up, all of which disasters and still more terrible ones than these have occurred many times before this, as everyone knows? And all these things happened because of the destructful error of the empty folly of those lawless men, when it oppressed their souls, and, we might almost say, weighed down the earth everywhere with its shameful deeds.'

After other remarks, he adds to these: 'Let them behold in the broad fields crops already flourishing and waving with ears of corn, and the meadows, thanks to the abundance of rains, glistening with plants and flowers, and the condition of the atmosphere, temperate and very mild, that has been granted us; in the future, let all rejoice that through our piety and sacrifices and worship of the most powerful and most cruel the air has been propitiated, and let them be happy that for this reason they are securely enjoying the most serene peace with quiet. And let as many as have been entirely rescued from that blind error and wandering return to a right and most noble frame of mind, and rejoice so the more, as if they had been torn away from an unexpected storm or severe disease, and had reaped a pleasant enjoyment of life for the future. But, if they should persist in that accursed vanity of theirs, let them be separated and driven very far away from your city and environs, as you have requested, in order that in accord with your praiseworthy zeal in this respect your city, freed of every stain and impiety and according to its natural inclination, may thus with due reverence attend to the sacred rites of the immortal gods.

'And that you may know how pleasing your request has been to us, and how our soul, without petitions and a request by its voluntary desire, is most eager for benevolence, we permit your Fidelity to ask whatever munificence you wish in return for this pious disposition of yours. And now ask so to do and to receive. You will obtain it without any delay. The granting of this request will furnish testimony for all time of your god-loving piety for the immortal gods, and it will be displayed to your sons and descendants as proof that you obtained worthy rewards from our benevolence for this your purpose of life.'

This was published against us in every province, shutting our lot off from every good hope, at least, as far as men are concerned, insomuch as, according to that divine oracle itself, to deceive [if possible] even the elect.[4] Now, then, when the expectation of the majority was almost failing,[5] suddenly, while those who were serving the writ promulgated against us were still on the road and had not finished their journey in some regions, God, the champion of His own Church, all but gagged the proud boasting of the tyrant against us, and displayed His heavenly aid in our behalf.

4 Cf. Matt. 24.24; also, 6.41, above.
5 Cf. Luke 21.26.

Chapter 8

Now, the customary rains and showers of the winter season
which then prevailed were withholding their usual down-
pour upon the earth, and an unexpected famine came upon
us, and besides these a plague, and an outbreak of another
disease—this was an ulcer, on account of its fiery appearance,
appropriately called an anthrax.[1] This crept over the whole
body and caused the sufferers serious danger, but especially
against the eyes did it direct its greatest attack, and it
deprived countless men, together with women and children,
of their sight.

In addition to this there was forced upon the tyrant the
war against the Armenians, men from of old friends and
allies of the Romans, whom also, since they were Christians
and zealous in the exercise of piety toward the Deity, he
tried to force to sacrifice to idols and demons; and he
thereby made them foes instead of friends, enemies instead
of allies. All these things coming together at one and the
same time utterly refuted the tyrant's insolent boasting against
the Deity; for he boldly bragged that because of his zeal
for the idols and his attack upon us neither famine nor
pestilence nor even war had taken place within his time.[2]
These things, then, coming together upon him at the same
time also included the prelude of his own overthrow. Thus

1 Lit., a precious stone of a dark red color, and thus used of a
malignant ulcer of similar appearance. Lactantius (*De mort. pers.*
37) refers to a famine at this time, but says nothing about it. Eusebius
alone tells of this famine and pestilence in the reign of Maximin.
2 Cf. 9.7.

he himself, together with his commanders, was worn out over the war against the Armenians, and famine as well as pestilence so exhausted the rest of the inhabitants of the cities under him that 2,500 Attic drachmas[3] was the cost of a single measure of wheat. Countless were those who then died in the cities, and more numerous than these in the country and villages, so that the registers which formerly showed an extensive rural population suffered almost complete reduction, almost all being suddenly destroyed by lack of nourishment and by pestilential disease. And some resolved to sell their dearest possessions to those better provided for the slightest bit of nourishment; others, selling off their goods little by little, were soon reduced to the last extremity of need; and some by chewing small wisps of hay and recklessly eating certain noxious herbs ruined their bodily constitutions and perished. And some of the women, the wellborn ladies in cities, were driven by their want to shameless necessity and went out into the market places to beg, displaying evidence of their past cultural training by their shamefacedness and by the decency of their apparel. And some, wasted away like ghostly corpses, at their last gasp, shaking and slipping here and there, because of their inability to stand fell down, and stretched out prone in the middle of the streets, earnestly begged that a small piece of bread be handed to them, and clinging to life with their last breath they shouted that they were hungry, having strength for this most distressing cry alone. Others, such as were regarded to be of the wealthier classes, astounded at

---

3 A silver coin worth eighteen or nineteen cents.

the multitude of beggars, after giving out immeasurable amounts, resorted henceforth to a hard and relentless disposition of mind, expecting that they themselves, also, before very long would be suffering the same as the beggars, so that in the middle of the market places and alleys corpses and naked bodies, scattered here and there and unburied for many days, furnished a most pitiful sight to those who looked upon them. Then, too, some became food for dogs; and for this reason, chiefly, the living turned to killing dogs lest these become mad and commence to devour men. And not the least serious was the pestilence which devoured entire houses, especially those whom hunger had not been able to bring low because they were well provided with food. Thus did men living in plenty, rulers and governors and countless officials, as if expressly left behind by the famine for the pestilential disease, suffer a quick and very speedy death. Thus all places were full of lamentations; in all alleys and market places and streets there was nothing to hear but funeral dirges, together with the flutes and noises[4] usually accompanying them. Waging war, then, in this manner, with the two aforesaid weapons of pestilence and famine, death in a short time wasted away entire families, so that one could see the bodies of two and three dead being carried out in one funeral procession.

Such were the rewards of the proud boasting of Maximin and of the decrees in the cities against us, when the testimonies of the zeal and of the piety of the Christians in all things became quite clear to all the heathen. For example, they alone in such evil surroundings exhibited their sympathy and humanity by actual deeds: all during the day some

---

4 Sometimes translated 'beating' (of breasts).

persevered diligently with the last rites and the burial of the dead (for there were countless who had no one to care for them); others gathered in one assemblage the multitude of those who throughout the entire city were wasting away from famine, and distributed bread to all of them, so that the matter became noised about among all men, and they glorified the God of the Christians, and, convinced by the facts themselves, they confessed that these alone were truly pious and religious.

After these things were accomplished in the aforesaid manner, the great and heavenly defender of the Christians, God, after displaying His threat of punishment and His anger against all men as we have shown, in return for the viciousness which they had displayed against us, again gave back to us the gracious and joyous radiance of His providence regarding us; most unexpectedly, as in a deep darkness, He caused the light of peace to shine upon us from Him, and He made it clear to all that God Himself had been watchful over our affairs always, now scourging His people at opportune moments by means of misfortunes, and again, after sufficient chastisement, displaying pity and goodwill to those who have hope in Him.

Chapter 9

Then Constantine, who we have mentioned before[1] was an emperor born of an emperor, a pious man born of a most pious and in every respect most prudent father, and Licinius after him, both honored for their intelligence and piety, were

---

1 On Constantine, Licinius, and Maxentius, cf. 8.13,14.

stirred up by the absolute Ruler, God of the universe and Saviour, against the two most impious tyrants, and when war was duly organized, God most wonderfully joined them as allies; Maxentius fell at Rome at the hands of Constantine, and the other in the East[2] did not survive him for a very long time, but he himself also met a most shameful death at the hands of Licinius who had not yet become insane.[3]

Now, Constantine, who was the superior both in dignity and imperial rank, was the first to take pity on those who were being tyrannized at Rome, and calling by prayer upon God in heaven and His Word and Him the Saviour of all, Jesus Christ, as his ally, went forward with his entire army,[4] seeking to procure for the Romans their ancestral liberty. Maxentius, indeed, since he put trust more in the devices of magic than in the good will of his subjects, and did not dare to proceed very far beyond the gates of the city, with a countless number of heavy-armed soldiers and with innumerable companies of legionaries fortified every place and region and city that had been enslaved by him in the neighborhood of Rome and in all Italy. The emperor, relying closely on the alliance of God, attacked the first and second and third armies of the tyrant and, capturing them all, very easily advanced over the greater part of Italy and presently was very near Rome itself. Then, that He might not be forced for the sake of the tyrant to make war on the Romans, God Himself, as if with some bonds dragged the tyrant very far

---

2 Maximin. On his defeat and death, cf. 9.10.
3 This clause was added later after Eusebius; also, the similar clause below.
4 Constantine's battle with Maxentius here described took place on October 27, 312, the sixth anniversary of Maxentius' accession. Cf. Lactantius, *De mort. pers.* 44 and 46.

from the gates, and confirmed the ancient threats against the impious, disbelieved by most as being in the nature of myth, but worthy of belief with believers since they were inscribed in the sacred books. He confirmed them, in short, by their very clarity with all, believers and unbelievers, who took in the marvels with their own eyes. For example, as in the time of Moses himself and of that ancient and pious race of the Hebrews, 'Pharao's chariots and his army he hath cast into the sea, chosen horsemen and captains; they were sunk in the Red Sea; the depths have covered them,' in the same way, also, Maxentius and the soldiers and armed guards about him 'were sunk to the bottom like a stone,'[5] when, turning his back on God's might that was with Constantine, he crossed the river that lay in his path, which he himself by joining boats had successfully bridged and so formed an instrument of destruction against himself. Therefore it were possible to say, 'He hath opened a pit and dug it, and he shall fall into the hole he made. His work shall turn on his own head, and his wickedness shall come down upon his own crown.'[6]

Thus, then, when the bridge over the river broke, the passage across collapsed, and suddenly the boats, men and all, went down into the deep, and he himself first, the most impious; then, too, the shield-bearers about him, as the divine oracles foretell, 'sank as lead in the mighty waters,'[7] so that fittingly, if not in words, then in deeds, like the followers of the great servant Moses,[8] those who by God's

5 Cf. Exod 15.4,5.
6 Cf. Ps. 7.16,17.
7 Cf. Exod. 15.10.
8 Cf. Exod. 14.31.

help won the victory might thus hymn in a manner the very words uttered against the impious tyrant of old and say: 'Let us sing to the Lord: for he is gloriously magnified, the horse and the rider he hath thrown into the sea. The Lord is my strength and protector, he is become salvation to me,' and 'Who is like to thee, among the gods, O Lord? Who is like thee, glorified among saints, marvelous in praises, doing wonders?'[9]

Constantine by his very deeds having sung to God, the Ruler of all and the Author of his victory, these words and such as were akin and resembling these, entered Rome with hymns of triumph. All the senators, together with very young children and women, and the most eminent otherwise, as well as with all the Roman people in a body immediately received him with beaming eyes and with their very souls as deliverer and saviour and benefactor, with praises and insatiable joy. But he, as if possessed of an inborn piety toward God, not at all stirred by their shouts nor elated by their praises, being very well conscious of his aid from God, straightway ordered that a memorial of the Saviour's Passion be set up in the hand of his own statue, and presently, when they had set him up in the most public place in Rome holding the Saviour's sign in his right hand, he commanded them to engrave upon it this very inscription in these words in the Latin tongue: 'By this saving sign, the true proof of bravery, I have saved and freed your city from the yoke of the tyrant; moreover, after freeing the senate and the people of Rome, I restored them to their ancient distinction and splendor.'[10]

---

9 Cf. Exod. 15.1,2,11.
10 Cf. Eusebius' *Life of Constantine* 1.28.

And after this, Constantine himself and with him the Emperor Licinius, whose mind at that time had not yet been directed to the madness into which he later fell,[11] having propitiated God as the author of all their blessings, both with one wish and determination fashioned in the fullest detail a most perfect law[12] in behalf of Christians, and they sent an account of the marvelous things that had been done for them by God, and the details of the victory over the tyrant, and the law itself to Maximin, who was still ruling the peoples of the East, and was making a pretense of friendliness toward them. And he, like a tyrant, becoming pained at what he learned, then not wishing to seem to yield to others, nor in turn to conceal what had been ordered out of fear for those who had commanded it, as if on his own authority by force wrote this first letter on behalf of the Christians to the governors under him, he himself falsely devising things against himself which had never been done by him.

Chapter 9A

Copy of a translation of the epistle of the tyrant 'Jovius Maximinus Augustus to Sabinus.[1]

'I am convinced that it is clear to your Firmness and to all men that our masters Diocletian and Maximian, our fathers, when they became aware that almost all men had abandoned the worship of the gods and had attached them-

---

11 This clause is a later addition; cf. note 3, above.
12 The famous Edict of Milan, issued in late January 313. The Latin original is given by Lactantius in his *De mort. pers.* 48; a Greek translation below, in 10.5.

---

1 Cf. 9.1.

selves to the nation of Christians, rightly decreed that all men who had abandoned the worship of the same gods, the immortal gods, be recalled by open chastisement and punishment to the worship of the gods. But when under favorable auspices I first came to the East, and learned that in some places a great many men able to aid the public good were being banished by the judges for the aforesaid cause, I gave orders to each of the judges that no one of these in the future deal roughly with the provincials, but rather recall them to the worship of the gods by flattery and exhortations.[2] At that time, then, when in accord with my command the orders which had been given were being observed by the judges, it happened that no one from the regions of the East was either banished or insulted, but rather, by reason of the fact that no harsh measures were taken against them, they were recalled to the worship of the gods. But afterwards, when within the past year[3] I went to Nicomedia under happy auspices and was sojourning there, citizens of the same city came to me with images of the gods, strongly entreating in every way that such a people by no means be permitted to dwell in their country. But when I learned that a great many men of the same religion dwelt in these very parts, I made reply to them as follows: that I was happily grateful for their request, but I noted that this was not made by all. If, then, there were some who persevered in the same superstition, that each one hold to his wish according to his personal choice, even if they should wish to acknowledge the worship of the gods. Nevertheless, to the Nicomedians of this same

2 This and the following statements are far from the truth.
3 In 311, after the death of Galerius; cf. Lactantius, *De mort. pers.* 36.

city and to the rest of the cities, who themselves have so very earnestly made a similar request to me, namely, that no Christian live in their cities, I was obliged to give answer in a friendly manner, because the emperors of old also observed this very thing, and it was pleasing to the gods themselves through whom all men and the government of the State itself endure, that I confirmed such a request as they presented in behalf of the worship of their deity.

'Therefore, although special messages have been sent by letter to your Devotedness before this time, and it has been likewise commanded by ordinances that no harsh measures be adopted against the provincials who were anxious to persevere in such a custom, but that they should be dealt with in a spirit of long-suffering and with moderation, nevertheless, that they may not suffer insults or extortions at the hands of the *beneficiarii*[4] or, by chance, others, I have thought it right to remind your Firmness by this letter that you should cause our provincials to recognize the care of the gods rather by flatteries and exhortations. Therefore, if anyone by his own choice should decide that the worship of the gods should be recognized, it is fitting to welcome these persons, but if some should wish to follow their own religion, you should leave it in their power. Therefore, your Fidelity should observe what has been enjoined upon you, and let power be given to no one to turn our provincials over to insults and extortions, when, as has been written already, it is fitting rather by exhortations and flatteries to recall our provincials to the worship of the gods. In order that this command of ours may come to the knowledge of all our provincials, you

---

4 Military officers of high rank in the entourage of the provincial governor.

ought to make known what has been commanded in an edict put forth by yourself.'

Since he was forced to this by necessity, but did not command it of his own free will, no longer was he truthful and worthy of trust in the eyes of all, because already on a former occasion, after a similar concession, his mind proved changeable and false. So, no one of our people dared to hold meetings or to present himself in public, because the letter did not even allow him this, yielding only this, our being preserved from harsh treatment, but not itemizing the holding of meetings or the erecting of church buildings or the practicing of any other of our customary activities. Yet, the advocates of peace and piety had written him to permit this, and had granted it by edicts and laws to all their subjects. However, the most impious person had determined not to yield in this, until, being forced by the divine justice, he was at last driven to this against his will.

Chapter 10

Some such causes as the following hemmed him in. He was unable to bear the magnitude of his office which had been unworthily entrusted to him, but, because of his lack of prudence and imperial understanding, managing his affairs without tact and above all being unreasonably uplifted in soul by a boastful arrogance even toward his colleagues in the Empire who were superior to him in every respect, in birth and in training and in education and in worth and intelligence and, most important of all, in prudence and in piety toward the true God, he rashly dared to act with insolence and to proclaim himself publicly as first in rank.[1] And pushing his mad actions to the point of insanity, he broke the treaty which he had made with Licinius,[2] and undertook an implacable war. Then in a little while, having thrown all into confusion and greatly agitated every city, and having brought together all the army, a multitude of countless thousands, he went forth in battle array to meet him, with his spirit elated by his hopes in demons, whom he thought gods, and by the myriads of his soldiers.

And having joined battle,[3] he now stands bereft of God's providence, victory being awarded by the one and only God of all Himself to him who was then ruling.[4] First, he lost completely the military force in which he had placed his trust, and, when the guards about him left him with no defence and divested of everything and took refuge with him who was then in power, the wretched man, ridding himself as quickly as possible of the imperial ensigns which did not befit him, in a cowardly and ignoble and unmanly manner slipped into the crowd, and then ran hither and yon, hiding himself in the fields and villages. Although he labored for his safety, he escaped the hands of the enemy with difficulty, by his very deeds proclaiming as trustworthy and true the divine oracles, in which it has been said: 'The king is not saved by a great army: nor shall the giant be saved

1 Actually, Maximin was Constantine's senior, and it is not surprising that he assumed first rank for himself.
2 The treaty made after Galerius' death in 311; cf. Lactantius, *De mort. pers.* 36.
3 For a more detailed and very imaginative account of this battle between Licinius and Maximin, fought on April 30, 313, at Adrianople in Thrace, cf. Lactantius, *De mort. pers.* 45f.
4 Licinius. These words were probably inserted later.

by his own great strength. Vain is the horse for safety:
neither shall he be saved by the abundance of his strength.
Behold the eyes of the Lord are on them that fear him, and
on them that hope in his mercy: to deliver their souls from
death.'[5] So, then, full of shame, the tyrant, after returning
to his own regions, first with frantic rage slew many priests
and prophets of the gods who were formerly admired by
him, because of whose oracles he had been incited to make
war, on the ground that they were sorcerers and cheats and,
above all, betrayers of his safety. Then, giving glory to the
God of Christians and drawing up a law for their freedom[6]
most completely and fully, straightway, with no respite being
given him, he ended his life by a lingering death.[7]

Copy of a translation of the edict of the tyrant in behalf
of the Christians, made from the Latin tongue into the
Greek.

'The Emperor Caesar Gaius Valerius Maximinus Germanicus, Sarmaticus, Pius Felix Invictus Augustus. We believe
that no one is ignorant [of this], but that everyone goes back
to what actually happened and everyone of mankind knows
and holds it within himself to be evident that we continuously
in every way care for the welfare of our provincials, and
wish to furnish them with that by which the advantage of all
is especially achieved, and such things as belong to their

---

5 Cf. Ps. 33.16-19.
6 Maximin's final edict of toleration was issued very soon after his
defeat. His motive is clear enough—to secure the loyalty of as many
of his subjects as possible that he might defeat Licinius. His real
attitude toward the Christians was not changed.
7 According to Lactantius (De mort. pers. 49), Maximin died at Tarsus,
probably several weeks after his defeat and the publication of his
edict of toleration. There are various accounts of how he died, none
of them reliable.

common welfare and advantage, and acquire the public advantage, and are really agreeable to the minds of all. When, then, before this, it became clear to our mind that on this pretext, that it had been commanded by our most divine fathers, Diocletian and Maximian, to abolish the assemblies of Christians, many extortions and robberies had taken place at the hands of the officials, and that this evil progressed as time went on to the misfortune of our provincials, for whom especially we are eager that due provision be made, while their personal property was wasting away, by writing letters to the governors of each province in the past year we ordained by law that, if anyone should wish to follow such a custom or the same observance of religion, he adhere without hindrance to his own purpose and not be hindered or prevented by anyone, and that they have a free hand, without fear and suspicion, to do that which pleases each. However, it could escape us even now that some of the judges failed to understand our orders, and caused our people to be uncertain about our commands, and made them rather reluctant to observe those religious rites which were acceptable to them.

'Therefore, in order that in the future all suspicion or hesitancy through fear may be abolished, we have ordained that this edict be promulgated, that it may be clear to all that it is permitted those who wish to follow this sect and religion, by virtue of this our bounty, so to observe this religion which he has chosen to follow according to his preference. It has also been granted them to build houses of the Lord. Moreover, that our bounty may be even greater, we have seen fit to ordain by law this, also: that if any houses and lands, which before this really belonged in justice

to the Christians, by the order of our fathers have fallen
into the right of the public treasury or have been seized by
any city, whether a sale of these took place or they were
given to some one at no cost—all these we have ordered to
be restored to the original possession of the Christians, that
also in this all may take notice of our piety and providence.'

These are the words of the tyrant, which came out less
than a full year later than the decrees against the Christians
he inscribed on tablets; to whom, a little while before, we
seemed impious and godless and destructive of all life, so
that we were not permitted to inhabit a city, rather, not
even a place in the country or deserts—by this man decrees
and ordinances in behalf of Christians were drawn up, and
those who a little while before were being destroyed before
his eyes by fire and sword, and as food for wild animals and
birds, and who were enduring every kind of chastisement and
punishment and loss of life most pitifully, as if godless and
impious, these he now admits to be observers of religion and
permits to build churches, and the tyrant himself confesses
that they share in certain rights.

And after making such admissions, as if having obtained
some blessing for these very deeds—suffering less, perhaps,
than he might, he was struck down by a sudden stroke of
God, and was destroyed in the second encounter of the war.
But the circumstances of his destruction were not such as
befall generals in battle who, again and again fighting bravely
in war for honor and friends, with good courage experience a
glorious end, but like some impious person and enemy of
God, remaining in hiding at home, while his line of battle
was still on the field, he suffered his due punishment, struck
down by a sudden lash from God against his whole body,

with the result that he fell prone, driven by terrible pains and torments, wasting away with hunger, his whole flesh being dissolved by invisible and God-sent fire, so that the entire appearance of the form which he once had wasted away and disappeared, and there remained only some dry bones like a phantom long since reduced to a skeleton, so that those present thought that his body was nothing but a tomb for his soul, which was buried in what was now a corpse and which was completely wasted away. And as the heat still more violently consumed him from the depths of his marrow, his eyes burst forth, and falling from their sockets left him blind. While still breathing in these circumstances, he confessed openly to the Lord, and asked for death, and, having confessed at the very last that he suffered this justly because of his violence against Christ, he gave up the ghost.

Chapter 11

When Maximin now had thus been put out of the way, who was the only remaining one of the enemies[1] of religion, and appeared to be the worst of all, efforts for the renewal of the churches from the foundations were set in motion by the grace of Almighty God, and the word of Christ, shining unto the glory of the God of the universe, received greater freedom than before, but the deeds of impiety of the enemies of religion were covered with the utmost shame and dishonor. Maximin himself was the first to be proclaimed by

---

1 Maximian died in 310 (cf. 8.13); Galerius in 311 (cf. 8.16); Maxentius in 312 (cf. 9.9); and Diocletian early in 313 (cf. 8, Appendix).

those in power as a common enemy of all, and was proclaimed on tablets through public decrees as a most impious
and most abominable and most God-hating tyrant. And as
for the portraits which were set up throughout the city to his
honor and that of his children, some were cast to the ground
from on high and were broken to bits; others were rendered
useless by having their faces blackened by dark-colored paint;
and all the statues that had been erected in his honor were
also cast down and smashed in the same way, lying there as
objects of laughter and joking for those who wished to insult
and abuse them.

Then, too, all honors were taken away from the other
enemies of religion, and all who were of the same mind as
Maximin were slain, especially those in high government
positions whom he had honored for their flattery toward
him and who had violently abused our doctrine. Such a one
was Peucetius,[2] the most highly honored of all by him, and
the most genuine of his companions, a consul for the second
and third time, and appointed by him general finance minister; and, likewise, Culcianus,[3] who had advanced through
every grade of office in government, the same one who had
gloried in the blood of countless Christians in Egypt; and,
besides these, not a few others through whom the activity
of Maximin's tyranny was strengthened and extended.

And then, too, Theotecnus[4] was summoned by Justice, who
by no means gave over to forgetfulness what he had done
against the Christians. After he had set up the idol at

---

2 Nothing further is known of him.
3 Culcianus was probably governor of Thebais; Eusebius is using the
  word Egypt in a general sense to include Thebais. According to 8.9,
  Phileas was martyred in Thebais.
4 Cf. 9.2.

Antioch,[5] he seemed to be prospering, and was already deemed worthy of governorship by Maximin, but Licinius, on entering the city of the Antiochenes and making a search for imposters, plagued the prophets and priests of the newly made idol with tortures, seeking by what means they were practicing their deceit. And when it was impossible for them when forced by tortures to continue the concealment, and they made it clear that the entire mystery was really a deceit devised by the art of Theotecnus, he meted out a just punishment upon them, also, and first gave over Theotecnus himself to death, and then, after a long succession of tortures, his confederates in the charlatanry.

To all these were also added the children of Maximin,[6] whom he had already made sharers both in the imperial dignity and in the paintings and pictures which had been set up. And those who formerly boasted of kinship with the tyrant and had been moved by pride to oppress all men suffered the same punishments, together with extreme dishonor, as those mentioned above, for they did not accept correction, nor did they know and understand the exhortation in the holy books which says: 'Put not your trust in princes: in the children of men, in whom there is no salvation. His spirit shall go forth, and he shall return into his earth: in that day all their thoughts shall perish.'[7] Thus, then, when the impious ones had been purged out of existence, the kingdom that belonged to them was preserved firm and undis-

---

5 Cf. 9.3.
6 According to Lactantius (*De mort. pers.* 50), Maximin left a wife, a boy eight years old, called Maximus, and a girl seven years old, betrothed to Candidianus.
7 Ps. 145.3,4.

puted for Constantine and Licinius alone. These, when first
of all they had purged the world of hostility against God, in
a manner conscious of the blessings bestowed upon them by
God displayed their love of virtue and of God, and their
piety and gratitude to the Deity by their legislation in behalf
of Christians.[8]

---

8 Cf. 10.5.

BOOK TEN

Chapter 1

O GOD ALMIGHTY AND KING of all we give thanks for everything, and the fullest thanks be to the Saviour and Redeemer of our souls, Jesus Christ, through whom we pray always that peace from the troubles that are without and those within the heart may be preserved for us firm and unshaken.

And with our prayers, having added herewith the tenth tome also to those that have gone before, we shall dedicate this tome to you, my most holy Paulinus,[1] calling upon you as the seal of the whole undertaking; and fittingly in a

---

1 Paulinus, Bishop of Tyre and later of Antioch, 328-329, was a native of Antioch (Eusebius, *In Marcell.* 1.4). He filled his office with great splendor and after the persecution came to an end rebuilt the cathedral with great magnificence. Eusebius elaborately describes it in an inaugural oration he delivered at its dedication (10.4). Paulinus was claimed by the church of the Antiochenes as their own, and was chosen their bishop. According to Philostorgius (*H.E.* 3.15), he held his new bishopric for only a half year before his death. Like his friend Eusebius of Caesarea, Paulinus was accused of being an Arianizer. In fact, Arius in his letter to Eusebius of Nicomedia (Theod., *H.E.* 1.5) claimed Paulinus as one of his sympathizers. Eusebius of Caesarea greatly admired him, and dedicated Book 10, as well as his *Onomasticon* to him. The present Book was probably completed in 324, or between the latter part of 323 and the early part of 325.

perfect number we shall arrange here the perfect and panegyrical discourse upon the restoration of the churches, obeying the divine Spirit who exhorts us in these words: 'Sing ye to the Lord a new canticle, because he hath done wonderful things; his right hand and his holy arm have saved him. The Lord hath made known his salvation; he hath revealed his justice in the sight of the gentiles.'[2]

And truly now in accordance with the Psalmist who bids us, let us sing out the new song, since, indeed, after those dreadful and gloomy sights and narratives, we are deemed worthy to see and to hymn such things as many of the just before us, indeed, and martyrs of God have desired to see on earth but have not seen, and to hear, but have not heard.[3] But they, hastening with all speed, obtained much better things in the very heavens, being caught up in a paradise of heavenly luxury,[4] while we, acknowledging that even the present things are greater than we deserve, stand in complete amazement at the graciousness of the munificence of the Author, and fittingly do we admire Him, worshiping Him with the power of our whole soul, and attesting to the truth of the written prophecies through which it is said: 'Come, and behold ye the works of the Lord, what wonders he hath done upon the earth, making wars to cease even to the end of the earth. He shall destroy the bow and break the weapons and the shield he shall burn in the fire.'[5] Rejoicing that these things have clearly been fulfilled in our day, let us enter upon our narrative.

---

2 Cf. Ps. 97.1,2.
3 Cf. Matt. 13.17.
4 Cf. Phil. 1.23; Heb. 10.34; 2 Cor. 12.4.
5 Ps. 45.9,10.

The whole race of the haters of God had indeed disappeared, as has been shown,[6] and thus had been blotted out
all at once from the sight of man, so that again a divine
saying has fulfillment,[7] which says: 'I saw the wicked highly
exalted and lifted up like the cedars of Lebanus, and I
passed by and lo, he was not; I sought out his place, but he
was not found.'[8] And now, henceforth, a day bright and
radiant, with never a cloud casting a shadow upon it, shone
down with rays of heavenly light upon the churches of Christ
throughout the whole world; nor were even those outside
our communion[9] begrudged, if not an equal share, at any
rate a share in the flow of the blessings sent us by God and
in their participation.[10]

Chapter 2

Accordingly, for all men there was freedom from the
oppression of tyrants, and one in one way and another in
another, released from his former ills, acknowledged as the
only true God, the Champion of the pious. But especially to us,
who had hung our hopes on the Christ of God, an unspeakable gladness was present, and a certain divine joy flourished
for all as we beheld every place, which recently had been laid

---

6 Cf. 9.10,11.
7 Cf. Luke 22.37.
8 Cf. Ps. 36.35,36.
9 Greek *thiasos* originally meant a Bacchic revel or rout. Gradually it
came to mean a religious guild or confraternity, and it is so used
here, being applied to the Christian society.
10 Not only Christians, but members of any creed or cult, received full
religious liberty through the edict of Constantine and Licinius.

waste by the impious acts of the tyrants, now reviving just as from a long and deadly pestilence, and temples again rising from their foundations to a limitless height, and taking on a splendor far superior to that of those which had been destroyed.

The most exalted emperor, also, by continuous legislation on behalf of Christians strengthened God's munificence to us for a long time and even to a greater extent; and personal letters from them continually came to the bishops, together with honors and gifts of money. And it may not be unfitting at the proper place[1] in this work to inscribe, as on a sacred monument, these documents translated from the language of the Romans into Greek, so that they may be borne in mind by all who come after us.

Chapter 3

In addition to this, there came to pass the spectacle prayed for and desired by us all: feasts of dedication in cities, and consecrations of the recently completed houses of prayer, assemblages of bishops for the same purpose, concourses of people from far-off foreign lands, deeds of kindness on the part of the people to the people, union of the members of Christ's body as they assembled with one accord. At any rate, in accordance with a prophetic prediction mystically signifying the event beforehand, there came together bone to bone and joint to joint,[1] and whatever the word in prophesy-

---

1 Cf. 10.5-7.

---

1 Cf. Ezech. 37.7.

ing through riddles truly foretold. One was the power of the divine Spirit running through all the members; and one soul possessed all,[2] and the same zeal for the faith, and from all one hymn in praise of the divinity of Christ; in very truth, the ceremonies of our leaders were perfect, likewise the sacrifices [of the Mass] by consecrated priests, and the sacred ordinances of the Church, here with the singing of psalms and with other recitations of the words given us from God, and with the performing of divine and mystic services, and the ineffable symbols of the Saviour's Passion. And altogether people of every age, both male and female, with all the power of the mind glorified God, the Author of their blessings, in prayers and thanksgiving with joyful heart and soul.

And every one of the rulers of the Church that was present, each to the best of his ability delivered panegyric orations, inspiring the assembly.

Chapter 4

And a certain one of moderate ability[1] advanced into the midst, having prepared a discourse as if for a church assembly, for a great many pastors were present giving orderly and quiet attention; and personally addressing one bishop,[2] in all respects most noble and beloved of God, through whose zeal and enthusiasm the temple in Tyre, the most splendid of all those among the people of Phoenicia, had been erected, he delivered the following sermon:

2 Cf. Acts 4.32.

1 Undoubtedly, Eusebius himself.
2 Paulinus, Bishop of Tyre; cf. 10.1.

Panegyric on the building of churches, addressed to Paulinus, Bishop of Tyre.

'O friends and priests of God who are clothed with the
holy robe[3] and the heavenly crown of glory, the inspired
unction and the priestly raiment of the Holy Spirit; and you,[4]
of youthful pride of God's holy temple, honored by God with
wisdom that is aged, but revealed in choice deeds and works
of a flourishing valor that is youthful, to whom God himself,
who encompasses the whole world, has given the distinguished
honor of building His house on earth and of restoring it for
Christ, His only-begotten and His first-born Word, and for
His holy and sacred Bride[5]—whether one indeed should wish
to call you a new Beseleel,[6] the builder of a divine tabernacle, or a Solomon,[7] king of a new and far better Jerusalem,[8]
or even a new Zorobabel[9] who bestowed far greater glory
than the former on the temple of God; and you, also, O
nursling of the sacred flock of Christ, fireside of blessed discourse, institution of moderation, a solemn and divinely
favored auditorium of godliness;[10] indeed, of old it was
permitted us, as through the divine readings we heard of the
incredible miracles and the benefaction to man from the

3 The Greek *podērēs* is used in the Septuagint for priestly attire. Cf.
   Exod. 29.5
4 Paulinus.
5 Cf. Apoc. 21.2.
6 Cf. Exod. 35.30,31.
7 Cf. 3 Kings 6-10; 2 Paralip. 3-6.
8 Apoc. 21.2.
9 Cf. Ag. 2.5.
10 It is interesting to note that Eusebius first addresses the assembled
   clergy in general, then Paulinus alone, and finally the people, using
   the terms 'nurslings,' 'fireside' or 'habitation,' 'institution' or 'school,'
   and 'auditorium.' The panegyric is an excellent example of the
   ecclesiastical rhetoric of the East at this time, embodying the
   artificial and turgid qualities of classic Asianism.

wonderous works of the Lord, to raise hymns and songs to
God, and to say as we were taught: "We have heard, O
God, with our ears; our fathers have declared to us the work
thou hast wrought in their days, and in the days of old."[11]
But now, in truth, no longer by hearing or by the words of
discourses do we learn of the mighty arm and the heavenly
right hand of our all-gracious God and universal King, but
by deeds, as it were, and by our very eyes as they see that
the things long ago committed to memory are faithful and
true, are we able to chant a second hymn of victory, raising
our voices clearly as we say: "As we have heard, so too have
we seen in the city of the Lord of hosts, in the city of our
God."[12] And in what kind of city other than this one, newly
built and made by God, which is a church of the living
God, a pillar and foundation of truth,[13] of which, also,
another divine oracle gives forth good tidings somewhat as
follows: "Glorious things are said of thee, O city of God."[14]
And since the all-gracious God has gathered us together in
this city, through the grace of His Only-begotten, let every
one of those who have been summoned sing, and all shout
and say: "I rejoiced at those who said to me: We shall go
into the house of the Lord"[15] and "I have loved, O Lord,
the beauty of thy house, and the place where thy glory
dwelleth."[16] And let us not only one by one, but all together
with one spirit and with one soul glorify and give honor with
a loud voice, saying: "Great is the Lord and exceedingly to

11 Ps. 43.2.
12 Cf. Ps. 49.9.
13 Cf. 1 Tim. 3.15.
14 Ps. 86.3.
15 Cf. Ps. 121.1.
16 Ps. 25.8.

be praised in the city of our God, in his holy mountain."[17] Indeed He is truly great, and great is His house, lofty and spacious,[18] and graceful in beauty above the sons of men.[19] Great is the Lord, who alone does wonderful things,[20] great is the One who does things great and incomprehensible, glorious and exceptional things of which there is no number;[21] great is the One who changes times and seasons, setting aside kings and setting them up,[22] "raising up the needy from the earth, and lifting up the poor out of the dunghill."[23] He hath put down the mighty from their seat, and hath exalted the humble from the earth.[24] He hath filled the hungry with good things, and hath broken the arms of the proud.[25] Since not only for believers, but also for unbelievers, He has confirmed the record of the ancient narratives, the Worker of great things, the Lord of the universe, the Fashioner of the whole world, the All-powerful, the All-gracious, the one and only God, let us sing to Him the new canticle,[26] supplying in thought the following: "to him who alone doeth wonders, for his mercy endureth forever; to him who smote great kings and slew strong kings, for his mercy endureth forever, for he remembered us in our low estate, and he redeemed us from our enemies."[27]

'And may we then never cease with these words to raise

17 Ps. 47.2.
18 Cf. Baruch 3.24,25.
19 Cf. Ps. 44.3.
20 Cf. Ps. 71.18.
21 Cf. Job 9.10.
22 Cf. Dan. 7.21.
23 Ps. 112.7.
24 Cf. Luke 1.52.
25 Cf. Job 38.15.
26 Cf. Ps. 97.1.
27 Cf. Ps. 135.4,17,18,23,24.

our voices in praise of the Father of the universe. But let us glorify the second Cause of our blessings, the Author of the knowledge of God, the Teacher of true piety, the Destroyer of the impious, the Slayer of tyrants, the Reformer of life, our Saviour when we were in despair, by bearing continually upon our lips the name of Jesus; for He alone, as the one and only all-gracious Son of an all-gracious Father, since the Father in His love for man so decided, willingly put on the nature of us who anywhere lay low in corruption, and, like some excellent physician who, for the sake of saving the sick, "though he sees their foul sores, yet touches the foul places, and reaps pain for himself for another's misfortunes," so He saved us for Himself from the very jaws of death, not only when we were sick and oppressed by grievous sores and wounds already become putrid, but even when we were lying among the dead; for none other of those in heaven possessed such strength as to minister without harm to the salvation of so many. Alone, then, did He take hold of the grievously afflicting corruption of our very selves, alone did He endure our troubles, alone did He assume the penalties of our impious deeds,[28] and not when we were half dead, but even when already altogether foul and stinking[29] in tombs and graves, He raised us up, and as of old so now, because of His earnest love for mankind, beyond all hope of anyone to be sure and even of ourselves, He saves us and He distributes an abundance of His Father's blessings, He the Creator of life, the Bringer of light, our great Physician and King and Lord, the Christ of God. But at that time, when once He saw the entire human race deeply entrenched in gloomy night

---

28 Cf. Isa. 53.4,5.
29 Cf. John 11.39.

and profound darkness through the deceit of sinful demons
and the operations of God-hating spirits, just as wax would
be melted by the rays of His light,[30] He loosed the many-
fettered cords of our impieties.

'And now, when at such great grace and kindness the envy
that hates the good, even the demon that loves the evil, was
all but torn asunder with wrath, and was marshaling against
us all his death-dealing forces, and at first, raging like a dog
that gnashes his teeth at the stones being hurled at him, and
expends upon the lifeless missiles his anger against those
who were driving him off, was directing his savage madness
against the stones of the houses of prayer and the lifeless
materials of the buildings, and was accomplishing, as he
thought to himself, at any rate, the destruction of the
churches; then he sent forth his terrible hissings and his
snake-like sounds, now by the threats of godless tyrants, again
by the blasphemous ordinances of impious rulers; moreover,
he vomited forth the death that was his, and infected the
souls which he captured by his baneful and soul-destroying
poisons, all but causing their death by his death-fraught
sacrifices to dead idols, and secretly arousing against us every
creature in human form and every kind of savage thing. Again
as of old the angel of great counsel,[31] the great prince of the
host of God,[32] after the greatest soldiers of his kingdom had
manifested sufficient training by patient endurance in all
things, by thus appearing all at once, routed into absolute
nothingness whatsoever was hostile and inimical, so that it
seemed never to have had a name, but whatsoever was

---

30 Cf. Ps. 57.9 (Septuagint).
31 Cf. Isa. 9.6 (Septuagint).
32 Cf. Josue. 5.14.

friendly and dear to Him He promoted with exceptional glory in the sight of all, not only of men, but also of the powers of the heaven, too, the sun and the moon and the stars and the entire heaven and earth, so that now, a thing never known before, the most exalted of all emperors, conscious of the honor which they had obtained from Him, spit upon the faces of the dead idols, trample upon the unholy rites of demons, and ridicule the old deceptions handed down by their fathers. But the one and only God Himself, the common Benefactor of all and of themselves, they recognize, and they acknowledge Christ, the Son of God, as the absolute King of the universe, and proclaim Him as Saviour on monuments, inscribing in an indelible record with imperial characters in the midst of the city that is empress of cities on earth His righteous acts and His victories over the impious ones, so that of those of all times only Jesus Christ is acknowledged even by the most exalted rulers on earth, not as having become a common king from among men, but is worshiped as the true Son of the God of the universe, and as Himself God.

'And rightly so. For, who of the kings at any time possessed so much excellence as to fill the ears and tongues of all men on earth with his name? What king, after he had arranged laws so sacred and so prudent, had sufficient power to publish them for the hearing of all men from the ends of the earth, even to the bounds of the whole inhabited world? Who abolished the barbarous and uncivilized customs of the uncivilized nations by his civilized and most benevolent laws? Who, though warred upon for whole ages by all men, manifested such superhuman valor as to flourish daily and remain youthful throughout his whole life? Who established a nation, unheard of from the beginning of time, not concealed anywhere in a corner of the earth, but extended throughout all the earth under the sun? Who so prepared his soldiers with the weapons of piety that in their souls they appeared harder than adamant in contests with their adversaries? Who of kings is so powerful, and continues his campaign after death, and sets up trophies over his enemies, and fills every place and country and city, Greek and barbarian, with consecrated objects of his royal houses and divine temples, such as the very beautiful adornments and consecrated objects here in this temple? These very things are truly sacred and great and worthy of wonder and amazement and such as to be clear proofs of the sovereignty of our Saviour, because even now He spoke and they were made; He commanded and they were created.[33] For, what was to resist the will of the absolute King and Ruler and the very Word of God himself? These matters really need leisure and a special discourse for careful examination and exposition. However, the zeal of those who have labored is not reckoned as so great and so noble in the judgment of Him who is called God, when He looks at the newly dedicated temple of all of you and beholds the house of living and moving stones,[34] well and safely "built upon the foundation of the Apostles and the prophets, Jesus Christ himself being the chief cornerstone,"[35] which stone the master builders, who were evil men of evil deeds, rejected, not only of the old temples, and that one no longer exists, but also of the building of the many men of today; but the Father, after approving

33 Cf. Ps. 32.9; 147.5 (Septuagint).
34 Cf. 1 Pet. 2.5,7.
35 Eph. 2.20,21.

it, both then and now made it the head of the corner of this our common Church. This living temple, then, of a living God, formed out of yourselves[36]—I speak of the greatest and truly holy sanctuary whose innermost shrine is not to be seen by the many and verily is holy and holy of holies—who, if he should see it, would dare describe? Who is able even to look within the sacred enclosures save only the great High Priest of the universe, for whom alone it is right to search through the mysteries of every rational soul?[37] Perhaps it is possible for another, also, for one only among equals, to be second after Him, namely, for this leader who presides over this army, whom the first and great High Priest Himself honored with second place in the sacred offices here, a shepherd of your divine flock, who has obtained your people by the allotment and the decision of the Father, as if He Himself had appointed him His minister and interpreter, the new Aaron or Melchisedech, made like to the Son of God, remaining and kept by Him forever by the common prayers of us all.[38] Therefore, to him alone let it be permitted after the first and greatest High Priest to see and observe, if not in the first place, at least in the second, the innermost recesses of your souls, for by experience and length of time[39] he has proved each one accurately, and by his zeal and care has disposed you all in pious order and doctrine, and is able better than anyone else to render the

36 Cf. 1 Cor. 3.16.
37 Cf. Heb. 4.14.
38 Cf. Heb. 7.3.
39 The implication is that Paulinus, though young, had been bishop for a long time.

account equal to the deeds, of those things which he with God's power has wrought.[40]

'Now, our first and great High Priest[41] says that what things soever He sees the Father doing, these things likewise the Son also does.[42] And this one,[43] too, with the pure eyes of the mind looking to the first One as to a teacher,[44] what things soever he sees Him doing, using these as originals and models, he has by his workmanship wrought the images of these as much as possible into the closest likeness, in no way falling behind that Beseleel, whom God Himself with the spirit of wisdom and understanding and with the knowledge of the other skills and sciences, and called him as a craftsman for the construction of the heavenly images of the temple through symbols.[45] In this way, then, this man, also, bearing in his soul the image of Christ entire, the Word, the Wisdom, the Light (nor is it possible to say with what liberal magnanimity and with what insatiate purpose and with what rivalry on the part of all of you, in the noblemindedness of your gifts, you strove nobly to be left behind him in no manner in this very purpose), built this magnificent temple of the most High God, responding in its nature to the pattern of the better, as the visible to the invisible. And this place he did not overlook, and it deserves to be mentioned first of all, since it was covered entirely with unclean rubbish according to the plans of the enemy, and, although he might have chosen another spot, for countless others were available in the

40 Cf. Heb. 13.17.
41 Cf. Heb. 4.14.
42 Cf. John 5.19.
43 Paulinus.
44 Cf. Heb. 12.2.
45 Cf. Exod. 31.2,3; 35.30,31; Heb. 8.5.

city, he did not concede to the malice of those responsible, so as to find ease from the labor and be released from trouble. Rather, he first aroused himself to the task, and then, after strengthening the entire people by his zeal, and after bringing them together into one great band from many, he fought the first contest, thinking that the very church that had been beleaguered by the enemy, the very one that had suffered ill beforehand and had endured the same persecutions as us and in our behalf, that this church, in the manner of a mother bereft of her children, ought to share in the enjoyment of the bounty of the Absolute Good. For, since the great Shepherd,[46] after driving away the wild beasts and the wolves and every cruel and savage creature, and after smashing the grinders of the lions,[47] as the divine oracles say, again considered it worthy to bring His children together again to the same place, it was most just that He also set up the fold of the flock to put to shame the enemy and the avenger,[48] and to bring forth a reproof to the daring acts of impious men, acts that fight against God. And now, these men, the haters of God, are no more, for they never were, but for a brief time they caused confusion and were thrown into confusion, and then, when paying a not contemptible penalty to Justice, they brought down to utter destruction both themselves and their friends and their houses, so that the predictions written of old on sacred records are acknowledged as trustworthy by the facts, through which the divine Word verifies other things, too, but this in particular it declares about them: "The wicked have drawn out the sword: they

---

46 Cf. Heb. 13.20.
47 Cf. Ps. 57.7.
48 Cf. Ps. 8.3.

have bent their bow, to cast down the poor and needy, to kill the upright of heart. Let their sword enter their own hearts and let their bows be broken";[49] and again: "Their memory hath perished with a noise";[50] and "Their name has been blotted out for ever and ever";[51] for, indeed, being also in trouble, "They cried, but there was none to save them: to the Lord, but He heard them not";[52] but as for them: "They are bound and have fallen: but we are risen, and are set upright";[53] and that which was predicted in these words: "O Lord, in thy city thou shalt bring their image to nothing,"[54] has been shown to be true in the eyes of all.

'But they, indeed, like giants, beginning a war against God, have obtained such a disastrous end to their lives, but of her who was deserted and rejected by men such things as we have seen are the results of her patient endurance in quest of God, so that the prophecy of Isaias calls aloud to her, saying: "Be glad, O thirsty wilderness, let the wilderness rejoice and blossom as a lily, and the desert places shall blossom forth and shall rejoice. Be strong, ye feeble hands, and ye weak knees; take courage, ye faint-hearted, be strong and fear not. Behold our God recompenseth judgment, and will recompense; He himself will come and will save us; because, he says, water has broken out in the desert, and a stream in the dry earth, and the dry land shall become marshes, and a spring of water shall be on the thirsty land."[55]

Ps. 36.14,15.
50 Ps. 9.7.
51 Cf. Ps. 9.6 (Septuagint).
52 Ps. 17.42.
53 Ps. 19.9 (Septuagint).
54 Ps. 72.20.
55 Isa. 35.1-4,6,7 (Septuagint).

'And these things, indeed, having been foretold long ago had been recorded by words in sacred books; the deeds no longer have been handed down to us by reports, but by actual fact. This desert, this dry land, this widowed and destitute place, whose gates they cut down as with axes in a wood of trees, (at once with axe and hatchet they have brought it down), whose books they also destroyed[56] and whose sanctuary of God they burned with fire, (on earth they have defiled the dwelling place of His name),[57] and after breaking down its hedge, all they who pass by the way do pluck thereof, and the wild boar out of the wood hath laid it waste, and a singular wild beast hath devoured it,[58] now by the marvelous power of Christ becomes as a lily when He wills it.[59] At that time, also, by His sanction, as by that of a thoughtful father, she was being chastised, "for whom the Lord loveth, he chastiseth, and scourgeth every son whom he receiveth."[60] Thereupon, after being duly corrected, she is enjoined once again to rejoice as formerly, and she blossoms forth as a lily[61] and breathes forth upon all men of her divine fragrance, "for," Scripture says, "waters are broken out in the desert, the streams of the divine regeneration of the laver of salvation,"[62] and now the desert of a little while ago, "has become a marsh, and upon the thirsty land springs of living water burst forth,"[63] and the hands that

---

56 Cf. 8.2. The first edict of Diocletian decreed the destruction of the sacred books of the Christians, as well as the churches.
57 Cf. Ps. 73.5-7.
58 Cf. Ps. 79.13,14.
59 Cf. Isa. 35.1.
60 Heb. 12.6.
61 Cf. Isa. 35.1.
62 Cf. Isa. 35.6; Tit. 3.5.
63 Cf. Isa. 35.7.

before were truly weak have become strong, and of the strength of the hands these great and manifest works are proof. But the knees that formerly were made feeble and relaxed have received again their familiar movement, and walk steadfastly on the road of the knowledge of God, hastening to the familiar flock of the all-good Shepherd.[64] But if also by the threats of the tyrants some have allowed their souls to become dull, not even these does the saving Word pass by as incurable, but very well does He heal them and urge them on to the calling of the divine, saying: "Take courage, ye faint-hearted, be strong, fear not."[65]

'When the Word prophesied that she who had become desert through God should enjoy these things, this our new and noble Zorobabel heard with the keen hearing of his mind after that bitter captivity and the abomination of desolation,[66] and, without noticing the fallen corpse, first of all with entreaties and prayers he made the Father propitious with the common consent of all of you, and, taking as an ally and co-worker Him who alone quickens the dead,[67] he raised up her who had fallen, after having cleansed and healed her ills, and he put a garment about her, not the old one which she had from the beginning, but such a one as he was again instructed by the divine oracles, which clearly speak as follows: "The last glory of this house shall be more than the former."[68]

'In this way, then, after entirely enclosing a much larger place, he strengthened the outer enclosure with the wall that

---

64 Cf. John 10.16.
65 Cf. Isa. 35.4.
66 Cf. Matt. 24.15.
67 Cf. Rom. 4.17.
68 Cf. Ag. 2.10.

surrounded the whole, so that it might be the safest defense of the entire work;[69] and a porch great and raised on high he spread out to the very rays of the rising sun, and even to those standing afar outside the sacred enclosures it afforded an abundant view of the things within, all but turning the sight even of strangers to the faith toward the first entrances, so that one might not pass by without his soul being struck by the memory of the former desolation and by the present incredible miracle; and by this he hoped that one might be struck, and would be led by the very sight to turn his steps to the entrances.

'But he who comes within the gates is not permitted to enter immediately within the holy places, if he has unholy and unwashed feet, for he left a very great space between the temple and the first entrances and adorned it round about with four transverse porticoes, fencing the place around into a sort of quadrangular shape by raising pillars on every side, shutting in the spaces in between with lattice work of wood reaching to a convenient height, and leaving the middle space open for a view of the heavens, thus providing a bright and airy space open to the rays of light. And here he has placed symbols of sacred purifications by erecting fountains directly opposite the temple, which afford purification by their abundant streams of running water for those who are advancing to the inner precincts. And this is the first resting place for those who enter, and provides, as well, adornment and splendor for the entire place and a convenient stopping place for those who need elementary instruction.

'But, passing by the spectacle of these things, by means of innermost porches in still greater numbers he constructed open

---

69 The description that follows (sections 37-45) is the oldest detailed picture that we have of the structure and furniture of a Christian church or basilica.

passages to the temple, again under the rays of the sun placing three entrances on one side, upon the middle one of which he was pleased to give honor far above the two on either side as regards height and breadth, brightening it especially with ornaments, with both iron-bound fastenings of bronze and varied embossed work; and thus he brought the other in subjection to this one, as bodyguards to a queen. In the same manner, also, he arranged the number of porches corresponding to the porticoes on each side of the entire temple, and higher up over these, to give still further light, he contrived openings to the building, effecting a varied adornment with fine workmanship in wood around these.

'The royal house[70] he built with abundant and even richer materials, manifesting an eager desire to spare no expense. So I think it to be superfluous for me to describe the length and breadth of the edifice, recounting in detail this brilliant beauty, the magnitude that defies description, and the brightly shining appearance of the workmanship, and the heights towering to heaven, and the costly cedars of Libanus placed above these, the mention of which not even the divine oracle passed over in silence, saying: "The trees of the Lord shall make merry, and the cedars of Libanus which he hath planted."[71]

'Why should I now describe in detail the pattern of the all-wise and masterful arrangement, and of the surpassing beauty of each part, when the testimony of the eyes leaves no place for instruction through the ears? However, having thus completed the temple, and having adorned it with thrones, very lofty for the honor of bishops, and similarly

---

70 Or, better, 'basilica.'
71 Cf. Ps. 103.16.

with benches conveniently in order throughout, and in addition to all these having placed in the midst[72] the holy of holies, the altar, again, so that they might not be trodden upon by the multitude, he surrounded these parts, also, with lattice-work of wood, finely wrought with the skill of the craftsman to the highest degree, so as to provide a wonderful sight for those who look upon it.

'Not even the floor, as one might think, lay unheeded by him. This, too, in fact, he brightened exceedingly with every adornment in marble, and then, finally, he went on to the outside of the temple, also, constructing very large chambers and dwellings on either side, skilfully joined together in the same way to the sides of the basilica[73] and connected by openings to the middle structure. And these, also, our most peace-loving Solomon,[74] who devised the temple of God, wrought for those who still need the cleansing and sprinkling that are through the water and the Holy Spirit,[75] so that the above-mentioned prophecy[76] is no longer a word but a fact, for the last glory of this house has become and now truly is greater than the former.[77]

'It was right and fitting that, as her Shepherd and Master once suffered death in her behalf, and after His Passion changed the foul body which He had put on for her sake into His resplendent and glorious body, and brought the

---

72 I.e., in the apse or chancel.
73 Large basilicas were regularly provided with additional rooms and adjacent buildings for various ecclesiastical purposes. These adjoined the church proper, and were often large enough to hold important synods.
74 Solomon means 'peaceful' in Hebrew.
75 Cf. John 3.5.
76 Cf. 10.4.
77 Cf. Ag. 2.9.

very flesh that had been destroyed,[78] from corruption to in-
corruption,[79] she also, in like fashion, enjoys the fruits of the
Saviour's husbandry. Indeed, after receiving from Him the
promise of far better things than even these,[80] she longs to
receive the far greater glory of the regeneration in the resurrection of an incorruptible body with the choir of angels
of light in the kingdoms of God beyond the heavens with
Christ Jesus Himself, the most beneficent Saviour, forever
into unending ages. Meanwhile, in the present time, the
deserted widow of long ago has been clothed by the grace of
God with these flowers, and has become truly like a lily,[81]
as says the prophecy; and having received again the bridal
garment and having put on the garland of comeliness, she is
taught by Isaias to dance, as it were, while presenting to
God the King her thank-offerings with words of praise. Let
us listen to her as she speaks: "Let my soul rejoice in the
Lord, for he hath clothed me with the garment of salvation
and the robe of gladness; he hath put a chaplet around me
as a bridegroom, and hath adorned me as a bride with
ornaments, and as the earth causing her flower to grow;
even as the garden causes its seeds to spring forth, so the
Lord God caused justice to spring forth and rejoicing before
all nations."[82]

'With these words, then, she danced, but with what words
even the Bridegroom, the heavenly Word, Jesus Christ Himself answers her, hear the Lord saying: "Fear not that you
were put to shame, nor linger because you were reproached,

78 Cf. Phil. 3.21; Heb. 2.9.
79 Cf. 1 Cor. 15.42.
80 Cf. Heb. 11.31,40.
81 Cf. Isa. 35.1.
82 Cf. Isa. 61.10,11.

for you shall forget thy lasting shame, and shall not remember the reproach of thy widowhood. For the Lord hath called thee not as a woman forsaken and faint-hearted, nor as a woman hated from her youth, saith thy God. For a small moment save I forsaken thee, but with great mercy I shall have mercy on thee. In a moment of indignation have I turned away my face from thee, but with everlasting mercy I shall have mercy on thee, saith thy Redeemer.[83] Awake, awake, thou who hast drunk at the hand of the Lord the cup of his wrath; for the cup of falling, the vessel of my wrath thou hast drunk to the bottom and drained. There was none who consoled thee among all your children whom you brought forth, and there was none who took hold of thy hand. Behold, I have taken out of thy hand the cup of falling, the vessel of my wrath, and thou shalt not take it again to drink it, and I will put it into the hands of them that have wronged thee, and of them that have humbled thee. Awake, awake put on thy strength, put on thy glory, shake off the dust and arise; loose the bond from off thy neck."[84] Lift up thy eyes round about, and see thy children that have gathered together; behold they were gathered and have come to thee. As I live, saith the Lord, you shall be clothed with all these as with an ornament, and thou shalt put them about thee as an ornament of a bride; for thy deserts and thy desolate places and the land of thy destruction shall now be too narrow for thee by reason of the inhabitants, and they that swallowed thee up shall be chased far from thee. For the children whom thou hast lost shall say in thy ears: "The place is narrow for me, make me room to dwell

---

83 Cf. Isa. 54.4,6-8.
84 Cf. Isa. 51.17,18,22,23; 52.1,2.

in." And thou shalt say in thy heart: "Who hath begotten
me these? I am childless and a widow, but who hath brought
up these for me? But I was left alone, and these, where were
they for me?"[85]

'These things Isaias prophesied; these things concerning us
had long ago been recorded in sacred books, and it was
fitting that somehow we receive the truthfulness of them at
some time by facts. Moreover, since the Bridegroom, the
Word, thus addresses His Bride, the sacred and holy Church,
fittingly did this bridal attendant,[86] stretching forth the hands
of you yourselves in the common prayers of us all awake and
raise up her who was desolate, who lay fallen, who was
despaired of by men, by the will of God, the absolute King,
and by the manifestation of the power of Jesus Christ, and
having raised her up he restored her to be such as he discovered from the record of the sacred oracles.

'A very great wonder, indeed, is this, and beyond all amazement, especially for those who attend only to the appearance
of external things, but of the wonderful things the more
wonderful are the archetypes and the rational prototypes and
the divine models[87] of these, I mean the revival of the divine
and rational building in our souls. This building the divine
Son Himself wrought in His own image entirely,[88] and in all
respects bestowed upon it the divine likeness, and incorruptible nature, incorporeal, rational, alien to all, earthly
matter, a being endowed with its own intelligence; and when

85 Cf. Isa. 49.18-21.
86 Paulinus is here referred to as the bridal attendant or friend of the
   Bridegroom (Christ) who assists the Bride (the Church).
87 I.e., as wonderful as the restoration of the Church is, even more
   wonderful is the restoration of the soul, for the spiritual is the
   archtype or prototype of the material.
88 Cf. Gen. 1.26.

once at first He had fashioned it from non-existence into
existence, He made it a holy bride and an entirely sacred
temple for Himself and for His Father. This He Himself
also plainly reveals when He says: "I will dwell in them and
walk among them, and I will be their God, and they shall
be my people."[89] And such, indeed, is the perfect and cleansed
soul, thus begotten from the beginning, so as to bear the
image of the heavenly Word.

'But when she of her own free choosing became sensual
and a lover of evil because of the envy and the jealousy of the
demon who is a lover of evil, and when the Divinity departed
from her, then, as if bereft of her divine Champion, an easy
prey and open to plots she has been captured by those who
long envied her, and, thrown down by the siege engines and
machines of her unseen foes and spiritual enemies, she has
fallen a headlong fall, so that not a stone upon a stone of her
virtue remained standing in her,[90] but she lay completely
dead stretched at full length upon the ground, entirely
deprived of her natural thoughts about God. Indeed, it was
not the wild boar coming forth from the wood as we looked
on that destroyed her as she lay fallen, even made in the
image of God,[91] but a destructive demon and spiritual wild
beasts, which after inflaming her with their passions, the
fiery darts of their own wickedness,[92] have set fire to the
truly divine sanctuary of God and have defiled the dwelling
place of IIis name on the earth.[93] Thereupon, they buried the

89 2 Cor. 6.16.
90 Cf. Luke 21.6.
91 Cf. Gen. 1.27.
92 Cf. Eph. 6.16.
93 Cf. Ps. 73.7.

wretched one in a great heap, and brought her into a condition without hope of salvation.

'But her Guardian, indeed, the divinely bright and saving Word, obedient to the benevolence of an all-good Father, took her up again, after she had paid the due penalty for her sins. Accordingly, having chosen the very souls of the highest rulers, through these most dear to God, he cleansed the whole inhabited world of the ungodly and destructive men and of the dreadful and God-hating tyrants themselves. And then those men well known to Him, those who for their entire lives had been consecrated to Him, yet were secretly concealed by His protection as in a storm of evils, He brought into the open, and He honored them worthily with the great gifts of the Father's bounty, and by these again He cleared away and cleansed with pickaxes and mattocks the penetrating instruction of His teaching, the souls which a short time before had been filthy with every sort of matter and rubbish of impious ordinances; and when He had rendered bright and clear the place of the intention of all of you, He thereupon handed it over for the future to this all-wise leader dear to God. And he, since he is able to judge and to be prudent in other respects, discerning well and distinguishing the minds of those committed to his care, from the first day, so to speak, even until now has never ceased to build and to fit in its place among all of you, at one time the radiant gold, at another time the tested and purified silver and the precious and very costly stones,[94] so as to fulfill anew by his deeds with respect to you the sacred and mystic prophecy, through which it has been said: "Behold I make ready for thee thy stone of garnet and thy foundations of sapphire and thy bulwarks of

94 Cf. 1 Cor. 3.12.

jasper and thy gates of stones, and all thy sons taught of God, and thy children in great peace, and thou shalt be founded in justice."[95]

'Building, then, in justice,[96] he duly distinguished the powers of all the people, for some fencing the outer enclosure alone, surrounding it with a wall of unerring faith (and such was the great mass of the people without the strength to bear a greater structure); to others entrusting the entrances to the building assigning them to wait at the doors and to guide those who enter, not unreasonably being considered gateways of the temple; but others he sustained with the first outer pillars about the quadrangular courtyard, introducing them to the first elements of the letter of the four Gospels; while others he joined closely on both sides to the royal house, these the while being instructed and in the stage of advancing and progressing, but not far off nor greatly separated from the divine vision of the innermost things possessed by the faithful. Then, taking from these the pure souls cleansed like gold in the divine laver, he sustains some with pillars much greater than the outermost ones from the innermost mystical doctrines of the Scriptures, and illumines others with the windows toward the light, adorning the entire temple with one very large gateway of the praise of the one and only absolute God, and providing on either side of the absolute power of the Father the second rays of the light of Christ and of the Holy Spirit. And of the remaining parts throughout the entire house he shows by a lavish and very varied effect the manifest splendor of the truth that is in each one, in that every-

95 Cf. Isa. 54.11-14.
96 Sections 63-68 contains a comparison of the material edifice with the spiritual Church, i.e., those who worship in it.

where and from every place he has selected the living and firmly set and solid stones of souls.[97] In this manner he builds the great and royal house of all, bright and full of light, both the inner and the outer parts, since not only the soul and the mind, but also the body had been splendidly arrayed with the many-blossomed adornment of chastity and prudence.

'There are also present in this holy place thrones and countless benches and seats, as many as are the souls on which the gifts of the divine Spirit rest, such as even of old appeared to the holy Apostles and their followers, "and there appeared to them cloven tongues, as it were, of fire, and it sat upon each of them."[98] But in the ruler of all, as is proper, Christ Himself entire sits, while among those occupying the second place after him, in due order according to his ability each advance by the apportioning of the power of Christ and of the Holy Spirit.[99] And the souls of some of those who had been devoted to instructing and guarding each person might be the seats even of angels, but of what nature would the consecrated and great and unique altar be than the pure and holy of holies of the common Priest of all?[100] And standing beside it on the right the great High Priest of the universe, Jesus Himself,[101] the only-begotten of God, receiving with glad countenance and with upturned hands the fragrant incense from all, and the bloodless and immaterial sacrifices through prayers, He sends them along to the heavenly Father

97 Cf. 1 Pet. 2.5.
98 Acts 2.3.
99 Cf. Heb. 2.4.
100 I.e., the sacred altar in the material edifice represents the spiritual sanctuary, the soul of Jesus Christ.
101 Cf. Heb. 4.14.

and God of the universe, for He Himself first adoring and alone assigning to the Father the reverence that is His due, thereupon beseeches Him to remain well disposed and propitious to us all forever.

'Such is the great temple which throughout the whole world beneath the sun the great maker of the universe, the Word, has constructed, even He having fashioned again this spiritual likeness on earth of the heavenly vaults beyond the realm, so that by all creation and by the rational living things on earth His Father might be honored and worshiped. But no mortal is able worthily to hymn the realm beyond the heavens and the models there of the things here, and the Jerusalem which is above,[102] and the heavenly mount Zion, and the supramundane city of the living of the living God, in which innumerable assemblies of angels and the church of the first-born, who are written in heaven,[103] glorify their Maker and absolute Ruler of the universe with unutterable words and praises to God that are incomprehensible to us, for, indeed, "eye hath not seen nor ear heard, neither hath it entered into the heart of man what things God hath prepared for them that love him."[104] Seeing that we have now in part been deemed worthy of these things, both men and children and women, small and great, let us all together with one spirit and one soul unceasingly acknowledge and acclaim the Cause of such great blessing of ours, "who forgiveth all our iniquities, who healeth all our diseases, who redeemeth our life from destruction, who crowneth us with mercy and compassion, who satisfieth our desire with good things,[105] for he hath not

102 Cf. Gal. 4.26.
103 Cf. Heb. 12.22,23.
104 1 Cor. 2.9.
105 Cf. Ps. 102.3-5.

dealt with us according to our sins, nor rewarded us according to our iniquities,[106] for as far as the east is from the west, he hath removed our iniquities from us; and as a father hath compassion on his children, so the Lord hath compassion on them that fear him."[107]

'Let us rekindle these thoughts in our memories both now and for all future time; indeed, let us keep ever in mind both night and day, through every hour, and, so to speak, in every breath, the Cause and Ruler of the present assembly Himself and of this joyous and most radiant day; and let us love and cherish with the whole power of our soul, and now let us arise and with a loud and sincere voice earnestly beg that He would shatter and spare us in His fold to the end, bestowing from Himself the unbroken and undisturbed eternal peace in Christ Jesus, our Saviour, through whom may glory be to Him unto all the ages of the ages. Amen.'

Chapter 5

Come now, let us finally quote also the imperial decrees of Constantine and Licinius as translated from the Latin.

A copy of the imperial ordinances as translated from the Latin tongue.

'When watching long ago that freedom of worship should not be denied, but that, according to the mind and purpose of each one, authority should be given of caring for divine

106 Cf. Ps. 102.10.
107 Ps. 102.12,13.

things according to his choice, we[1] had issued orders to the Christians . . . to guard the faith of their own sect and worship;[2] but since many different conditions seemed clearly to have been set forth in that decree, in which such authority was granted to the same persons, it seems likely that some of them after a while were repelled from such observance.

'When under happy auspices I, Constantine Augustus, and I, Licinius Augustus, had come to Milan and held an inquiry about all matters such as pertain to the common advantage and good, these things along with the others that seemed to benefit the many, or rather, first and foremost, we resolved to issue decrees by which esteem and reverence for the Deity might be procured, that is, that we might give all Christians freedom of choice to follow the ritual which they wished, so that whatever is of the nature of the divine and heavenly might be propitious to us and to all those living under our authority. Accordingly, with sound and most correct reasoning we decided upon this our plan: that authority is to be refused no one at all to follow and to choose the observance or the form of worship of the Christians, and that authority

1 The quotation from section 2-14 is the famous so-called Edict of Milan. It is strictly not an edict but a rescript, since it is addressed to an individual, namely, a governor by whose edict it was to be promulgated among the people under his jurisdiction. Constantine and Licinius drew up this set of instructions late in 312, after Constantine's victory over Maxentius (cf. 9.9). It was the first pronouncement of the doctrine of freedom of conscience for all religions. In this regard it was an advance over the edict of Galerius which granted conditional liberty to a single religion. One version was translated by Eusebius, another was transcribed by Lactantius (*De mort. pers.* 48).

2 The reference here is to the edict of Galerius and not to a lost edict of Constantine and Licinius, as was formerly supposed. In other words, we are dealing not with three edicts but with two: that of Galerius, Constantine, and Licinius (311), and the present one of Constantine and Licinius (312).

be given to each one to devote his mind to that form of worship which he himself considers to be adapted to himself,[3] in order that the Deity may be able in all things to provide for us His accustomed care and goodness. And so it was natural for us to send a rescript that this is pleasing to us, in order that, when those conditions had been altogether removed which were contained in our former letters sent to your Devotion concerning the Christians, those things, also, which seemed to be very unfavorable and foreign to our clemency might be removed, and that now each one of those who had the same inclination to observe the ritual of the Christians might without any hindrance engage in this very observance freely and simply. And we resolved to present these matters in the fullest measure to your Grace, that you may know that we have granted to the same Christians free and unlimited authority to look after their own ritual. And when you observe that we have granted this unlimited authority to them, your Devotion will see that authority has been given to others, also, who wish to continue their own observance and ritual, a condition which is clearly accommodated to the peacefulness of our times, so that each one may have authority to choose and to observe whatever ritual his spiritual inclination wishes. This, then, we have done, so that we may seem to have detracted nothing from any honorable ritual.

'And this, also, besides the rest, we resolve with respect to the Christians: that their places at which they were formerly accustomed to assemble, concerning which, also, in the former letter sent to your Devotion a definite ordinance had been

---

3 A simple and clear statement that every one is permitted either to follow the religion of his ancestors or to choose another.

laid down for that time,[4] to the effect that if some had manifestly bought these places either out of our own treasury or from some other source, be returned to the same Christians without payment or any other demand for compensation, putting aside all negligence and ambiguity; furthermore, if any perchance have received them as gifts, that they should restore them as quickly as possible to the same Christians, with the understanding that, if either those who have bought these same places or those who have acquired them as gifts demand something from our generosity, they go to the prefect of the district, in order that thought may be taken through our beneficence in their behalf, also. All these things must be handed over to the body of Christians immediately and without any delay.

'And since the same Christians had not only those places in which they used to assemble, but are known to have had others, also, which belonged not to individuals among them, but to the rightful claim of their whole body, that is, of the Christians, all these, in accordance with the law which we have just mentioned, you are to order to be restored without delay to the same Christians, that is, to their group and to each assembly, guarding clearly the aforementioned statement, that whoever restore the same places without compensation, even as we have already said, may hope for indemnification from our own generosity.

'In all these matters you should exercise the utmost care for the aforementioned group of Christians, so that our order

---

4 From this passage it seems clear that, according to the last rescript, Christians were obliged to pay something for their restored property, either to the persons then holding it or to the State.

may be carried out as quickly as possible, and that also in this forethought may be exercised through our beneficence for the common and public peace. For by this means, as has been mentioned before, the divine zeal in our behalf, which we have already experienced in many things, will remain steadfast forever. And that the scope of this our decree and generosity may be brought to the knowledge of all, it is fitting that these matters as decreed by us be declared everywhere, and brought to the knowledge of all by being published at your order, so that the decree of this our generosity may escape the notice of no one.'

Copy of another imperial decree[5] which he also made, pointing out that the favors have been made to the Catholic Church alone.

'Greetings, Anulinus, our most honorable Sir. This is the manner of our benevolence, to will that those things which belong to another by right not only suffer no harm but even be restored, most honorable Anulinus. Wherefore, we wish that when you receive this letter, if any of those things which belonged to the Catholic Church[6] of the Christians in the several cities, or even in other places, should now be possessed

---

5 This communication is a sample of special letters sent out soon after the publication of the Edict of Milan to the governors of the various provinces. It gives instruction on the execution of certain of the provisions of the edict. Of Anulinus we know only what is stated here. He was proconsul of the Roman province of Africa, of which Carthage was the capital, and which was heavily populated with Christians.

6 According to the heading of this letter it would seem that Eusebius took this to mean the Catholic Church as distinguished from the Donatist schismatics, to whom he refers in another epistle quoted in the next chapter. This is improbable. The reference is to the Church in Africa as it was prior to the persecution and the schism, the Christian Church as a whole.

either by citizens or by any others, you should have them
restored immediately to these same churches, since we have
determined that these things which these same churches
formerly possessed should be restored to them as their right.
Since, then, your Devotion sees that the order of this our
command is most clear, make haste to restore to them as
quickly as possible all things, whether gardens or buildings or
whatever belonged by right to these same churches, so that
we may learn that you have rendered most careful obedience
to this order of ours. Farewell, Anulinus, our most honored
and beloved friend.'

Copy of an imperial letter, in which he commands that a
synod of bishops be held at Rome in behalf of the unity and
harmony of the churches.[7]

7 The Donatist schism is responsible for this and the following letter.
It arose soon after the end of the persecution of Diocletian and split
the Church in North Africa for more than a century. Like Nova-
tianism, it was a conflict between the rigorists and the more lenient.
The Novatian schism was concerned with the rebaptism of the lapsed;
the Donatist schism with the validity of the sacraments when performed by unholy clergymen. Nearly a century later, Augustine, as
a result of this schism, felt obliged to develop his doctrine of the
Church and the Sacraments. The election of Caecilian, who followed
the orthodox view, as Bishop of Carthage in 311 was the immediate
cause of the schism. It was charged that Bishop Felix of Aptunga, by
whom Caecilian was ordained, had been a *traditor,* i.e., had sur-
rendered the Scriptures to the pagan authorities during the persecutions, and so that Caeilian's ordination was invalid. The bishops of
Numidia, who had not been invited to the election, accordingly held
a synod of their own, and elected Majorinus as bishop, and thus the
schism was established. The schism at first took its name from
Majorinus, but in 315 he was succeeded by Donatus the Great, and
thenceforth the sect took its name from him. Information about this
schism comes from the works of St. Augustine (the anti-Donatist
writings and a few letters) and Optatus' *Contra Parmenianum
Donatistam.* Constantine was unwilling to meddle in the controversy,
but the Donatists, through the proconsul Anulinus, appeal to him

'Constantine Augustus to Miltiades,[8] Bishop of Rome, and to Mark.[9] Since such documents and many of them from Anulinus, the most illustrious proconsul of Africa, have been dispatched to me, in which it is clear that Caecilian,[10] Bishop of the city of Carthage, is censured on many counts[11] by some of his colleagues in Africa, and since this seems to me a very serious matter in these provinces, which Divine Providence has freely entrusted to my Devotedness, and where there is a great multitude of people, the many are found set upon the worse course, splitting up into two parties, as it were, and the bishops at odds among themselves, I resolved that

in 313 (cf. Augustine's Letter 88, in which Anulinus communicates the request to the emperor). In reply, Constantine in the present epistle summons both parties before a Roman synod held in October 313. The Donatists lost their case. They then demanded that they be heard a second time, and at a council held in Gaul at Arles in the following year they again lost the decision (cf. the next letter quoted in this chapter). An appeal was now made to the emperor himself, who upheld the decisions of the two councils and threatened the Donatists with the banishment of their bishops and the confiscation of their property. But he soon abandoned all persecution, and adopted a policy of toleration. The condition of the Donatists now went from bad to worse until they disappeared with the devastation of the Church in North Africa by the Vandal invasion in 428.

8 Also called Melchiades, Bishop of Rome from July 2, 310, to January 10 or 11, 314.

9 Otherwise unknown; some identify him with the presbyter of Rome who became Bishop of Rome for about eight months in 336.

10 Archdeacon of the church of Carthage under Bishop Mensuris, and an active supporter of his against the Donatists. He became bishop in succession to Mensuris in 311, and died in 345. He was universally acknowledged by all in and outside of North Africa, except by the Donatists themselves.

11 The most important charge brought against Caecilian was that he was ordained by Felix of Aptunga, a *traditor,* and so his ordination was invalid. This charge, after careful investigation at the Council of Arles, was declared without foundation. All the other charges against Caecilian, such as tyranny, bloodthirstiness, and others were also shown to be groundless.

Caecilian himself, with ten bishops of those who seem to censure him, and ten of the others whom he himself may consider necessary to his cause, should set sail for Rome, so that these in the presence of you and, moreover, of Reticius[12] and Maternus[13] and Marinus,[14] your colleagues, whom I have ordered to hasten to Rome for this purpose,[15] may hear him as you may judge to be in harmony with the most sacred law. Yet, in order that you may have the fullest knowledge of all these matters, I have attached to my letter copies of the documents sent to me by Anulinus, and have sent them to your colleagues previously mentioned. And when your Constancy reads these, he will determine in what manner it is necessary to carry on a most careful investigation of the case mentioned above, and to reach a decision in keeping with justice, since it does not escape the notice of your Grace that I give such respect to the lawful Catholic Church, as to wish to leave behind no schism or division in any place. May the divinity of the great God protect you for many years, most honored Sir.'

Copy of an imperial letter, by which he orders a second synod to be held for the purpose of removing every dissension among the bishops.

---

12 Bishop of Autun in Gaul. Except for the legendary account by Gregory of Tours, little else is known of him.
13 Bishop of Cologne, the first one in that see known to us. He is mentioned by Optatus (1.22), and was present at the Council of Arles. Nothing else is known of him.
14 Bishop of Arles, present in 314 at the council held in that city.
15 This council assembled in the house of Fausta in the Lateran on October 2, 313. It was attended by nineteen bishops—the three just mentioned from Gaul, Miltiades, and fifteen Italian bishops. The party of Caecilian was completely victorious.

'Constantine Augustus to Cherstus,[16] Bishop of Syracuse. Already on a former occasion, when some basely and perversely had begun to cause divisions concerning the form of worship of the holy and heavenly Power and the Catholic faith, wishing to cut off such rivalries among them, I had issued orders that certain of the bishops be sent from Gaul, and, indeed, that those be called from Africa who were of opposite sides contending so stubbornly and so persistently that, with the Bishop of Rome present, this problem which seemed to have been raised might by their presence receive a proper and careful examination. But when, as it happens, some, forgetting even their own salvation and the reverence due their most holy religion, even now still do not cease to continue their personal enmities, being unwilling to abide by the decisions already rendered, and affirming that even then it was a few who had rendered their opinions and decisions, or even that they hurried to pass a quick and a sharp judgment without first examining everything that ought to have been investigated carefully, and as a result of all this it comes about that these very ones, who ought to be of one mind in brotherly love, are rather shamefully separated from one another, and furnish for the men who have souls foreign to this most holy religion the occasion for scoffing; wherefore it has become a matter of conscience with me to insist that what should have ceased by voluntary agreement after the judgment had been rendered, even now may possibly be ended in the presence of so many. Since, therefore, we have ordered that very many[17] bishops from diverse and numberless places

16 Nothing further is known of him.
17 The number of bishops present was in all probability no more than thirty-three, the number given in the only extant lists of the members of the synod.

come to the city of Arles[18] by the first of August, we have thought to write you also to obtain from the very brilliant Latronianus,[19] the "corrector"[20] of Sicily, a public vehicle, and to add to your group any two of the second rank,[21] whomever you yourself decide to choose, and also to take along three servants who shall be able to serve you along the way, and be present on the same day at the place mentioned above, so that both by your Constancy and by the complete agreement of mind and soul of the rest who assemble, even this dissension which until now has kept up a disgraceful existence, when all has been heard that likely will be said by those now at variance with one another, whom we have likewise ordered to be on hand, may possibly be recalled, even if slowly, to a due condition of religion and to brotherly faith and harmony. May Almighty God keep you in good health for many years.'

---

18 A city of Southern France, not far from the mouth of the Rhone, it was the seat of several important synods, of which the present one is the first known. This was convened by Constantine on August 1, 314. Although twenty-two canons of this synod are extant in a letter addressed to Sylvester of Rome, comparatively little about it is known. If these canons are genuine, the synod was concerned about many matters other than the Donatists schism.

19 Otherwise unknown.

20 The title of the governors of certain provinces in the fourth century.

21 I.e., presbyters, commonly called 'priests of the second order.'

Chapter 6

Copy of an imperial letter in which money is granted to the churches.[1]

'Constantine Augustus to Caecilian, Bishop of Carthage. Since it has indeed given pleasure among all the provinces, that is, the African, the Numidian, and the Muretanian, that a contribution be made to certain specified ministers of the lawful and holy Catholic religion for expenses, I have given a letter to Ursus,[2] the most distinguished finance minister of Africa, and I have indicated to him that he exercise care to pay to your Constancy 3,000 *folles*.[3] Do you, then, when you have received the aforesaid sum of money, order it to be distributed to all those mentioned above according to the plan sent you by Hosius.[4] But if you now should discover some lack for fulfilling this my desire as regards them all, you should ask unhesitatingly whatever you discover is necessary from Heraclides[5] the administrator of our possessions. For, when he was here, I truly issued orders to him that, if your Constancy asked of him any money, he deem it wise to pay it to you without any hesitancy. And since I learned that some people, who, perchance, are not of sound mind, wish to

---

1 This is the earliest instance of financial support being furnished the clergy by the State.
2 Otherwise unknown.
3 A *follis* was originally a bag of small coins. Later it was used for a small coin worth, in all probability, a double denarius.
4 Hosius is doubtless to be identified with the famous Bishop of Corduba, capital of the province of Baetica in Spain. In the controversies of the first half of the fourth century, he took a leading part on the Catholic side. Eusebius (*Vit. Cons.* 2.63,73) says: 'He was approved for the sobriety and genuineness of his faith, had distinguished himself by the boldness of his religious profession, and his fame was wide spread.' He died shortly before 360, when over a hundred years old. Cf. *Catholic Encyclopedia*, art. 'Hosius.'
5 Otherwise unknown.

turn astray the people of the holy and Catholic Church by some vile deceit,[6] know that I have given such orders as these to Anulinus, the proconsul, and to Patricius,[7] also, the vicar of the prefects,[8] when they were here, to the effect that in all remaining matters and especially in this they bestow fitting attention, and not allow such an event to be disregarded. Wherefore, if you should observe that some such men are continuing in this madness, without any hesitation proceed to the above-mentioned judges and bring this matter before them, so that they (as I ordered them when they were here) may turn these people from their error.[9] May the divinity of the great God protect you for many years.'

Chapter 7

Copy of an imperial letter in which he commands that the presidents of the churches be relieved of all services to the State.[1]

---

6 Probably a reference to the Donatists.

7 Otherwise unknown.

8 The Greek phrase is for the Latin *'vicarius praefectorum,'* vicar or deputy of the prefects. The vicar was the governor of a 'diocese' or group of provinces. The prefect was in control of an even larger administrative area.

9 This is the first instance of Constantine attempting to suppress schismatics. Later he tried it again in connection with the Arians. In both cases he relaxed his policy of repression. His successors were much less tolerant with heretics and schismatics.

---

1 Holding municipal offices and magistracies was a great burden in the later Roman Empire. It amounted essentially to paying a heavy tax to the government. Granting an exemption from this obligation to any group naturally aroused the resentment of all others not so exempted. However, in granting this privilege to the African clergy, Constantine was granting only what had already been enjoyed by the pagan priesthood and some of the learned professions. This privilege was later extended to the clergy of other provinces.

'Greeting, Anulinus, our most honorable Sir. Since from very many circumstances it appears that religious worship, in which the highest reverence for the most holy and heavenly [Power] is preserved, when once disregarded, has brought the gravest dangers to public affairs, and that this, when once it has been lawfully restored and preserved, has brought the greatest good fortune on the Roman name and exceptional prosperity on all the affairs of men (for Divine Providence bestows this), it has seemed good that those men who, with fitting holiness and constant observance of this law, provide their services for the ritual of divine worship, receive the rewards of their individual efforts, most honored Anulinus. For this reason I wish that those within the province which is under your guidance in the Catholic Church, over which Caecilian has been placed,[3] who bestow their services on this holy worship, and whom they call clerics, be held once and for all completely exempt from all the public services, so that they may not be drawn away by any error or sacrilegious lapse from the worship due to the Divinity, but, rather, may without any hindrance devote themselves entirely to their own law. For, while rendering the greatest service to the Deity, they seem to render a correspondingly great service to the common good. Farewell, Anulinus, our most honored and very dear friend.

---

2 I.e., the proconsular province of Africa.

3 The bishop of Carthage was the metropolitan of the province, and was looked upon as the leading bishop of North Africa, and in a sense the head of the Church of that entire section of the country.

Chapter 8

Such gifts, then, did the divine and heavenly grace of the appearance of our Saviour bestow upon us, and such abundance of blessings for all men was procured by our peace. And thus were our affairs fulfilled in rejoicing and in festive assemblies. But the sight of what was seen was not bearable to the envy that hates good and to the demon who loves evil, just as the events the befell the aforementioned tyrants[1] were not sufficient to bring Licinius to sound reason. He who was deemed worthy of sharing the rule and held the second position of honor to the great Emperor Constantine, and was related by marriage and was of the noblest kinship with him, abandoned the imitation of the good and eagerly sought the evil manners and the wickedness of the impious tyrants; and he chose to follow the judgment of those whose destruction he had witnessed with his very eyes rather than to abide with the friendship and association of the nobler man. Filled, indeed, with envy of the common benefactor, he carried on against him an impious and very dreadful war, with no regard for the laws of nature, unmindful of oaths and of ties of blood and of agreements.[2] Constantine, the wholly good emperor, furnishing him with the tokens of true good will, did not envy him kinship with himself, and did not deny him the enjoyment of an illustrious marriage with his sister; instead, he deemed him worthy to become a partaker of the

---

1 Maxentius and Maximin.
2 To make Licinius alone responsible for the war between himself and Constantine is, of course, a gross exaggeration. The occasion of the war has never been made entirely clear. A final struggle for sole supremacy was inevitable, and Constantine, not Licinius, was certainly the aggressor.

nobility of his fathers and of his imperial blood and origin, and provided the right of enjoying the supreme rule[3] as a brother-in-law and joint-emperor, favoring him with the direction and administration of no inferior part of the peoples under the rule of the Romans, while Licinius, to the contrary, was engaged in the opposite conduct, contriving daily all sorts of schemes against Constantine, and meditating all manner of plots that he might reward his benefactor with evils. At first, then, while trying to conceal his intrigue, he feigned friendship, and hoped that by frequently resorting to trickery and deceit he might most easily attain his expectations.[4] But, for Constantine, God was Friend, Protector, and Guardian, who brought to light for him the plots devised in secret and darkness, and reproved them.[5] Of such power is the great weapon of godliness to ward off the attack of the enemy, and to strengthen the protection of its own safety. Armed then with this, our emperor, most beloved of God, escaped the plots of this hateful one. And Licinius, when he saw that his covert scheme was by no means progressing as he wished (for God exposed to the emperor, whom He loved, every trickery and wickedness), since he no longer was able to conceal himself, chose open warfare.[6] Thereupon, intending to war at close quarters with Constantine, even now he was hastening to array himself against the God of all, whom he knew Constantine worshiped; and so he set about to attack his pious subjects quietly and in silence, although

3 The reference here is to the treaty of December 314, when the Empire was divided anew, five of the European provinces passing from Licinius to Constantine.

4 Licinius was no more guilty than Constantine in this respect.

5 Cf. Eph. 5.11-13.

6 This is a direct contradiction to what Eusebius himself says in his *Life of Constantine* 2.3, and is in all probability incorrect.

they had never at any time done any harm to his rule.[7] And he did this, being forced by his innate wickedness into a terrible blindness. Thus, he placed before his eyes neither the memory of those who persecuted Christians before him nor of those whom he himself murdered and punished for the impious deeds they had performed, but turned aside from sound reasoning, and, becoming quite mad, determined to war on God Himself, as the Helper of Constantine, instead of on him who was being helped.

First, he expelled every Christian from his house; thus he himself deprived himself, wretched man, of the prayers to God in his behalf, which they were taught by their ancestral custom to make for all men.[8] And then he gave orders that the soldiers in the cities be singled out and deprived of their rank of honor unless they chose to sacrifice to demons.

These matters were yet small when judged by comparison with more serious actions. But why is it necessary to mention separately and distinctly the things done by this God-hater, namely, how this most lawless man invented laws devoid of law? Indeed, he laid down a law that no one should treat humanely those who were suffering in prison by distributing food among them, that no one should take pity on those perishing from hunger in bonds, and that no one should be kindly at all or do them any kindly service, even when drawn on by a natural sympathy for their neighbors. And of his laws this one, at any rate, was most openly shameless and

---

7 Licinius began to change his policy toward Christians in 319, for he had become more and more suspicious of them as the friends of Constantine. Whether he had any grounds for these suspicions is not known, but he certainly took an unwise step in openly showing his hostility.

8 Cf. 1 Tim. 2.1,2.

most severe in disregarding every gentle impulse, according
to which punishment was even placed upon those showing
mercy, that they suffer equally with the ones being shown
mercy, and that they be delivered over to bonds and imprisonment, and that those ministering humane acts suffer punishment equally with those undergoing it. Such were the decrees
of Licinius. Why is it necessary to enumerate his new regulations pertaining to marriage, or his revolutionary changes
with regard to those who were departing this life, in which
he dared to annul the ancient laws of the Romans, which
were established well and wisely, and introduce in their stead
certain barbarous and crude regulations, lawless laws that
were really contrary to law; and the countless injunctions he
devised against his subject peoples, and all sorts of taxes of
gold and silver, and revaluation of land, and the harmful
exactions from men in the country districts no longer living
but long since departed? And what banishments this man-
hater invented for those who had done no wrong, what arrests
of noble and highly esteemed men, whose wedded wives he
separated from them and gave over to certain lewd characters
of his household for insult; and with how many married
women and unmarried girls this drunken old sot satisfied the
unbridled lust of his soul, why should one dwell upon these
things, when the excesses of his last deeds prove the first to
be of small and of no account?

At any rate, in the final course of his madness he went
against the bishops, and, deeming them the servants of the
God of all, and opposed to what he was doing, he plotted
against them not yet openly, to be sure, from fear of his
superior, but again secretly and craftily, and he destroyed the
most highly respected among them through the connivance

of the governors. And the manner of their death was strange, such as was never known before. For instance, what was done at Amasea[9] and the other cities of the Pontus exceeds every excess of cruelty. There some of the churches of God were torn apart from top to bottom; others they closed, so that none of the accustomed worshipers might gather or return to God the services due Him. For he did not think that the prayers were being offered up for him (this being the reckoning of an evil conscience), but he had been persuaded that we did everything and appeased God in behalf of the God-beloved emperor. Therefore he set forth to vent his wrath upon us. Indeed, the flatterers among the governors, being convinced that they were doing what pleased the impious man, inflicted on some of the bishops in the usual manner the penalties of evil-doers, and those who had done no wrong were led away and punished without disguise like murderers. And some now endured a novel death, their bodies being cut into many pieces, and, after this cruel and most frightening spectacle, being hurled into the depths of the sea as food for fishes. Thereupon, flight became the watch-word of God-fearing men, and again the fields, again the deserts and valleys and mountains received the servants of Christ. And when the impious man thus made progress in these measures, he cast about in his mind the idea of stirring up the persecution against all. He would have succeeded in his purpose, and there would have been nothing to stop him from attaining his aim, had not God, the Champion of souls of His own, very quickly foreseen what would take place, and caused to shine forth immediately, as if in deep darkness

9 Amasea (Amaseia or Amasia), an important city of Pontus on the Iris River.

and gloomy night, a great luminary and savior for all, guiding into those regions with a mighty hand, His servant Constantine.

Chapter 9

To him, accordingly, from heaven above as the worthy fruit of piety did He grant the trophies of victory over the impious ones, but the guilty one with all his counselors and friends He threw down prone under the feet of Constantine.

When Licinius had carried his madness to the last extreme against him, the emperor, the friend of God, thinking that he was no longer to be endured, summoned his prudent reasoning, and, tempering the firm manner of justice with benevolence, decided to aid those in sore distress under the tyrant, and hastened to save the greater part of the human race by putting insignificant spoilers out of the way. When he employed benevolence alone during the time before this and showed mercy on him who was unworthy of any sympathy, nothing further came of it, because Licinius did not give up his evil ways, but rather increased his madness against the subject peoples; while for those who were being ill treated, no hope of safety was left, as they were being oppressed by a tyrannical wild beast. Wherefore, mingling his hatred of evil with his love of good, the defender of the good went forth together with his son Crispus,[1] a most benevolent emperor,

---

1 Crispus Flavius Julius, the eldest son of Constantine by his first wife, Minervina, was born in the beginning of the fourth century, appointed Caesar in 317. He gained great distinction in a campaign against the Franks and in the war with Licinius. But he excited the jealousy of his stepmother Fausta, and was put to death by his father in 326 (cf.

extending his saving right hand to all who were perishing. Thereupon, with the aid of God, the universal King and the Son of God, the Saviour of all, as guide and ally, the father and son encircled the array of the haters of God, and easily bore off the victory,[2] for everything in the attack was made smooth for them by God in accordance with His plan. Indeed, suddenly and sooner than it can be spoken, those who yesterday and the day before were breathing out slaughter and threatenings[3] were no more, nor was there any remembrance of their names, and their pictures and honors received the disgrace that they deserved, and the things that Licinius had seen with his own eyes happen to the impious tyrants of old, these he himself similary suffered, since he neither received instruction himself nor did he acquire wisdom from the strokes that befell his neighbors, but he continued along the same road of impiety as they did, and justly was hurled over the same precipice.

Thus, then, was Licinius cast down and laid prostrate; but Constantine, the greatest conqueror, excelling in every virtue that comes from godliness, with his son Crispus, an emperor most dear to God and in every way like his father, recovered their own East, and rendered as one united realm the Empire of the Romans, as of old, bringing under their peace all of it from the rising of the sun on both sides of the inhabited earth, north and south, even to the farthest limits of the

---

Sozomen, *H.E.* 1.5). His execution is a very dark blot on the memory of Constantine. Eusebius in his *Life of Constantine* discreetly makes no mention of it.

2 Licinius met defeat first at Adrianople on July 3, 323, and later on September 18 and 20, 234, when he fled to Byzantium and was forced to cross the straits, at Chrysopolis, now Scutari. He was shortly afterwards put to death by Constantine.

3 Cf. Acts 9.1.

declining day. Thus, then, men were relieved of all fear of those who formerly oppressed them, and they set about celebrating with bright and festive days of feasting, and all things were filled with light, and with smiling countenances and gleaming eyes; those who formerly looked at each other with downcast expressions now danced and sang throughout the cities and countryside alike, honoring first of all God, the universal King, for so they had been instructed, and then the devout emperor with his sons dear to God; thus, there was oblivion of past evils, and a forgetfulness of every impious deed, and an enjoyment of present blessings and expectation of those yet to come. Thus, then, were put forth in every place from the hand of the victorious emperor[4] decrees full of benevolence and laws that provided evidence of munificence and true piety. Thus, in truth, when every vestige of tyranny had been cleansed away, the foundation of their rightful kingdom was kept secure and without reproach for Constantine and his sons alone.[5] And when they, as the first of all their actions, cleansed the world of hatred for God, mindful of the blessings bestowed on them by God, they manifested their love of virtue and love of God and their piety and gratitude with respect to the Deity by the deeds which they performed openly in the sight of all men.

---

4 Eusebius has given some of these laws in his *Life of Constantine* 2.
5 This statement and the references to Crispus made previously seem to indicate that Eusebius completed the *History* before the execution of Crispus.

INDEX

Agrippinus, *1*: 251
Akhmin, *2*: 23
Albinus, *1*: 129, 130, 134, 156
Alburnus, *1*: 90
Alce, *1*: 241
Alcibiades, *1*: 290, 320; *2*: 63
Alexander, the Alabarch, *1*: 95
Alexander, Decian martyr, *2*: 74, 113
Alexander, Bishop of Alexandria, *1*: 7-10; *2*: 18
Alexander, Bishop of Constantinople, *1*: 8, 207, 210, 295; *2*: 42
Alexander, Bishop of Jerusalem, *1*: 304, 306, 319; *2*: 17, 20-22, 24, 27, 39, 40, 51, 65, 66, 89, 95
Alexander Jannaeus, King, *1*: 57
Alexander Polyhistor, *1*: 19
Alexander Severus, Emperor, *2*: 39, 40, 42, 43, 47, 52, 102
Alexandria, *1*: 3, 4, 8, 9, 15, 18, 93, 94, 96, 111, 113, 130, 131, 143, 163, 168, 185, 207, 208, 211, 212, 215, 223, 226, 246, 251, 300, 302-304, 308, 332, 339; *2*: 3, 5, 7-9, 13-17, 28, 32, 34, 36, 40, 46, 47, 51, 54, 56, 58, 60, 67, 68, 70, 82, 86, 89, 99, 106, 109, 112, 120-123, 137, 138, 140, 151-154, 156, 159, 161, 180, 185, 189, 197, 215; Bishop of, *1*: 7, 163, 207, 332; *2*: 5, 38, 51, 65, 67, 91, 106, 120, 140, 142, 152, 189
Alexas, *1*: 67

Alphaeus, *1*: 85
Amalpae, *1*: 138
Amasea (Amaseia, Amasia), *2*: 285
Amastris, *1*: 258; Bishop of, *1*: 334
ambassadors, *1*: 35
Ambrose, St., *1*: 216, 310; *2*: 44, 52
Ambrose, of Alexandria, *2*: 32
Ammia, *1*: 320, 321
Ammon, *2*: 75, 137
Ammonarion, *2*: 74
Ammonius Saccas, *2*: 34-37, 189
Anacletus, 1: 139, 224
Ananias, *1*: 77
Ananus, *1*: 129, 130
anathema, *1*: 11
Anatolius, Bishop, *2*: 152-158
Anchialus, *1*: 316, 327
Ancyra, Bishop of, *1*: 15, 18, 313
Andrew, St., *1*: 137, 138, 180, 203
Anencletus, *1*: 139, 163, 169, 295
angels, *1*: 38, 41, 44, 65, 68, 101, 102, 181, 185, 240, 308; *2*: 146
Angoria, *1*: 313
Anicetus, *1*: 223, 226, 230-232, 251, 253, 254, 295, 338
Annas, *1*: 71, 72, 129
Annianus, *1*: 111, 131, 163, 168
Anteros, *2*: 53
Anthimus, *2*: 173
anthrax, *2*: 220
Antichrist, *1*: 165, 298, 299; *2*: 15, 136
Antigonus, *1*: 58
Antinoites, *2*: 21

Antinous, 1: 219, 253
Antinoöpolis, 1: 219; 2: 21
Antioch, 1: 7, 9-12, 75, 86, 91, 92, 99, 104, 142, 182, 196, 198, 215, 234, 260, 261, 304, 326, 332; 2: 22, 42, 43, 45, 51, 66, 78, 79, 89, 95, 115, 138-143, 146-149, 151-153, 158, 185, 186, 189, 211, 215, 237, 239; Bishop of, 1: 9-12, 169, 195, 199, 260, 261, 326, 332; 2: 42, 45, 54, 66, 70, 86, 88, 138, 147, 239
Antiochus Epiphanes, 1: 158
Antipater, 1: 56, 57, 62, 68, 69
antipope, 2: 40, 65, 87
Anti-Sabellians, 1: 15
Anti-Trinitarians, 1: 342
Antonianus, 2: 78
Antoninus, 1: 106, 219, 270, 292, 301, 306; 2: 17, 31, 41, 42
Antoninus Pius, 1: 212, 215, 222, 223, 226-230, 233, 248, 249, 251, 294, 314
Antoninus Verus, see Aurelius, Marcus
Antony, 1: 54, 63
Anulinus, 2: 272-275, 279, 280
Apamea (Cibotus) 1: 318, 319
Apelles, 1: 308-310
Apion, 1: 94, 95, 158, 202, 307, 341
Apocalypse, of John, see Scripture; of Justin, 1: 178; of Peter, 1: 179; 2: 26
apocrypha, 1: 256; 2: 158
Apolinarius, 1: 252, 266, 267, 293, 312, 316, 326, 327

Apollo, 1: 57, 62, 158
Apolloniades, 1: 346
Apollonis, virgin, 2: 71
Apollonius, 1: 313, 322, 323, 325, 326, 330, 331
Apollophanes, 2: 35
apologists, 1: 20, 29, 38, 44, 200
Apology, of Athanasius, 1: 12; of Justin, 1: 44, 106, 219, 227, 229, 244, 246, 248, 249, 293; of Miltiades, 1: 321; for Origen, 1: 5; 2: 45, 59; of Tertullian, 1: 89, 193
Apostles, 1: 23, 35, 37, 72, 75-77, 79, 80, 83-86, 88, 91, 99, 100, 103, 104, 106, 108, 110, 112-114, 116, 119, 122-125, 132, 133, 137, 140, 142-145, 154, 157, 161-163, 165, 168-170, 172-174, 177, 179, 180, 186-189, 190, 192, 195, 196, 199-201, 203-205, 207, 211, 212, 215, 219, 224, 231, 232, 250, 251, 255, 260, 261, 268, 269, 271, 295, 296, 299, 302, 304-307, 312, 321, 323, 324, 326, 328, 329, 332, 338-340, 342; 2: 23, 25, 41, 48-50, 63, 119, 120, 129, 131, 132, 163, 250, 266
April (Xanthikus), 1: 155, 156
Aptunga, Bishop of, 2: 273
Aquila, 1: 119, 142, 300; 2: 9, 13, 29-31, 111
Arabia, 1: 56; 2: 38, 40, 58, 62, 95, 184
Arabia Nabataea, 1: 73
Arabians, Bishop of, 2: 40

Arabianus, *1*: 341

Arcadia, *1*: 219

archangels, *1*: 41

archdeacon, *2*: 42, 274

Archelaus, *1*: 59, 69, 73

Ardaban, *1*: 314

Aretas Aeneas, King, *1*: 73

Arianism, *1*: 7-15, 29, 30, 31, 77; *2*: 239, 279

Aristarchus, *1*: 123, 142

Aristides, *1*: 209, 210; *2*: 56

Aristion, *1*: 203, 204, 206

Aristobulus, *1*: 58, 62, 92; *2*: 25, 156, 157

Ariston, of Pella, *1*: 214

Ariston, of Chios, *2*: 36

Aristotle, *1*: 234, 345; *2*: 35

arithmetic, *2*: 33, 36, 158

Arius, *1*: 3, 4, 7-15, 28; *2*: 239

Arles, *2*: 274, 277; Bishop of, *2*: 275

Armenia, *1*: 82, 253, 292; *2*: 89, 174, 220

Armenicus, *1*: 229

Arnuphes, *1*: 293

Arsinoë, *2*: 129

Artaxerxes, *1*: 159, 301

Artemon (Artemas), *1*: 342; *2*: 147, 148

Ascalon, *1*: 57, 62

Ascension, *1*: 45, 83-85, 88, 106, 137, 145, 187, 205

asceticism, *1*: 108, 111, 180, 267, 312, 325

Asclepiades, *1*: 304, 346; *2*: 21, 42

Asclepiodotus, *1*: 344

Asia, *1*: 119, 137, 138, 141, 169, 185, 189, 195, 196, 204, 221, 223, 228-233, 239, 243, 244, 252, 262, 263, 265, 272, 276, 291, 298, 300, 307, 311, 312, 314, 325, 327, 329, 333-336; *2*: 133, 134, 149; Common Council of, *1*: 228-230

Asphaltites, Lake, *1*: 67

Assyria, *1*: 19, 63, 105, 245, 305

Asterius, *1*: 7, 15

Asterius Orbanus (Urbanus), *1*: 318

Astyrius, *2*: 117, 118

Athanasius, *1*: 12-15, 31; *2*: 67, 97, 120, 160

atheism, *1*: 217, 235, 237, 250, 345

Athena, Temple of, *1*: 324

Athenagoras, *1*: 305

Athenodore, *2*: 55, 115, 138, 140

Athens, *1*: 144, 209, 210, 219, 257, 265, 304, 324; *2*: 36, 57; Bishop of, *1*: 144, 209, 257, 320

athletes, *2*: 3

Attalus, *1*: 274, 276, 281, 283, 285, 290

Attica, *2*: 160

Atticus, *1*: 191, 192; *2*: 40

Augusti, *2*: 107, 108, 191

Augustine, St., *1*: 40, 82, 134, 180, 205; *2*: 20, 186, 273, 274

Augustus, Caesar, *1*: 13, 54-58, 69, 70, 95, 101, 158, 228, 264,

283, 293; 2: 156, 192, 195, 201, 204, 227, 269, 274, 276, 278
Aurelian, Emperor, 2: 36, 141, 148, 149
Aurelius Cyrenius, 1: 327
Aurinitis, 1: 69
Auriolus, 2: 105
Auses, 1: 47
Autolycus, 1: 260
Autun, Bishop of, 2: 275
Axamea, 2: 63

Babel, Tower of, 1: 43
Babylas, 2: 45, 54
Babylon, 1: 57, 110; 2: 48
Bacchius, 1: 228
Bacchylides, 1: 258, 332
Bacchyllus, 1: 332, 334
Baetica, 2: 278
Balbinus, 2: 53
Banias, 2: 118
baptism, 1: 10, 70, 73, 87, 145, 181, 184; 2: 12, 14, 64, 82, 84, 85, 93, 97-101
Baptists, 1: 255
barbarians, 1: 50; 2: 163, 172, 194, 250
Bar Cabbas, 1: 216
Bar Chochebas (Bar Choziba), 1: 213, 220
Bar Coph, 1: 216
Bar Manu, Prince, 1: 270
Bardesanes, 1: 269, 270
Barnabas, 1: 75, 85, 91, 92, 99, 104, 110, 142, 179, 205, 299; 2: 134

Baronius, 1: 304
Barsabas (Joseph), 1: 75, 204, 205
Bartholomew, St., 1: 137, 303
Basantide, 1: 64
Basil, St., 2: 160
basilica, 1: 6, 13; 2: 257-259
Basilicus, 1: 309
Basilides, 1: 215, 216; 2: 13, 14, 137
Basilidians, 1: 225, 255
Bassianus, Varius Avitus, 2: 41
Batanea, 1: 69
Bathsheba, 1: 60
Benedict XIV, 1: 304
beneficiarii, 2: 229
Benjamin, Bishop, 1: 212
Benson, Archbishop, 2: 90
Berenice (Bernice), 2: 137
Bergellus, 2: 40, 58, 59, 62
Berytus, 2: 55
Besa, 1: 219
Besas, 2: 74
Beseleel, 2: 244, 252
Bethlehem, 1: 54, 55, 65, 68
Beththera, 1: 213
Bibbas, 1: 278
Biblias, 1: 274
bishops, 1: 9, 15, 84, 142, 170-172, 185, 195, 197, 207, 211, 212, 214, 254, 257, 259, 279, 313, 327, 333, 335, 336, 344; 2: 17, 20, 21, 39, 45, 55, 58, 65, 66, 76, 78, 80-82, 84, 85, 89, 91, 95, 98, 99, 105, 114, 115, 120, 121, 128, 137-139, 141, 149, 151-153, 158-160, 168, 175,

180, 188-190, 215, 239, 242, 243, 273-276, 280, 284

Bithgiria, *1*: 138, 141, 219; *2*: 95, 171

Black Sea, *1*: 137, 138, 223, 327

Blandina, *1*: 274, 276, 277, 281, 282, 285

blasphemy, *1*: 278, 323; *2*: 97

Blastus, *1*: 253, 311, 327

Bolanus, *2*: 142

Bosphorus, *1*: 303

Bostra, *2*: 40, 58, 64, 140

Britain, *1*: 271

Brucheium, *2*: 153

Bruttius, *1*: 166

Bubalia, *2*: 91

Burckhardt, J., *1*: 26

Byzantium, *2*: 287

Caecilian, Bishop, *2*: 273-275, 278, 280

Caesar, *1*: 237, 238; *2*: 192, 286; *see also* individual emperors

Caesarea, *1*: 4, 6, 11-13, 19, 29, 91, 100, 101, 190, 306, 332, 334; *2*: 4, 17, 32, 39, 45, 51, 52, 54, 55, 57, 58, 61, 95, 112, 113, 115 116, 138, 140, 158, 159, 189, 237; Bishop of, *1*: 4, 6, 7, 306, 334; *2*: 17, 39, 51, 52, 116, 139, 153, 158

Caesarea Philippi, *2*: 118

Caiaphas, *1*: 71, 72

Caius (Gaius), *1*: 132, 133, 185, 189

Caius, Caesar, *1*: 92-96, 98, 99, 101, 103, 118

Caligula, Emperor, *1*: 73, 93, 119

Calixtus, St., *2*: 93

Callirhoe, *1*: 67

Callisti Nicephorus, *1*: 211

Callistus, *1*: 343; *2*: 41, 42, 97, 151

Candace, Queen, *1*: 87

Candia, 1: 142

Candidianus, *2*: 237

Candidus, *1*: 341

cannibalism, *1*: 218

canons, *1*: 17, 37, 111, 155, 179; *2*: 7

Caparattaea, *1*: 182

Capito, *1*: 306, 307

Capitolinus, *1*: 293

Cappadocia, *1*: 138, 141, 292, 304, 306; *2*: 20, 21, 32, 51, 89, 95, 96, 115, 143, 184

Caracalla, *1*: 270, 343, *2*: 21, 39, 41

Caria, *1*: 138

Caricus, *1*: 326; *2*: 22

Carinus, *2*: 149

Carnutum, Congress of, *2*: 192

Carpocratians, *1*: 108, 216, 217, 255, 296

Carpophorus, *2*: 41

Carpus, *1*: 243

Carthage, *1*: 89; *2*: 93, 94, 103, 273, 274; Bishop of, *2*: 273, 274, 278, 280

Carus, Emperor, *2*: 149

Caspian Sea, *1*: 137, 138

Cassian, *1*: 307; *2*: 25

Cassius, Bishop, *1*: 339

Castor, *1*: 19

336; 2: 53, 93, 95, 138, 147, 151; in Sardis, 1: 230; at Smyrna, 1: 195, 198, 231, 234; and State, 2: 168, 278, 279; structure of, 2: 257, 259; theology of, 1: 16, 18, 248; 2: 55

Cilicia, 2: 89, 95, 96, 99

circumcision, 1: 44, 52, 53, 56, 141, 195, 212, 214, 255, 306; 2: 63

Clarus, Bishop, 1: 339

Claudius, Emperor, 1: 89, 92, 93, 99, 103, 104, 106, 108, 111, 115, 118-120; 2: 141, 149

Clement of Alexandria, 1: 19, 20, 44, 54, 75, 84, 85, 87, 100, 110, 125, 128, 132, 140, 143, 169, 170, 173, 175, 179, 180, 187, 188, 201, 202, 216, 217, 225, 254, 263, 302, 304, 305, 315, 320, 326, 343; 2: 15, 22, 24, 25, 27, 47

Clement, Bishop of Rome, 1: 139, 163, 164, 168, 194, 259, 295, 299; 2: 24, 50

Clement VIII, 1: 304

Cleobius, 1: 255

Cleopatra, 1: 54

Cleopatra, wife of Herod, 1: 69

Cletus, 1: 139, 224

Clopas, 1: 162, 190-192, 254

Cnossians, 1: 258

Cochaba, 1: 64

Coele-Syria, 1: 305

Colluthion, 2: 109

Cologne, Bishop of, 2: 275

Commodus, Lucius Ceionius, 1: 228, 264, 301, 318, 329, 332, 340; 2: 15

communion, 1: 7, 14; 2: 77, 87, 241

confession, 1: 14

Constantia, Empress, 1: 19

Constantine, Emperor, 1: 7, 9, 12-16, 19, 22-27, 31, 205, 230; 2: 15, 59, 151, 174, 192-195, 204, 205, 223-227, 231, 238, 241, 268, 269, 274, 276-279, 281-283, 286-288

Constantinople, 1: 8, 13-17, 27, 28, 138, 142, 179; 2: 82; Bishop of, 1: 8

Constantius Chlorus, 2: 149, 191, 192, 204

continence, 1: 187

Coracion, 2: 130

Corban, 1: 97

Corduba, Bishop of, 2: 278

Corinth, 1: 17, 75, 133, 134, 144, 164, 201, 252, 254, 256, 259, 295; Bishop of, 1: 133, 252, 254, 258, 332, 334

Cornelius, 1: 91, 199, 251; 2: 65, 66, 73, 78, 79, 82, 85, 86, 92, 93

Cornutus, 2: 36

Costabarus, 1: 67

Covenant, New, 1: 224, 308, 313

Creation, 1: 39, 52, 263, 267, 310

Creed, Apostles', 2: 100; Caesarean, 1: 10, 11; Nicene, 1: 9, 11, 31

Crescens, 1: 142, 243-245

Crete, *1*: 142, 252, 257; Bishop of, *1*: 252
Crispus, *2*: 286-288
Crivelucci, *1*: 25
Cronius, *2*: 35
crucifixion, *1*: 282, 334
Crusades, *1*: 101, 137, 138
Culcianus, *2*: 236
Cumane, *1*: 318
Cumanus, *1*: 119, 120
Curubis, *2*: 67
Cuspius Fodus, *1*: 95, 104
Cyprian, *1*: 41, 84, 224; *2*: 51, 53, 64, 65, 67, 73, 78-80, 82, 93-95, 98-100, 102, 103
Cypros, mother of Herod, *1*: 56
Cyprus, *1*: 86, 223
Cyrenaico, *2*: 137
Cyrenius, *1*: 54, 55; *2*: 114
Cyrene, *1*: 208, 213
Cyril, *2*: 120, 151, 152
Cyzicus, *1*: 30

Dalmatia, *1*: 142; *2*: 191
Damos, Bishop, *1*: 197
Damascus, *2*: 214
Danube, *1*: 138
David, *1*: 47, 49, 56, 57, 60, 61, 127, 162, 166, 167, 191, 266; *2*: 47
Daza, *2*: 195
deacons, *1*: 84, 186; *2*: 32, 40, 78, 82, 90, 103, 106, 125, 142, 143, 146, 152; sub-deacons, *2*: 82
Dead Sea, *1*: 56, 74
Debeltum, Bishop of, *1*: 327
Decapolis, *1*: 64

Decius, *1*: 165, 193, 273; *2*: 54, 59, 64-66, 68, 70, 89, 91, 110, 112, 126, 140, 141, 170
Deity, *2*: 35, 165, 176, 190, 209, 220, 270, 280, 288
Demetrian, *2*: 89, 95, 115, 138, 147
Demetrius, *1*: 332; *2*: 5, 8, 10, 16, 17, 25, 28, 38-40, 51, 54, 111, 114
demons, *1*: 227, 312; *2*: 118
deposyni, *1*: 64
De Rossi, *2*: 151
Devil, *1*: 105, 108, 109, 182, 198, 214, 259, 278, 279, 281, 286, 289, 315, 316; *2*: 136, 150, 170; as Adversary, *1*: 273, 283; as Enemy, *1*: 311; as Serpent, *1*: 282; *see also* Satan
Diatessaron, *1*: 268; *2*: 35
Didache, *1*: 303, 323; *2*: 100
Didius Julianus, *1*: 340; *2*: 5
Didymus, *1*: 312; *2*: 28, 110, 112, 120
Dio Cassius, *1*: 63, 87, 99, 131, 166, 168, 208, 209, 293, 330
Dioceses, *1*: 131, 142, 162, 163, 168, 189, 195, 196, 206, 212, 251, 256-258, 262, 291, 294, 325, 332-334, 336, 338, 339
Diocletian, *1*: 5, 24, 273; *2*: 70, 112, 149, 151, 152, 158, 160-162, 164, 167, 168, 170-173, 180, 186, 188, 191, 195, 203, 204, 227, 233, 235
Diodorus, *1*: 19
Dionysia, *2*: 74

Egyptians, *1*: 19, 21, 121, 122, 184, 293; *2*: 74, 75, 122, 124, 156, 177, 189

Elagabalus, *2*: 41, 42, 56

Elcesaites, *2*: 63

Eleutherius, *1*: 226, 252-254, 271, 291, 294, 295, 332

Eli, *1*: 61, 62, 64

Eliezer, *1*: 71

Elpistus, *1*: 258

Emesa, *2*: 188, 189, 214

Empire, Roman, *1*: 13, 44, 80, 119, 165, 193, 228, 264, 300, 340; *2*: 3, 103, 107, 113, 127, 141, 171, 174, 190, 191, 204, 230, 279, 282, 287

Encratites, *1*: 245, 267

Enoch (Henoch), *2*: 158

Enon, *1*: 176

Epaphroditus, *1*: 158

Ephesus, *1*: 138, 142, 168, 170, 171, 189, 197, 204, 230, 232, 298, 300, 324, 326, 332, 335; *2*: 134; Bishop of, *1*: 142, 189, 322

Ephraem, *1*: 77

Ephres (Ephrem), Bishop of Jersualem, *1*: 212

Epimachus, *2*: 74

Epiphanius, *1*: 18, 54, 64, 107, 111, 128, 145, 175, 179, 180, 194, 212, 215, 217, 223-225, 251, 255, 268, 313, 314, 323, 328; *2*: 30, 54, 97

Epirus, *2*: 30

episcopacy, *1*: 64, 85, 125, 139, 143, 196, 211, 222, 252, 257, 262, 294, 295, 302, 306, 332; *2*: 5, 21, 53, 55, 56, 60, 65, 66, 80, 81, 89, 92, 120, 148, 151, 152, 159

Epistle, Catholic, *1*: 256; *2*: 26, 132, 133, 135

Epistles, of Barnabas, *1*: 205; *2*: 25, 26; of Clement, *1*: 254; *2*: 25; of Ignatius, *1*: 195, 196, 201, 230, 233; of James, *1*: 130, 178; of John, *1*: 130, 177, 178, 206, 299; *2*: 49, 132, 133, 135; of Jude: *1*: 130, 178; *2*: 25, 26; of Paul, *1*: 140, 174, 178, 188, 224, 268, 341; *2*: 41, 136; of Polycarp, *1*: 233

equinox, *2*: 156-158

Erastus, *1*: 142

Eros, Bishop, *1*: 251, 252

Esau, *1*: 56

Esdra, *1*: 301

Esdras I (Ezra), *1*: 159

Esdras II (Nehemias), *1*: 159, *2*: 48

Essenes, *1*: 255

Estha, *1*: 61, 62

Ethiopia, *1*: 87, 88

ethnarch, *1*: 59, 69

Etruscus Herennius, *2*: 91, 92

Eucharist, Holy, *1*: 196, 338; *2*: 77, 82, 85, 87, 273

Euclid, *1*: 342, 345, 346

Euelpis, *2*: 39

Eumanes, Bishop, *1*: 212, 226

Eumeneia, *1*: 319, 326, 335

eunuch, *1*: 335; *2*: 16, 152

Eunus, *2*: 73

Euphranor, 2: 137
Euphrasion, 1: 19
Euphrates River, 1: 77
Euphronius, 1: 12
Eupolemus, 2: 25
Euporus, 2: 137
Eusebians, 1: 13
Eusebius Pamphili, life and career, 1: 3-16; works 1: 17-27; style, 1: 28; *Chronicon*, 1: 19-22, 82, 166, 169, 170, 306; 2: 56
Eusebius of Emesa, 1: 3
Eusebius of Laodicea, 2: 106, 111, 112, 152-155, 158
Eusebius of Nicomedia, 1: 3, 4, 7-9, 13; 2: 239
Eusebius of Samosata, 1: 3
Eustathius, Bishop of Antioch, 1: 10-12
Eutychianus, 2: 151
Eutychius, 2: 142
Euzoius, 1: 14
Evangelists, 1: 69, 70, 74, 85, 91, 153, 165, 169, 175, 176, 178, 200, 201, 203, 303; 2: 56, 132, 133
Evarestos, Bishop, 1: 194, 207, 295
Evodius, 1: 169, 195
excommunication, 1: 252, 258; 2: 8, 58, 141, 147
exorcists, 2: 82, 83
Ezra, 1: 266

Fabian, 2: 45, 53, 54, 62, 65

Fabius, 2: 65, 66, 70, 78, 79, 86, 88, 89, 115
Fadus, 1: 103, 104, 119
famine, 1: 99, 104, 147-153; 2: 220
Fathers, the, 1: 8, 9, 11, 41, 44, 50, 108, 110, 138-140, 143, 171, 175, 179, 180, 186, 193, 196, 202, 210, 214, 215, 232, 262, 299, 303, 314, 337; 2: 29, 30, 56, 64, 150, 186; Ante-Nicene, 1: 60, 139, 170, 180; 2: 153, 161
Fausta, 2: 275, 286
Faustinus, 2: 111
Faustus, 2: 70, 106, 107, 111, 112, 189
Feast, of Unleavened Bread, 1: 155; of Pentecost, 1: 156; of Tabernacles, 1: 156; *see also* Passover
Felix, 1: 120-122, 157; 2: 114
Felix, Bishop of Aptunga, 2: 273
Felix, Bishop of Rome, 2: 149, 151
Festus, 1: 122-124, 129
Firmilian, 2: 51, 89, 95, 96, 99, 115, 138, 139, 143
Flavia Domitilla, 1: 166
Flavia Neapolis, 1: 226, 228
Flaviopolis (Flaviadis) , 2: 20
Flavius, 2: 120
Flavius Clemens, 1: 166
Florinus, 1: 253, 311, 327-329
forgers, 1: 70
fornication, 1: 187, 268; 2: 196, 197

303

Forty Hours, *1*: 337
Forum Trebonii, *2*: 91
Franks, *2*: 286
Friday, *1*: 334; Good, *1*: 338
Fronto, *2*: 36

Gaius, Pope, *2*: 151
Gaius of Derbe, *1*: 142, 205
Gaius of Eumeneia, *1*: 319, *2*: 69
Gaius of Macedonia, *1*: 142, *2*: 40, 111
Gaius of Jerusalem, *1*: 307
Gaianus, *1*: 307
Galatia, *1*: 138, 141, 185, 313; *2*: 96, 99, 211
Galba, *1*: 144
Galen, *1*: 345
Galerius, *2*: 149, 164, 170-172, 174, 195, 199-201, 204, 209, 231, 235, 269
Galilee, *1*: 55, 69, 119, 120, 134, 176, 255
Gallienus, *2*: 67, 92, 102, 103, 105-107, 113, 114, 116, 126, 127, 140, 141
Gallus, *2*: 65, 91, 92, 102
Gamala, *1*: 55
Gamaliel, *1*: 103, 104, 130
Gaul, *1*: 15, 73, 92, 99, 252, 272, 273, 276, 284, 291, 294, 334, 336; *2*: 274-276
Gaulonite, *1*: 55
Gaza, *1*: 57; *2*: 189
Gelasius, *1*: 30
genealogy, *1*: 59, 60, 63, 64
Genistae, *1*: 255
Gentiles, *1*: 35, 44, 45, 47, 53, 57,

58, 86, 87, 123, 127, 135, 141, 145, 154, 157, 214, 216, 306, 308, 343; *2*: 11, 26, 49, 240; Bishop of the, *1*: 133, 306
geometry, *1*: 345; *2*: 33
Gerisem, Mt., *1*: 98
Germanicus, *1*: 234, 306
Germany, *1*: 292-294; *2*: 105
Germanion, *2*: 20
Germanus, *2*: 67, 68, 106, 110
gers, 1: 63
Gessius Florus, *1*: 129, 134
Geton, *2*: 122
Gittho, *1*: 106
gladiators, *1*: 281
gluttony, *1*: 323
Gnosticism, *1*: 87, 106, 107, 181, 184, 215-217, 223-225, 227, 232, 245, 253, 290, 307-310, 328
God, 1: 35-45, 49-54, 56, 57, 62, 65, 66, 70, 71, 73, 78, 87, 88, 90, 91, 95, 97, 101, 102, 108, 112, 114, 115, 117-119, 121, 123, 126, 128, 131, 132, 145, 146, 148, 149, 154-156, 159, 160, 165, 171, 172, 182, 184, 185, 194, 198-200, 215, 224, 227, 229, 234, 238, 240, 243, 248, 249, 251, 255, 266-268, 273, 274, 276, 277, 280, 282-285, 287-293, 297-301, 305, 308-312, 315, 316, 318, 321, 327-331, 336, 337, 343, 345; *2*: 3, 4, 6, 9, 10, 12, 14, 17, 19-21, 48, 50, 68, 69, 74, 75, 80, 83, 88, 92, 95, 97, 100-108, 111, 112, 117, 118, 132, 133, 135,

139, 143, 145, 147, 150, 155, 159, 160, 163, 164, 167, 170, 179, 181, 183, 184, 186, 188, 189, 192, 196, 199, 202, 207, 209, 210, 213, 219, 223-227, 230-236, 238-256, 259-265, 267, 275, 277, 279, 282-288; Almighty, *1*: 40; *2*: 26, 97; as Creator, *1*: 39, 91, 201, 227, 251; *2*: 170; as Father, *1*: 11, 38-42, 44, 45, 48-50, 54, 80, 81, 88, 128, 157, 225, 227, 234, 240, 248, 273, 280, 281, 289; *2*: 58, 97, 133, 135, 136, 139, 247, 250-252, 256, 263-267; as Guardian, *1*: 43; *2*: 264, as Maker, *1*: 39, 227; *2*: 267; Providence of, *1*: 90, 108, 118, 154; *2*: 5, 22, 177, 199, 274, 280; as Ruler, *1*: 39; *2*: 267, 268; as Wisdom, *1*: 42; *2*: 252; *see* also Christ, Holy Spirit, Lord; Trinity; Word

Gordiaean Mountains, *1*: 105

Gordian, *2*: 45, 53, 57, 59, 64

Gordius, *1*: 306; *2*: 20

Gorgonius, *2*: 164, 173

Gorthaeus, *1*: 255

Gortyna, Bishop of, *1*: 142, 257, 261

Gospels, *1*: 18, 29, 49, 59, 60, 64, 65, 70, 72, 73, 75, 88-90, 97, 110, 114-116, 139, 141-143, 162, 173-180, 191, 200, 202, 206, 216, 224, 245, 253, 255, 257, 260, 268, 269, 298, 303, 313, 323, 335; *2*: 11, 23, 27, 31, 37,

46, 48-50, 52, 53, 61, 63, 82, 117, 119, 129, 132, 133, 161, 265; Apocryphal, *1*: 89, 216; *2*: 23

Gothicus, *2*: 141

Goths, *2*: 91, 92

Graecia, Magna, *1*: 305

Greece, *1*: 113, 138, 304, 332; *2*: 45

Greek, *1*: 24, 29, 74, 90, 171, 209, 217, 249, 270, 338, 341, 346; literature, *1*: 3, 90, 93, 126, 158, 175, 181, 203, 219, 221, 223, 234, 300, 302; *2*: 36, 120, 202, 211, 232, 242

Greeks, *1*: 19, 21, 28, 50, 63, 91, 94, 99, 150, 208, 218, 227, 245, 249, 265, 266, 269, 274, 298, 340; *2*: 8, 24-26, 33, 35, 37, 38, 136, 152, 154, 163, 172

Gregory Nazianzen, *1*: 142

Gregory of Nyssa, *1*: 42, *2*: 55

Gregory (Thaumaturgus), *2*: 4, 55, 62, 115, 138, 140, 142

Gregory of Tours, *2*: 275

Gregory VII, *2*: 98

Guirinius, *1*: 54

Hades, *1*: 81

Hadrian, Emperor, *1*: 105, 199, 208-215, 219-222, 230, 265, 294, 306; *2*: 21, 40, 214; Epistle of, *2*: 203

Hebrew, *1*: 20, 21, 28, 64, 111, 128, 175, 206, 212, 225, 255, 303, 305; *2*: 26, 29-31, 48, 152

305

Hebrews, *1*: 17, 19, 44, 48, 50, 52, 55, 63, 74, 79, 114, 141, 159, 160, 174, 179, 184, 201, 206, 211, 255, 256, 268, 269, 298, 340; *2*: 26, 41, 47, 50, 157, 158, 225

Hegesippus, *1*: 36, 84, 85, 125, 126, 128, 130, 162, 164, 166, 191, 192, 215, 217, 219, 226, 252, 253, 255, 271

Heikel, I. A., *1*: 26

Helen, Queen, *1*: 104, 105

Helena, *1*: 106, 107

Helenus, *2*: 89, 95, 96, 140, 142

Heli, *1*: 62

Heliodorus, *2*: 95

Helkesaites, *2*: 63, 64

Helleninians, *1*: 255

Hellenism, *1*: 29

Hemerobaptists, *1*: 255

Henoch, Book of, *2*: 158

Heraclas, *1*: 226, 302; *2*: 8, 29, 38, 51, 54, 56, 60, 67, 98, 101

Heraclides, *2*: 12, 278

Heraclitus, *1*: 340

Herais, *2*: 12

Hercules, *1*: 222

Herenius Etruscus, *2*: 91, 92

Heresiarch, *1*: 308

Heresy, *1*: 7, 29, 31, 87, 105, 107, 133, 165, 169, 184-187, 196, 205, 215, 216, 223, 224, 227, 250, 252, 254, 255, 257, 260, 266-270, 308, 311, 313, 314, 319, 320, 322, 326-328, 342-344; *2*: 23, 31, 32, 44, 62, 63, 78, 79, 131, 140, 141, 147, 150

Heretics, *1*: 23, 87, 105, 108, 143, 179, 180, 191, 192, 223, 227, 232, 257, 261, 316, 329, 341; *2*: 7, 32, 38, 51, 67, 93, 96-101, 113, 138, 147, 279

Hermammon, *2*: 92, 102, 126

Hermo, Bishop, *2*: 160

Hermas, *1*: 140, 141, 225, 299, 342

Hermogenes, *1*: 260

Hermophilus, *1*: 346

Hermopolitans, *2*: 88

Hero, *1*: 252; *2*: 74

Herod, *1*: 54, 56-59, 62, 63, 65-69, 72, 92, 101, 102, 167, 237, 241

Herod Agrippa, *1*: 59, 85, 92, 96, 99-103, 119, 129, 130, 145, 158, 161

Herod Antipas, *1*: 59, 63, 69, 70, 72-74, 88, 92, 103, 176

Herodians, *1*: 255

Herodias, *1*: 72-74, 92

Herodotus, *2*: 76

Heros, Bishop, *1*: 199

Hesychius, *2*: 180, 189

heterodoxy, *2*: 62, 140-142

Hexaemeron, *1*: 310, 341; *2*: 43

Hexapla, *2*: 29-31

Hierapolis, *1*: 189, 190, 204, 262, 266, 312, 314, 316, 326, 327, 335; Bishop of, *1*: 101, 195, 262, 266, 293, 327

Hierax, *2*: 121, 124, 142

Hierocles, *1*: 18

Hippo, Bishop of, *2*: 20; Council of, *1*: 139

306

Hippolytus, *1*: 106, 139, 215, 217, 223, 225, 310, 322, 328, 342, 343; *2*: 40, 41, 43, 44, 63, 64, 90, 96, 97

Holofernes, *1*: 63

Holy Spirit, *1*: 38, 39, 84, 185, 189, 240, 275, 316, 335, 346; *2*: 7, 54, 97, 98, 100, 136, 139, 150, 243, 244, 259, 265, 266; as Paraclete, *1*: 311, 312, 323; *2*: 150; *see also* Spirit

homooúsion, *1*: 11

Honorius, *2*: 103

Hoshea, *1*: 47

Hosius, *2*: 278

Hostilianus, *2*: 91, 92

Hungary, *1*: 292

Hyginus, *1*: 222-225, 295

Hymenaeus, Bishop, *2*: 115, 140, 142, 160

hymns, *1*: 113, 114, 116; *2*: 128

hypostasis, *2*: 139

Hypotyposes, *1*: 75, 84, 100, 110, 304; *2*: 24, 26

Hyrcanus, *1*: 56-58, 62

hyssop, *1*: 116

Hystaspes, Bishop of Edessa, *1*: 269

Iconium, *2*: 39, 99, 140

idols, *1*: 44, 46, 216, 219, 285; *2*: 73, 108, 184, 195, 196, 212, 213, 220

Idumaea, *1*: 56, 57, 59, 62, 69

Ignatius of Antioch, *1*: 169, 195-197, 199, 201, 202, 230, 231, 233, 234, 300

Illyricum, *1*: 118, 138, 141; *2*: 49

Illyrium, *2*: 105

immoralities, *1*: 15, 245

impiety, *1*: 66, 118, 239

Incarnation, *1*: 36, 43, 45, 54, 196

incest, *1*: 218

India, *1*: 137, 300, 303

Indus, River, *1*: 137

Ingenuus, *2*: 75

Irenaeus, *1*: 54, 84, 87, 88, 106, 107, 138, 139, 142, 143, 165, 169, 175, 178, 181, 184, 186, 188, 195, 198, 202, 203, 205-207, 212, 215-218, 222, 223, 225, 226, 230-233, 243, 250-252, 256, 261, 267, 268, 271, 273, 291, 294, 296, 298-301, 320, 327-330, 334, 336, 337, 339, 340, 343; *2*: 26, 29, 30, 48

Isaac, *1*: 42, 52

Ischyrion, *2*: 76

Ishmael, *1*: 71, 120

Isidore, *2*: 74, 82

Isola Tiberiana, *1*: 106

Israel, *1*: 40, 52, 60, 64, 121; *2*: 122, 165

Israelites, *1*: 63, 255

Issus, Gulf of, *2*: 23

Italy, *1*: 137, 138, 144; *2*: 79, 147, 149, 224

Izates, *1*: 104

Jacob, *1*: 40, 42, 61, 62, 64

James, St., *1*: 76, 84, 85, 99, 100, 125-130, 145, 154, 161, 162,

166, 203, 212, 254, 305; *2*: 120, 132, 134

James, the Just, *1*: 84, 85, 100, 125-129, 254

Jasper, *2*: 265

Jehosaphat, Valley of, *1*: 128

Jericho, *1*: 41, 67, 121; *2*: 31

Jerome, St., *1*: 25, 30, 31, 76, 82, 89, 93, 111, 123, 130, 131, 134, 141-143, 163, 166, 175, 180, 204, 212, 216, 219, 225, 251, 252, 260, 261, 303, 304, 307, 313, 320, 322, 323, 326, 331, 333, 334, 337, 339-341; *2*: 4, 15, 28-30, 32, 43, 44, 46, 47, 53-59, 62, 78, 79, 88, 139, 141, 151, 152, 160, 180, 215

Jerusalem, *1*: 13-15, 17, 26, 27, 57, 58, 73, 78, 85, 91, 96-98, 101, 104, 118-122, 125, 129, 134, 137, 138, 141, 144-146, 148, 151-154, 156-158, 161, 162, 169, 185, 190, 195, 208, 211, 213, 300, 306, 322, 326, 332, 334; *2*: 17, 20, 21, 40, 49, 65, 66, 115, 120, 134, 140, 160; Bishop of, *1*: 84, 125, 154, 161, 190, 195, 211, 212, 214, 255, 304, 306, 334, 341; *2*: 17, 39, 51, 65, 89, 115, 120, 160; Council of, *1*: 85

Jesus of Ananias, *1*: 156

Jesus of Dammaeus, *1*: 130

Jesus, son of Nave, *2*: 47

Jesus, son of Sirach, *2*: 25

Jews, *1*: 4, 20, 47, 48, 50, 56-59, 61, 63-65, 67-69, 73, 74, 78, 86, 92-98, 100, 118, 119, 121, 122, 124, 126, 128, 129, 134, 135, 137, 138, 144, 146, 148, 151, 152, 154, 157-160, 162, 184, 191, 194, 208, 209, 211-214, 220, 239, 241, 242, 249, 250, 254-256, 266, 294, 301, 306, 317, 321, 333, 336; *2*: 25, 29, 37, 41, 156

John, St., the Apostle, *1*: 84, 85, 99, 125, 137, 138, 145, 165, 168-177, 180, 186, 188, 189, 195, 203, 204, 206, 232, 260, 298, 305, 323, 326, 329, 335, 338; *2*: 27, 46, 49, 53, 102, 131-134

John the Baptist, St., *1*: 69, 70, 72-74, 175, 176, 274

John, Bishop of Jerusalem, *1*: 212

John Chrysostom, St., *1*: 84; *2*: 10, 54, 60

John V, of Portugal, *1*: 304

Jonathan, *1*: 121

Joppa, *1*: 57

Jordan River, *1*: 67, 104, 145, 151, 214; *2*: 118

Joseph, *1*: 60-62, 64, 84, 162, 192, 300; *2*: 31

Joseph (Barsabas), *1*: 205, 212

Josephus, *1*: 19, 20, 55, 56, 58, 63, 66, 68-74, 85, 92, 94, 95, 97, 101-104, 119-122, 128, 129, 134, 135, 144-146, 148, 153, 157-161; *2*: 156

Jotapata, *1*: 158

Jubaionus, *2*: 100

Juda, *1*: 54, 56, 58

Judaea, *1*: 17, 55, 56, 59, 62, 64, 67-70, 76, 86, 95, 97-99, 101, 103-105, 108, 109, 119, 120, 125, 129, 134, 144-146, 157, 190, 209, 213; *2*: 51

Judaism, *1*: 184, 224, 308; *2*: 3, 22, 48, 63

Judas, the betrayer, *1*: 75, 83, 205, 317, 321

Judas, Bishop of Jerusalem, *1*: 212, 255

Judas, brother of the Lord, *1*: 167

Judas, the Galilean, *1*: 55

Judas, a Gaulonite, *1*: 55

Judas (Thomas), *1*: 79

Judas, a writer, *2*: 15

Julia Domna, *2*: 41, 42

Julia Mamaea, *2*: 42

Julian, Emperor, *1*: 302, 307, 318, 332; *2*: 5

Julian, martyr, *2*: 73

Juliana, *2*: 32, 52

Julius Caesar, *1*: 54, 56, 70, 238

Jupiter, *1*: 293

justice, *1*: 53; *2*: 236, 253, 265

Justin Martyr, *1*: 41, 43, 52, 87, 88, 105, 106, 143, 178, 180, 181, 184, 205, 210, 213, 218-221, 226-228, 235, 243-251, 267, 268, 293, 300, 320, 343

Justus (Barsabas), *1*: 204, 205

Justus of Alexandria, *1*: 211

Justus (Judas) of Jerusalem, *1*: 212

Justus of Tiberias, *1*: 160, 161, 194

Kallistio, *1*: 310

Kamithus, *1*: 71

Katharoi, *2*: 78

Kenites, *1*: 128

Kephro, *2*: 67

king, *1*: 38, 48, 50, 238, 242, 248; *2*: 239, 247, 249, 250, 260, 262, 287, 288

kingdom, of God, *1*: 45; *2*: 129; of Heaven, *1*: 109

Kingdoms, Books of, *1*: 266; *2*: 47

Kuryet Jit, *1*: 106

Lacedaemonians, *1*: 256

Laetus, *2*: 5, 9

Lactantius, *1*: 26, 82, 175, 260; *2*: 164, 167, 171, 174, 184, 192, 200, 201, 204, 210, 211, 213, 220, 224, 227, 231, 232, 237, 269

Lagus, *1*: 300

Lake, K., *1*: 32

Lake Marsia (Mareotis), *1*: 113

Laodicea, *1*: 8, 189, 263; *2*: 89, 95, 152, 153, 155, 158; Bishop of, *1*: 8; *2*: 106, 112, 152, 158

Laranda, Bishop of, *2*: 39

Larisians, *1*: 265

Lateran, *2*: 275

Latin, *1*: 90, 158, 212, 221, 252, 253, 277, 283, 285, 293, 296; *2*: 114, 120, 202, 232, 268

Latronianus, *2*: 277

Law, *1*: 65, 130, 159; *2*: 31, 35; of Moses, *1*: 310, 327; *2*: 257;

309

and Prophets, *1*: 118, 184, 224, 254, 265, 268, 310, 347; *2*: 129
Lawler, H. J., *1*: 32
Lawrence, St., *2*: 103
Lebanon, *1*: 305; Cedars of, *2*: 241, 258
lectors, *2*: 82, 83
Leir, Bishop of Jerusalem, *1*: 212
Lent, *1*: 337
Leo, St., *1*: 337
Leonides, *2*: 4
Leontius of Antioch, *2*: 60, 141
Leptis, *2*: 36
Leudefredus, *2*: 82
Levi, tribe of, *1*: 301
Levite, *1*: 128
Libbaeus, *1*: 76
Libellus synodicus, *1*: 333
Liberian Catalogue, *2*: 138, 151
Liberius, *2*: 45
libraries, *1*: 29, 158; *2*: 36, 40
Libya, *2*: 36, 107, 109, 111, 137
Licinius, *1*: 7; *2*: 192, 195, 201, 204, 205, 210, 211, 223, 224, 227, 231, 232, 237, 238, 241, 268, 269, 281, 282, 284, 287
Linus, *1*: 139, 143, 163, 169, 295
Lipsius, *1*: 89
Loeb, C. L., *1*: 32
Logos, *1*: 27, 39, 40, 83, 200; *2*: 139
Longinus, *2*: 35
Lord, *1*: 21, 36, 38-42, 47-51, 54, 64, 72, 76, 80, 83-85, 101, 105, 106, 123-125, 128, 153, 154, 161, 162, 166-170, 172, 174, 187-189, 191, 192, 195, 199, 203, 204, 206, 212, 214, 224, 231, 232, 234-236, 241-243, 245, 250, 251, 254, 259, 272, 274, 276, 279, 296, 298, 300, 315, 316, 323-325, 328, 329, 333, 335, 336, 338, 344, 345; *2*: 13, 14, 18, 22, 26, 43, 56, 58, 71-74, 82, 88, 100, 101, 129, 133-135, 143, 145, 165, 179, 181, 186, 213, 226, 232, 235, 240, 245-247, 254, 255, 260, 261, 267
Lord's Day, *1*: 334, 337
lots, *1*: 76, 281
Lucerne, Lake, *1*: 99
Lucian, *1*: 7, 325; *2*: 80, 102, 188, 215
Lucianus, *2*: 161
Lucius, martyr, *1*: 247, 248
Lucius Quietus, *1*: 209; *2*: 105
Lucius Verus, *1*: 228, 233, 243, 262; *2*: 93, 111, 143, 151
Lucuas, *1*: 208, 209
Lugdunum, *1*: 92
Lupus, *1*: 208
Lycaonia, *2*: 99, 140
Lycus, *1*: 105
Lydia, *1*: 138
Lyons *1*: 73, 272, 276, 290, 291, 294; *2*: 41; Bishop of, 252, 279
Lysanias, *1*: 69, 70, 103

Macar, *2*: 74
Macedonicans, *1*: 300; *2*: 156
Macharius, Bishop, *2*: 160
Macherus, *1*: 74

310

Macrianus, 2: 103-105, 114, 116, 121, 126, 127

Magi, 1: 65; 2: 103

magicians, 1: 121; 2: 195

Magnesia, 1: 197

Malalas, John, 1: 196

Malchion, 2: 138, 141, 143

Malchus, 2: 113

Malthace, 1: 59, 69

Mamaea, 2: 42

Mambre, oak of, 1: 40

Manethus, 1: 19

Manichaeans, 1: 18, 224, 267; 2: 150

Mantinea, 1: 219

Marcella, 1: 313; 2: 13

Marcellinus, 2: 34, 151

Marcellus, Bishop of Ancyra, 1: 15, 16, 18, 313, 316; 2: 107

March, 2: 167

Marcia, 1: 330

Marcianus of Rhossus, 2: 23, 42

Marcion, 1: 108, 223, 224, 226, 227, 232, 242, 248, 250, 253, 255, 257, 260, 261, 267, 268, 270, 300, 307-310, 319, 340; 2: 23, 44, 113

Marcosians, 1: 225

Marcus, 1: 214, 225, 226, 228, 306

Marcus Aemilius, 1: 90

Marcus Aurelius, Emperor (Antoninus Verus), 1: 209, 228, 230, 233, 243, 248, 252, 262-264, 267, 271, 283, 292, 293, 301, 313, 330

Marcus Opellius Macrinus, 2: 41

Marcus Turbo, 1: 208

Mareotis, 2: 67, 109, 111

Marinus, 2: 95, 116, 275

Marjorinus, Bishop, 2: 273

marriage, 1: 60, 225, 322

martyrs, 1: 23, 24, 84, 189, 226, 235, 240-243, 252, 263, 267, 271, 272, 277, 278, 283, 287-292, 295, 306, 319, 324, 326, 327, 331, 335; 2: 9, 12, 42, 57, 66, 71, 73, 77, 80, 85, 117, 174-178, 181, 183, 184, 186, 188-190, 240

martyrdom, 1: 6, 7, 17, 24, 36, 124, 128, 133, 134, 138, 161, 162, 166, 190, 191, 193, 195-198, 212, 222, 231, 233, 234, 237, 241-244, 246, 247, 254, 257, 263, 268, 271, 273, 274, 276, 280, 288, 294, 319; 2: 3, 5-8, 12, 14, 32, 52, 65, 70, 78, 86, 88, 89, 112, 116, 125, 149, 151, 159, 162, 173, 175, 178, 181, 184, 188, 195

martyrologies, 1: 31, 131, 304

Mary, Virgin, 1: 64, 84, 283; 2: 31, 32

Mary, beyond Jordan, 1: 151

Mary of Clopas, 1: 191

Masbothei, 1: 255

Mass, 1: 231; 2: 82

Maternus, 2: 275

mathematics, 1: 345; 2: 6, 33, 36, 158

Matthan, 1: 61, 64

Matthias, 1: 75, 83, 180, 205

Montanism, *1*: 133, 189, 252, 271, 291, 311-316, 320-327, 337, 343, 344

Montanus, *1*: 266, 290, 311, 312, 314-317, 321-325

Moors, *2*: 175

Moses, 1: 26, 39-42, 46, 47, 52, 53, 56, 57, 64, 98, 117, 119, 159, 266, 269, 301, 310, 327; *2*: 34, 85, 122, 157, 225

Moses Chorenensis, *1*: 77

Muratorian fragment, *1*: 143

Musaeus, *2*: 156

Musanus, *1*: 252, 267

Mysia, *1*: 138, 314

Nablus, *1*: 106

Narcissus, *1*: 306, 332, 339; *2*: 17-21

Natalius, *1*: 344

Nathan, *1*: 60, 61, 64

Nave, *1*: 47

Nazarenes, *1*: 255

Nazareth, *1*: 64

Nebuchadnezzor, *1*: 63, 301

Necephorus, *1*: 111

Nehemias, *1*: 159

Nemesion, *2*: 75

Neo-Caesarea, *2*: 55; Council of, *2*: 82

Neo-Platonism, *2*: 35, 36

Neon, *2*: 39

Nepos, *2*: 128, 129

Nero, Emperor, *1*: 106, 111, 119, 122-124, 129-134, 138, 144, 164, 165, 168, 190, 264, 293; *2*: 36

Nerva, *1*: 168

Newman, John Henry, Cardinal, *1*: 196, 296

Nicea, Council of, *1*: 9, 11, 12, 14-16, 28, 30, 314; *2*: 21; Second, *1*: 30; *2*: 82, 152

Nicephorus, *1*: 142, 266, 306

Nicetes, *1*: 237, 241

Nicodemus, Gospel of, *1*: 88

Nicolaus, *1*: 186, 187

Nicomachus, *2*: 36

Nicomas, *2*: 140, 142

Nicomedia, *1*: 16, 179, 257; *2*: 171, 172, 174, 188, 215, 228; Metropolitan of, *1*: 179; palace at, *2*: 164

Nicopolis, *2*: 30

Nile River, *1*: 87, 219; *2*: 21, 76, 129

Nilopolis, *2*: 76

Nilus, Bishop, *2*: 189

Nisan, *1*: 333

Noe, *1*: 52; *2*: 122

Noetus, *2*: 97

nomads, *1*: 43

Noricum, *2*: 103

Novatian (Novatus), *1*: 289; *2*: 51, 65, 67, 78-81, 86-90, 94, 95, 99, 100

Numerianus, *2*: 149

Numenius, *2*: 35

Numidia, *2*: 273, 278

Nun, *1*: 47, 266

Oblias, 1: 126

Odenathus, *2*: 105

Oedipodean, *1*: 276

oikonomia, 1: 36

313

oil, *1*: 49, 50, 126, 306
oligarchy, *1*: 57
Olives, Mount of, *1*: 121, 122
Olympiads, *1*: 99
Onesimus, *1*: 197, 265
Ophites, *1*: 108
oracles, *1*: 46; of the Lord, *1*: 202
ordination, *1*: 84
Orient, *1*: 123, 245; *2*: 103
Origen, *1*: 4, 5, 12, 18, 28, 30, 41, 43, 50, 73, 107, 129, 132, 138, 139, 174, 175, 178-180, 184, 195, 216, 226, 238, 302, 310, 315, 332, 341; *2*: 4-9, 12, 15-17, 28, 29, 31, 32, 34-39, 42, 43, 61, 63, 64, 66, 67, 89, 92, 115, 128, 161
Orosius, *1*: 54, 209
Orphaus, *1*: 324
orthodoxy, *1*: 8, 11, 15, 28, 30, 256, 258, 333; *2*: 7, 62, 67, 82, 97, 148
Ortona, *1*: 137
Osrhoenes, *1*: 85, 334
Ostian Way, *1*: 133
Otrous, Bishop of, *1*: 314
Oulton, J. E. L., *1*: 32

Pachymius, *2*: 180, 190
Pacianus, *1*: 327
paganism, *1*: 5, 29, 121, 245; *2*: 37, 64, 213
Palatine Hill, *1*: 158
Palestine, *1*: 4, 17, 24, 62, 88, 89, 91, 101, 119, 134, 213, 228, 254, 305, 306, 332, 334, 339; *2*: 17, 39, 45, 55, 65, 89, 103,

112, 115, 116, 118, 153, 158-160, 175, 189; Bishop of, *2*: 17; Council of, *1*: 339
Palladius, *2*: 13, 32, 52
pallium, *2*: 38
Palmas, Bishop, *1*: 258, 334
Palmyra, *2*: 36, 138, 144
Pambouk Kelessi, *1*: 189
Pamphilus, *1*: 3-6, 17, 24, 25; *2*: 4, 45, 57, 59, 61, 159, 189
Pamphylia, *1*: 318; *2*: 134
Paneas, *2*: 118
panegyric, *1*: 10, 15, 16, 26, 28
Paneion, *2*: 118
Pannonia, *2*: 64, 91
Pantaenus, *1*: 175, 302-305; *2*: 15, 24, 27, 38
Papa (Pope), *2*: 98
Paphos, *2*: 134
Papias, *1*: 110, 175, 195, 202-206
Papirius, *1*: 335
Papylas, *1*: 243
Paraetonium, *2*: 111
Parthia, *1*: 58, 137; *2*: 63
Pasch, *1*: 119, 126, 127, 130, 146, 155, 175, 231, 237, 252, 258, 262, 263, 306, 327-339; *2*: 24, 25, 43, 44, 120, 121, 145, 153-156
Pasquali, G., *1*: 25
Passion, of Christ, *1*: 70, 72, 83, 92, 116, 146, 154, 185, 191; *2*: 167, 243, 259
pastor, *1*: 252; *2*: 78
Patmos, *1*: 165, 170; *2*: 133
Patricius, *2*: 279
Paul, *2*: 70, 111

314

Paul, St., the Apostle, *1*: 73, 75, 76, 85, 86, 88, 91, 92, 99, 104, 105, 110, 114, 118, 119, 122-124, 132-134, 138-144, 169, 170, 174, 177-179, 184, 188, 199, 201, 223, 257, 268, 269, 295, 298, 305, 341; *2*: 26, 49, 50, 71, 108, 119, 134, 136

Paul, Antiochene heretic, *2*: 7

Paul of Samosata, *1*: 342; *2*: 51, 67, 89, 115, 138, 140-148, 152, 153, 158

Paulinus, Bishop, *1*: 6, 8, 10; *2*: 239, 243, 244, 251, 262

Paulinus, layman, *2*: 39

Pausanius, *1*: 105

Pelagius II, *1*: 30

Peleus, Bishop, *2*: 189

Pella, *1*: 145, 214

penance, *2*: 60

Pentapolis, *2*: 97, 137

Pentecost, *1*: 156

Pepuza, *1*: 311, 322, 325

Peraea, *1*: 69, 119, 120, 145, 214

Perennius, *1*: 331

Pergamon, *1*: 243, 276

Perge, *2*: 134

Perigrinus, *1*: 325

Peripsema, *2*: 125

persecutions, 1: 5, 6, 23, 24, 86, 190, 193, 213, 214, 216, 234, 242, 252, 259, 270, 271, 273, 276, 282, 318, 326, 330; 2: 3, 5, 8-10, 12, 15, 22, 45, 52-54, 64, 66, 68, 70, 77, 84, 103, 110, 112-114, 116, 121, 138, 151, 152, 158, 160, 162, 163, 165-168,

171, 174, 175, 178, 184-195, 198-204, 214, 215, 239, 272, 274, 283

Persian Gulf, *1*: 137

Persians, *1*: 159, 301; *2*: 105, 113, 150

Persius, *2*: 36

Pertinax, *1*: 340

pestilence, *2*: 123, 220, 222

Peter, *2*: 70, 111, 173

Peter St., the Apostle, *1*: 75, 76, 84, 85, 87, 91, 100, 109-111, 125, 132-134, 137-141, 143, 169, 180, 188, 196, 198, 202, 203, 206, 224, 233, 260, 295, 298, 305, 326, 342; *2*: 23, 26, 27, 45, 48, 49, 119, 133, 134

Peter, Archbishop of Alexandria, *2*: 161, 189, 215

Petra, *1*: 56, 73

Phabi, *1*: 71

Pencetius, *2*: 236

Phaeno, *2*: 189

Phamenoth, *2*: 156

Pharao, *2*: 122, 225

Pharisees, *1*: 55, 126, 127, 129, 255

Philadelphia, *1*: 197, 198, 242, 320, 321; *2*: 58

Philaster, *1*: 180, 217, 223

Phileas, Bishop, *2*: 180, 181, 190, 236

Philetus, *2*: 42, 45

Philip, St., the Apostle, *1*: 335

Philip of Arabia, Emperor, *2*: 59, 61, 62, 64, 70, 72, 102

315

Philip, the Asiarch, *1*: 239, 252, 261, 321

Philip, deacon, *1*: 86-88, 137, 188, 189-200, 203, 204

Philip, son of Herod, *1*: 69, 70, 72; *2*: 118

Philip and Lysanias, *1*: 92, 103, 119

Philippus Severus, Emperor, *2*: 59, 91

Philistines, *1*: 57

Philo, *1*: 93, 95-97, 111, 113-117; *2*: 25, 156

Philocalia, *2*: 57

philology, *1*: 27, 29

Philomelium, *1*: 234

Philoromus, *2*: 179

Philostorgius, *1*: 10, 138; *2*: 119, 239

Philomene, *1*: 308

Philotheos Bryennios, *1*: 179

Phoenicia, *1*: 4, 86, 106; *2*: 118, 175, 188, 214, 243

Photius, *1*: 30, 111, 133, 253, 302

Phrygia (Paroreios), *1*: 234, 235, 266, 272, 273, 290, 291, 307, 311, 314, 319, 322, 335; *2*: 41, 99, 184

physicians, *1*: 67, 142, 284

Pierius (Hierius), *2*: 159, 161

Pilate, *1*: 69, 70, 71, 74, 88, 95-98, 297; Acts of, *1*: 88; Memoirs of, *2*: 213, 216

Pinnas, *2*: 114

Pinytus, Bishop, *1*: 252, 258

Pionius, *1*: 242

Pirucheum, *2*: 154

Pisidia, *1*: 318

Pius I, *1*: 223, 225, 226, 295, 338

plagues, *1*: 43, 121; *2*: 220

Plato, *1*: 21, 44, 93, 220, 223, 245; *2*: 10, 35, 47

Pliny, *1*: 87, 193, 194, 218, 331

Pliny the Younger, *1*: 221

Plotinus, *2*: 33

Polycarp, *1*: 170, 186, 195, 197-199, 202, 203, 230-239, 242, 252, 294, 328-330, 335, 338

Polybius, *1*: 197, 234

Polycrates, *1*: 189, 262, 263, 319, 326, 332-335

polytheism, *1*: 91, 342

Pompey, *1*: 57, 58, 62, 224

Pontia, *1*: 166

Pontianus, *2*: 45, 53

Ponticus, *1*: 274, 285

Pontifex Maximus, *1*: 229

Pontius, *1*: 326; *2*: 22

Pontus, *1*: 138, 141, 223, 224, 226, 258, 300, 309, 334; *2*: 29, 55, 95, 115, 140, 186, 285; Bishop of, *2*: 159

Pope, *2*: 98, 139, 151

Poppaea, *1*: 131, 134, 157

Porphyrius, *1*: 19, 22

Porphyry, *1*: 18; *2*: 33, 35, 37

potentiality, *1*: 107

Pothinus, *1*: 252, 274, 279, 294

Potamiaena, *2*: 13, 14

Potitus, *1*: 308, 309

Praxeas, *1*: 343

preaching, *1*: 85, 139

Pre-millenarians, *1*: 312

presbyters, *1*: 11, 139, 140, 163, 168, 169, 171, 203, 206, 242, 291, 292, 297, 299, 314, 328, 329, 338; *2*: 22, 26, 27, 40, 52, 78, 80, 82, 84, 85, 87, 96-98, 106, 111, 112, 121, 125, 129, 140, 142, 143, 146, 159, 175, 188, 189, 274, 277

presbyterate, *1*: 311; *2*: 17, 39, 45, 142, 152, 159, 161

priests, *1*: 4, 46, 48, 50, 58, 120, 128, 170, 189, 196, 252, 269, 335; *2*: 244, 266

Priest, High, *1*: 46, 48, 50, 58, 59, 71, 72, 120, 121, 129, 130, 189, 240; *2*: 251, 252, 266

primacy, *1*: 196, 314

Primus, *1*: 207, 211, 254

principles, *1*: 308-310

Priscilla (Prisca), *1*: 119, 142, 312, 315, 323, 327; *2*: 164

Priscus, *1*: 228; *2*: 113

Probus, *2*: 149, 151

Proclus, *1*: 132, 133, 189; *2*: 41, 142

Procopius, *2*: 57

procurator, *1*: 56, 59, 69

prophecy, *1*: 38, 51, 53, 54, 56-59, 65, 190, 253, 290, 308, 309, 315, 321, 322, 325; *2*: 132, 133, 259, 260

Prophetess, *1*: 190, 266, 308, 311, 323, 324

Prophet, *1*: 20, 39, 45-48, 50-53, 74, 92, 112-114, 118, 126, 146, 159, 216, 219, 224, 250, 255, 262, 266, 269, 290, 296, 315,

316, 321, 323-325, 341; *2*: 57, 61, 127, 132

Prophets, Book of, *1*: 17

proselytes, *1*: 63, 300

Protectetus, *2*: 52

Protogenes, *2*: 142

Prudentius, *1*: 134

Psaltes, *1*: 249

Ptolemais, *1*: 113; *2*: 97, 178; Bishop of, *1*: 339

Ptolemy, *1*: 54, 247, 300, 301; *2*: 75, 156, 157

Publius, *1*: 307

Publius Quadratus, *1*: 257

Pupienus, *2*: 53

purification, *1*: 74; *2*: 257

Purim, *1*: 237

Puritans, *2*: 78

Pythagoras, *1*: 44, 93, 216; *2*: 36

Quadratus, *1*: 200, 209, 210, 320

Quadratus, Bishop of Athens, *1*: 209, 257

Quartodeciman, *1*: 252, 262, 237, 333, 338

Quinquennalia, *1*: 101

Quinta, *2*: 71

Quintus, *1*: 235

Quirinius, *1*: 71

rebaptism, *2*: 92, 95, 96, 98, 99

Rechab, *1*: 128

Rechabim, *1*: 128

Red Sea, *2*: 122, 225

Resurrection, *1*: 45, 76, 77, 85, 88, 182, 185, 198, 205, 333, 336, 341; *2*: 46

317

Revelation, *1*: 139, 204
Reynolds, H. R., *1*: 88
Rhaetia, *2*: 103
Rhoda, *1*: 307-310, 313
Rhodes, *1*: 229
Rhone River, *1*: 272, 287
Rhossus, *1*: 326; *2*: 23
righteousness, *1*: 52, 74, 117, 126
Romans, *1*: 19, 56-59, 73, 89, 95,
    109, 118, 119, 122, 124, 133,
    140, 148, 150, 157, 158, 161,
    195, 197, 211, 213, 222, 226-
    230, 249, 258, 259, 264, 276,
    283, 291-293, 300, 320, 338,
    346; *2*: 28, 38, 41, 53, 59, 92,
    116, 153, 154, 156, 167, 184,
    190, 201, 208, 214, 220, 224,
    226, 242, 282, 284, 287
Rome, *1*: 58, 89, 93-96, 98, 106,
    108, 110, 111, 118, 119, 123,
    124, 132-134, 138, 139, 143,
    144, 153, 157, 158, 163, 164,
    166, 189, 195-197, 207, 210,
    222-227, 230-232, 245, 252, 254,
    259, 269, 291, 298, 304, 307,
    308, 310-312, 327, 330, 334,
    336, 338, 342, 343; *2*: 27, 28,
    33, 36, 41, 42, 45, 53, 63-65, 78,
    79, 81, 85, 86, 89, 90, 93, 96,
    97, 99-103, 106, 115, 117, 148,
    193-195, 197, 224, 226, 273,
    275, 277; Bishop of, *1*: 9, 133,
    139, 143, 163, 164, 169, 189,
    194, 196, 207, 210-212, 223,
    224, 251, 262, 270, 271, 291,
    294, 342, 343; *2*: 39, 41, 42, 45,
    50, 53, 62, 66, 67, 78, 79, 95,

100, 138, 148, 149, 151, 274,
    276
Rufinus, *1*: 24, 137, 221, 263; *2*:
    4, 11, 13; 46, 53, 67, 90, 184,
    197
Rufus, *1*: 199, 213
Russia, *1*: 138
Rusticus, *1*: 243
Ruth, *1*: 63, 159, 266; *2*: 47

Sabbath, *1*: 44, 52, 237
Sabellianism, *1*: 12, 15; *2*: 97,
    137
Sabellius, *2*: 67, 96, 97, 137
Sabinus, *2*: 68, 110, 207, 227
Sadducees, *1*: 129, 255
Sadduchus, *1*: 55, 255
Sagaris, Bishop, *1*: 263
Salim, *1*: 176
Salome, *1*: 67, 68
salvation, *1*: 37, 58, 77; *2*: 167
Samaria, *1*: 59, 69, 86, 120
Samaritans, *1*: 98, 106, 180, 181,
    255
Samuel, Books of, *1*: 159
sanctuary, *1*: 126
Sanctus, *1*: 274, 276, 277, 281,
    282
San Lazzoro, *1*: 210
San Paolo, Church of, 1: 133
Sapor, *2*: 64, 113
Saracens, *2*: 76
Sardinia, *2*: 41, 45
Sardis, *1*: 197, 230, 262, 335;
    Bishop of, *1*: 230, 262
Sarmatians, *1*: 292

318

320

Simon Bar-Jona, 2: 133
Simon Magus, 1: 86, 87, 105-109, 180-182, 254, 317
Simonians, 1: 87, 108, 254, 296
Sinai, Mount, 1: 210
Sinope, Bishop of, 1: 223; 2: 29
Sion, 2: 165
Sirmium, 2: 141
slave, 1: 118, 120
Smyrna, 1: 170, 197, 198, 231, 233, 234, 239, 241, 242, 252, 335; Bishop of, 1: 170, 195, 231, 241, 335
Socrates, historian, 1: 12, 30, 31, 137, 326, 337; 2: 58, 78
Socrates, philosopher, 1: 245
Socrates of Laodicea, 2: 152
Sodom, and Gomorrha, 1: 40, 150, 344
Solomon, 1: 42, 60, 61, 64, 127, 256, 266, 299, 340; 2: 25, 48, 259
Sopater, 1: 142
Sophronia, 2: 197
Sophronius, 1: 331
sorcerers, 1: 122, 214
Sosthenes, 1: 75
Sotas, 1: 316, 327
Soter, 1: 226, 251, 254, 259, 270, 271, 295, 300, 338; 2: 95
Sozomen, 1: 10, 22, 31; 2: 54, 119, 287
Spain, 1: 92, 123
Spartianus, 2: 3
Spatian, 1: 208, 209
Spirit, divine, 1: 45, 49, 51, 110, 170, 174, 176, 280, 290, 297, 315; 2: 27, 54
Statius Quadratus, 1: 235
Stephen, St., 1: 84, 86, 91, 145, 186, 288; 2: 51, 93-95
Stephen of Laodicea, 2: 158
Stoic, 1: 93, 303
Strabo, 1: 63, 87, 101
Strabo's Tower, 1: 101
substance, of God, 1: 11, 38, 40
succession, 1: 23, 35, 37, 200, 207, 211, 212, 224, 251, 254, 306, 307, 315, 326, 328, 339; 2: 162, 163
Suetonius, 1: 131, 158, 166, 168
suicide, 1: 67; 2: 186
Sunday, 1: 312, 333
superstitions, 1: 53, 91
Susanna, 2: 56
Sylvester, 2: 277
symbols, 1: 46-52
Symeon of Jerusalem, 1: 161, 162, 191, 194, 212, 254
Symmachus, 2: 29, 31, 32
Syncellus, George, 1: 173
Syneros, 1: 309
Synnada, 2: 39, 99
Synods, 1: 12-14, 333; 2: 62, 67, 78, 79, 89, 99, 138, 139, 141, 152, 158, 259, 273, 276
Synoda, Bishop of, 2: 39
Synoptists, 1: 175
Syracuse, Bishop of, 2: 276
Syria, 1: 8, 54, 55, 71, 98, 135, 195-197, 199, 215, 223, 269, 304; 2: 23, 35, 95, 105, 112, 153, 154, 158, 168, 174, 177

Syriac, *1*: 24, 77-79, 82, 210, 270; *2*: 120

Tacitus, *1*: 99, 131; *2*: 149
Tanais, *1*: 138
Taposiris, *2*: 68
Tarsus, *2*: 51, 89, 95, 140, 143, 195, 232; Bishop of, *2*: 89, 140
Tatian, *1*: 20, 108, 143, 244, 245, 267-269, 307, 310, 320, 343; *2*: 25
Teachings of the Apostles, *1*: 179
Telesphorus, *1*: 212, 222, 295, 338; *2*: 137
Temples, *1*: 17, 57, 95, 96, 119, 126-128, 130, 146, 149, 155, 156, 219
Tertullian, *1*: 44, 54, 82, 88-90, 106, 132, 138, 165, 168, 175, 179, 181, 193, 194, 205, 217, 218, 223, 235, 238, 239, 264, 282, 293, 294, 308, 312, 313, 315, 317, 320, 322, 328, 337; *2*: 3, 41, 48, 83
Testament, New, *1*: 31, 72, 84, 92, 97, 111, 129, 140, 141, 164, 177, 178, 224, 320, 321; *2*: 26 82; Old, *1*: 19, 38, 40, 57, 159, 184, 224, 253, 265, 266, 308, 310, 320; *2*: 29, 30, 37, 47, 63, 82, 158
Testeri, *1*: 140
Tetrapla, *2*: 31
tetrarch, *1*: 63, 69, 70, 73
Thaddaeus, *1*: 76, 77, 79-81, 85, 137

Thebais, *1*: 5, 219; *2*: 4, 175, 178, 189,. 236
Thebouthis, *1*: 254
Thelymidres, *2*: 89, 95
Themiso, *1*: 318, 323, 324
Themistius, *1*: 209
Theoctistus, *2*: 17, 39, 52, 89, 95, 115
Theodore of Mopsuestia, *1*: 10
Theodore (Synnada), *2*: 39, 55, 142
Theodoret, *1*: 10, 12, 13, 31, 41, 107, 215, 255, 322, 342; *2*: 54, 152
Theodorus, Bishop, *2*: 180, 190
Theodotian, *1*: 300; *2*: 29-31
Theodotus of Laodicea, *1*: 8
Theodotus, Montanist, *1*: 290, 317, 342-344, 346
Theodotus, Passion of Saint, *2*: 106, 158, 211
Theonas, Bishop, *2*: 160, 161
Theophania, *1*: 16, 18
Theophanies, *1*: 27, 40, 41
Theophilus, *1*: 178, 251, 260, 261, 306, 332, 334, 339; *2*: 75, 120, 142
Theophrastus, *1*: 345
Theotecnus, *2*: 115-117, 140, 142, 153, 158, 159, 211, 236, 237
Therapeutae (Therapeutrides), *1*: 112, 113
Theudas, *1*: 103, 104, 223
Thomas, St., the Apostle, *1*: 77, 85, 137, 180, 203
Thrace, *1*: 326, 327; *2*: 231
Thraseas, *1*: 319, 326, 335

323

Thucydides, 2: 125
Thumis, 2: 180, 181; Bishop of, 2: 180
Thundering Legion, 1: 293
Thurston, Herbert, 1: 337
Thyestean feasts, 1: 276
Tiber River, 1: 106
Tiberius Caesar, 1: 69-73, 88-98, 102, 104, 158, 284, 324
Tigris River, 1: 105, 137
Timaeus, Bishop, 2: 147, 151
Timothy, 1: 123, 124, 139, 142, 143, 295; 2: 68, 69
Tischendorf, 1: 89
Titus, Bishop, 1: 142, 144, 257
Titus, Emperor, 1: 144, 148, 149, 158, 161-163
Tobias, 1: 79, 80, 212
Trachontis, 1: 69
Tradition, apostolic, 1: 12, 298
traditor, 2: 274
Trojans, 1: 90, 138, 168-170, 188, 190-194, 199, 207-209, 211, 213, 218, 230, 251, 294, 331; 2: 38
Trallians, 1: 197, 239
Trechontis, 2: 64
Tricennalia, 1: 10, 13, 15, 16, 26
Trinity, Blessed, 1: 40, 328
Tritheism, 2: 67
Troas, 1: 198
Trophimus, 1: 142
Trypho, 1: 249, 250
Tuebingen School, 1: 173
Tychichus, 1: 142
Tymion, 1: 322
types, 1: 46-50
Tyrannion, Bishop, 2: 188

Tyrannus, 2: 151, 152
Tyre, 1: 5, 6, 8, 10, 12-15, 19, 106, 339; 2: 33, 95, 152, 175, 177, 188, 216, 239, 243, 244; Bishop of, 1: 8, 338; 2: 188, 239, 244

Ur of the Chaldees, 1: 77
Ural, 1: 138
Urban, 2: 42, 45, 80
Urbanus, 1: 318; 2: 45
Urbicius, 1: 247, 248
Ursus, 2: 278
usury, 1: 325

Valens, 1: 307
Valentinus, 1: 223, 225, 232, 255, 268, 270, 328; 2: 32
Valeria, 2: 164
Valerian, 2: 67, 68, 78, 93, 102-105, 107, 110, 112-114, 126, 127, 138, 140, 141, 152, 167, 168, 170
Valerius Gratus, 1: 71, 314
Valesius, 1: 31
Vandal, 2: 274
Vaphris, 1: 212
Vatican, 1: 106, 133
Venice, 1: 210
Verissimus, 1: 228
Verona, 2: 64, 91
Vettius Epagathus, 1: 274, 275
Vespasian, Emperor, 1: 98, 128, 134, 144, 153, 157, 158, 161, 162, 165, 294
Vicennalia, 1: 10, 19

Victor, Bishop of Rome, *1*: 189, 252, 253, 262, 263, 320, 332, 334, 336-339, 342-344
Vienne, *1*: 73, 99, 272, 273, 276
Vigils, *1*: 116; *2*: 18
Virgins, *1*: 115, 187, 189, 192, 254, 335; *2*: 71, 74, 139, 196
virginity, *1*: 196, 312; *2*: 13
virtue, *1*: 52, 53, 196
Vitalis, *2*: 152
Vitellius, proconsul, *1*: 71, 98, 144, 162, 324; *2*: 274, 279
Volusian, *2*: 102

Wendland, P., *1*: 27
widows, *1*: 61, 324; *2*: 260
Wood, Simon P., *2*: 24
Word, of God, *1*: 28, 35, 38, 39, 42, 43, 45, 50, 53, 54, 86, 91, 108, 109, 116, 165, 194, 217, 226, 254, 257, 265, 303, 314, 343; *2*: 4, 12, 27, 38, 45, 97, 135, 143, 167, 191, 197, 214, 224, 244, 250, 252, 256, 262, 263, 264

Xerxes, *1*: 159
Xystus, *1*: 211, 295, 338; *2*: 39, 95, 100, 101, 103, 115, 138

Zabdas, Bishop, *2*: 160
Zacchaeus, Bishop, *1*: 212
Zacharias, *1*: 274, 275
Zebedee, *1*: 85, 145, 177; *2*: 132
Zebenus, *2*: 42, 45, 54
Zefyrinus, *1*: 133, 342-345; *2*: 28, 41, 42, 53
Zeno, *2*: 75
Zenobia, *2*: 36, 138, 144, 147
Zenobius, *2*: 188, 189
Zephyrinus, *2*: 96, 97
Zeus, *1*: 96; *2*: 211, 217
Zion, Mount, *2*: 267
zodiac, *2*: 156, 157
Zoroastrian, *1*: 216
Zorobabel, *2*: 244, 256
Zosimus, *1*: 199; *2*: 72
Zoticus, *1*: 314, 318, 325

THE FATHERS OF THE CHURCH SERIES

(A series of approximately 100 volumes when completed)

ADVANTAGE OF BELIEVING (trans. by Sr. Luanne Meagher)

ON FAITH IN THINGS UNSEEN (trans. by Deferrari and Sr. Mary Francis McDonald)

VOL. 5: ST. AUGUSTINE (1948)

THE HAPPY LIFE (trans. by Schopp)

ANSWER TO SKEPTICS (trans. by Kavanagh)

DIVINE PROVIDENCE AND THE PROBLEM OF EVIL (trans. by Russell)

SOLILOQUIES (trans. by Gilligan)

VOL. 6: ST. JUSTIN MARTYR (1948)

FIRST AND SECOND APOLOGY (trans. by Falls)

DIALOGUE WITH TRYPHO (trans. by Falls)

EXHORTATION AND DISCOURSE TO THE GREEKS (trans. by Falls)

THE MONARCHY (trans. by Falls)

VOL. 7: NICETA OF REMESIANA (1949)

WRITINGS (trans. by Walsh and Monohan)

SULPICIUS SEVERUS

WRITINGS (trans. by Peebles)

VINCENT OF LERINS

COMMONITORIES (trans. by Morris)

PROSPER OF AQUITANE

GRACE AND FREE WILL (trans. by O'Donnell)

VOL. 8: ST. AUGUSTINE (1950)

CITY OF GOD, Bks. I-VII (trans. by Walsh, Zema; introduction by Gilson)

VOL. 9: ST. BASIL (1950)

ASCETICAL WORKS (trans. by Sr. M. Monica Wagner)

VOL. 10: TERTULLIAN (1950)

APOLOGETICAL WORKS (vol. 1), (trans. by Arbesmann, Sr. Emily Joseph Daly, Quain)

MINUCIUS FELIX

OCTAVIUS (trans. by Arbesmann)

VOL. 11: ST. AUGUSTINE (1951)

COMMENTARY ON THE LORD'S SERMON ON THE MOUNT WITH SEVENTEEN RELATED SERMONS (trans. by Kavanagh)

328

VOL. 18: ST. AUGUSTINE (1953)
LETTERS 83-130 (vol. 2), (trans. by Sr. Wilfrid Parsons)

VOL. 19: EUSEBIUS PAMPHILI (1953)
ECCLESIASTICAL HISTORY, Bks. 1-5 (trans. by Deferrari)

VOL. 20: ST. AUGUSTINE (1953)
LETTERS 131-164 (vol. 3), (trans. by Sr. Wilfrid Parsons)

VOL. 21: ST. AUGUSTINE (1953)
CONFESSIONS (trans. by Bourke)

VOL. 22: ST. GREGORY OF NAZIANZEN and ST. AMBROSE (1953)
FUNERAL ORATIONS (trans. by McCauley, Sullivan, McGuire, Deferrari)

VOL. 23: CLEMENT OF ALEXANDRIA (1954)
CHRIST, THE EDUCATOR (trans. by Wood)

VOL. 24: ST. AUGUSTINE (1954)
CITY OF GOD, Bks. XVII-XXII (trans. by Walsh and Honan)

VOL. 25: ST. HILARY OF POITIERS (1954)
THE TRINITY (trans. by McKenna)

VOL. 26: ST. AMBROSE (1954)
LETTERS 1-91 (trans. by Sr. M. Melchior Beyenka)

VOL. 27: ST. AUGUSTINE (1955)—Treatises on Marriage and Other Subjects:
THE GOOD OF MARRIAGE (trans. by Wilcox)
ADULTEROUS MARRIAGES (trans. by Huegelmeyer)
HOLY VIRGINITY (trans. by McQuade)
FAITH AND WORKS, THE CREED, IN ANSWER TO THE JEWS (trans. by Sr. Marie Liguori Ewald)
FAITH AND THE CREED (trans. by Russell)
THE CARE TO BE TAKEN FOR THE DEAD (trans. by Lacy)
THE DIVINATION OF DEMONS (trans. by Brown)

VOL. 28: ST. BASIL (1955)
LETTERS 186-368 (vol. 2), (trans. by Sr. Agnes Clare Way)

331

VOL. 42: ST. AMBROSE (1961)
     HEXAMERON, PARADISE, AND CAIN AND ABEL (trans. by Savage)

VOL. 43: PRUDENTIUS (1962)
     POEMS (vol. 1), (trans. by Sr. M. Clement Eagan)

VOL. 44: ST. AMBROSE (1963)
     THEOLOGICAL AND DOGMATIC WORKS (trans. by Deferrari)

VOL. 45: ST. AUGUSTINE (1963)
     THE TRINITY (trans. by McKenna)

VOL. 46: ST. BASIL (1963)
     EXEGETIC HOMILIES (trans. by Sr. Agnes Clare Way)

VOL. 47: ST. CAESARIUS OF ARLES (1964)
     SERMONS 81-186 (vol. 2), (trans. by Sr. Mary Magdeleine Mueller)

VOL. 48: ST. JEROME (1964)
     HOMILIES 1-59 (vol. 1), (trans. by Sr. Marie Liguori Ewald)

VOL. 49: LACTANTIUS (1964)
     THE DIVINE INSTITUTES, Bks. I-VII (trans. by Sr. Mary Francis McDonald)

VOL. 50: OROSIUS (1964)
     SEVEN BOOKS AGAINST THE PAGANS (trans. by Deferrari)

VOL. 51: ST. CYPRIAN (1965)
     LETTERS (trans. by Sr. Rose Bernard Donna)

VOL. 52: PRUDENTIUS (1965)
     POEMS (vol. 2), (trans. by Sr. M. Clement Eagan)

VOL. 53: ST. JEROME (1965)
     DOGMATIC AND POLEMICAL WORKS (trans. by John N. Hritzu)

VOL. 54: LACTANTIUS (1965)
     THE MINOR WORKS (trans. by Sr. Mary Francis McDonald)

VOL. 55: EUGIPPIUS (1965)
LIFE OF ST. SEVERIN (trans. by Bieler)

VOL. 56: ST. AUGUSTINE (1966)
THE CATHOLIC AND MANICHAEAN WAYS OF LIFE
(trans. by Donald A. and Idella J. Gallagher)

VOL. 57: ST. JEROME (1966)
HOMILIES 60-96 (vol. 2), (trans. by Sr. Marie
Liguori Ewald)

VOL. 58: ST. GREGORY OF NYSSA (1966)
ASCETICAL WORKS (trans. by Virginia Woods
Callahan)

VOL. 59: ST. AUGUSTINE (1968)
THE TEACHER, THE FREE CHOICE OF THE WILL,
GRACE AND FREE WILL (trans. by Russell)

VOL. 60: ST. AUGUSTINE (1968)
THE RETRACTATIONS (trans. by Sr. Mary Inez
Bogan)